GENERATIONS

By E. A. Alexander

For more information visit
www.eaalexander.com

Cover design and text layout: Magic Graphix, West Fork, AR
Printed in the United States of America

ISBN: 978-0-9825649-0-5

For my brother Steve, who made me believe I could.
But mostly for my children, Jennifer, Joey , Jeffrey, and Jessica
who brought so much joy to my life everyday.
It has always been a privilege and an honor to be their mother.

TABLE OF CONTENTS

THE BEST JOB IN THE WHOLE WIDE WORLD, FOREVER AND EVER

Typically, our view of our mothers depends on our own chronological age. As children, we see our mother as an angel, a vision, the most beautiful woman in the world. She has her own unique scent, and no one ever smells as wonderful as she does. No one can cook as well as she does either. She is our advocate, the one who makes the monsters go away, the one who heals all our boo-boos. She is our protector, the one person in the world we can count on and who loves us unconditionally.

As teenagers, we discover that our mothers really can't cook after all, and we wonder what we were thinking. We find that she can't really drive a car either without scaring those in and around the car half to death, and she is single-handedly responsible for the downfall of our society, high taxes, war, rising unemployment, and the problems of the world. We question her sense of fairness, her love, and her loyalty. We wonder how in the world she ever made it to the age she is, because she obviously doesn't have a brain in her head. We believe we are much more sophisticated, and she could never fathom the decisions and temptations we face on a daily basis. We sincerely believe she doesn't have a clue what it is like being a teenager, because she has always been a mother — a fuddy-duddy grownup. We truly wonder who could possibly find her interesting.

1

As young adults, our mother has become our friend and confidant. She forgives everything without question. We call her for advice almost on a daily basis. She is the one person who always rejoices in the smallest of our triumphs and consoles us in the agony of our defeats. She will take our side every time. We wonder how she could still possibly love us after treating her so disrespectfully through those teenage years. We discover her patience knows no bounds. She is wise beyond her years.

As older adults, we discover that we have become the parent and our mother has become the child. We scold her for eating too many brownies topped with vanilla ice cream and not eating enough vegetables. We constantly remind her to take a sweater because she always gets cold, and we get impatient with her when she leaves the sweater in the car because she wasn't cold in the car. She has become stubborn, and we find she taxes our patience. We begin to worry that she can no longer make wise decisions, so we see a need to take control of her life and she become rebellious.

My own mother is 80 years of age. She can't cook and she can't drive. She is stubborn and rebellious. She is also my friend and confidant. She still loves me unconditionally, and I can't imagine my life without her. She raised five children who have grown up to be self-sufficient and successful adults against all odds. She is the grandmother of eighteen and the great-grandmother of twenty-one. She is an incredible woman, and she is one of the funniest people I know. I love being around her.

My mother wrote a book about her life a couple of years ago that was not for publication but just for her family. Her children and some of her grandchildren wrote stories of memories we have of her to include in the book as a tribute and surprise for her. Reading those stories, I realized for the first time just how wildly crazy and mischievous my mother was when I was a young girl. I called her after reading her book to tell her just that.

"Mom," I said, "you were so cool when we were young."

"I was?" she asked, completely surprised. "Did you think I was cool at the time?"

"No," I sighed. "I guess I was just a typically ungrateful child who just never fully appreciated you until I had kids of my own," I said, feeling really sad that although I was teasing when I made the statement, it was probably very true.

Most teenagers are not nice people. I have known educated adults who have said that they never had any children because they didn't want to deal with teenagers. I really understood that feeling. I wasn't proud of my teenage years. I made good grades in school and never got into any trouble, but I seldom showed my mother the respect she deserved. Reading those stories written about my mother, I saw a side of her I had long forgotten, and I realized there was never a mother born who was as hip and cool as my mother had been. She was awesome. But it made me think about my own motherhood and how I wasn't like her.

When I was a young child, I asked my mother if I could go across the street to a friend's house. It was early evening but in the winter when it got dark early. My mother rejected my request to go to my friend's house because of the darkness. I pleaded with her again. I mean, it was just across a residential street, after all, and hardly more than twenty steps. Asking her a second time was a big mistake on my part. My father came out of nowhere. It was as if he magically appeared out of thin air. I didn't even know he was home. Never in a million years would I have ever asked my mother twice for anything knowing my father was home. I just closed my eyes and started praying. My father's thundering voice could be heard on the next block as he told me to NEVER ask my mother twice for anything. This was something I already knew not to do when he was around, but, like I said, I didn't know he was home. I made a mental note to always make sure my father wasn't home whenever I asked my mother for something when it might be questionable that she would say yes.

My parents divorced when I was nine years old, and by the time I was ten, I took advantage of the fact that my father was not around to back my mother up. I could pretty much get whatever I wanted by badgering her until she gave in to the exhaustion of it all. When I was a young teenager, I argued with my mother over everything. I remember thinking at the time that I would never allow my children to speak to me the way I spoke to my mother. I didn't want to be like her. I was so naïve in thinking that I could do a better job. I have since told my mother many times how sorry I am for being such a difficult daughter and for causing her such grief. She is always great when I call to apologize for something I did as a child. She usually laughs at the memory and graciously accepts my apology. She is still awesome.

I was a mother of four by the time I was 23 years old. Jennifer was the oldest, followed by Joey, Jeffrey, and Jessica. I had a tight rein on my children — for a while. It wasn't too hard when they were small, but once they hit their teens, I lost control. I was outnumbered, and my sons were bigger than me. The *"Terrible twos"* were nothing compared to the *"Terrible teens"*. My sister, Mary, was visiting during this time, and my house was in chaos. Young teenagers were everywhere. Mary looked at me, her mouth wide-open in shock, and all I could do was shrug my shoulders.

Jennifer tried my patience beyond all limits. When she was 14, she asked me if she could get her hair cut. "Great! Just don't get anything too funky," I requested. When she came home, I looked at her and almost burst into tears.

"The side of your head is shaved!" I yelled in disbelief.

"No it's not. They just cut it really short," she responded.

"What? Do I have 'Stupid' written on my forehead? Don't you think I know the difference between a shave and a cut?" I asked incredulously.

Jennifer's hair was naturally blonde, and, as a typical teenager, she tried to find her own identity through her hairstyles. When she was 16 years old, I came home from work to find that she had dyed her hair jet black. I felt like Fred Sanford from *Sanford and Son* or Marie from *Everybody Loves Raymond*. I clutched at my chest and asked her if she was trying to kill me.

"Just start digging my grave now," I whimpered.

A couple of days later, she decided to remedy my disapproval of her black hair by dyeing it so blonde that it was almost white. I began making my own funeral arrangements. I'm sure Jennifer decided sometime during those years that she was not going to be the kind of mother I was, that somehow she could do a better job. To my delight, she is a much better mother than I was, and I'm very proud of that.

Anyone can be a mother. But being a good mother is the hardest job there is. I never got promoted to "World's Greatest Mother" or even made "Honorable Mention". Some mothers strive to be their children's best friend. They give them everything their little hearts desire in hopes of gaining their children's love and loyalty and are afraid that if they say no, their children won't love them. Others rule with an iron fist, and their children obey out of fear more than anything else. Still others ignore their children and allow them to make their own decisions when they are much too young to do so. As a mother, I was a combination of all of these. My forte was inconsistency, and I was great at it. One day I would declare to the entire household that things were getting out of hand and I was "laying the hammer down".

"We're getting back to basics. You will use your manners and respect me as your mother. You will do as I say, not question my authority, or ask me twice for anything. If I say no, I mean no. You will do your chores without me reminding you and pick up after yourselves. I'm not your slave, and I refuse to live in a pigsty! Do I make myself clear?" I demanded.

The next day, my son Jeffrey would ask if he could go to his friend's house after school, and I would bribe him to stay home.

"If you stay home, I'll make cookies."

My sister, Mary, told me once that I was really messing up my kids with my inconsistency.

Jennifer subscribes to the theory that she is not her children's friend. Her job as a mother is to teach, direct, discipline, and love her children so they will grow up to be self-sufficient adults and leave home someday whether they like it or not. Jennifer didn't come to this way of thinking while she was planning her family. She learned by trial and error. She found out, as did I, that it wasn't as easy at it looked. She is a tireless mother of three, and after so many years, she has recognized her own strengths and knows her weaknesses. She is continually searching for her own way in motherhood, but it changes daily and is a never-ending struggle. Jennifer has envisioned the kind of people she wants her children to become, and she gently nudges them in that direction by example, encouragement, strength, love, and above all — consistency.

Grandmotherhood — now that's a whole different ballgame. Motherhood is all the work and sacrifice. Grandmotherhood is the long-awaited reward. My grandchildren tell me that I am the best grandmother in the whole wide world, forever and ever.

Okay, so I make them say that before I give them chocolate, but they always say it. In fact, they say it with such enthusiasm that anyone in the house can hear them. Sometimes they even say it without being prompted. Olivia, or Livvy as we call her, has on occasion said to me, "You're the best Grandma in the whole wide world, forever and ever."

I bend over, give her a big hug, and kiss and thank her for being such a wonderful granddaughter. Again, I hear with a slight impatient tone to her voice,

"Grandma! You're the best Grandma in the whole wide world, forever and ever!"

It's then I realize that Livvy, in her own subtle way, is asking for a sweetie. As always, Livvy receives her reward.

I love being a grandmother. It's what I was born to do. I've looked forward to being a grandmother ever since the day my husband realized he needed to permanently nip the whole baby making process in the bud, so to speak. He knew me so well. I would have just kept popping babies out every couple of years until the first one hit their teens and I saw what the future held. When it hit me that Jessica was my last baby, I began dreaming what it would be like when I became a grandmother. In my own mind, Grandmotherhood was the ultimate achievement. My grandchildren would love me completely, and I wouldn't have to dole out the punishment. I would be a fun Grandmother, have the answers to all the questions of the universe, and they would be in awe of my wisdom. My oldest granddaughter, Morgan, once told my daughter Jennifer that she was so lucky to have grown up with me as her mother.

Jennifer's jaw almost fell to the floor. "That's not the woman I grew up with!" she exclaimed. "Grandma was strict and tough! We were spanked, had bedtimes and rules, and NEVER got candy!" but Morgan didn't believe it.

Grandma has very few rules: Respect is number one, and they must always say please and thank you. Other than that, I'm pretty easy. There are no bedtimes. I let my grandkids fall asleep on the couch or in bed while watching cartoons. I let them have chocolate after they have just brushed their teeth. If they don't eat all their dinner, I still let them have dessert. Grandma always has sweeties: ice cream with chocolate syrup, popsicles, cookies, and, of course, candy. I believe it's the law.

I have many grandchildren now, and I always find it amusing when they come over and tell their parents to leave. Morgan used to come over and immediately tell her mother Jennifer to go away, "Go far, far away."

Morgan is in middle school now, and Grandma's magic has worn off for her, but there are others. Livvy is at the age of magic, and she tells her mother Jessica the same thing, "You can leave now, Mommy. Just go away."

Livvy is a little bolder than Morgan, though. When Jessica announces that it is time to leave, Livvy is the first to say, "I'm not going; I'm staying here." Rachel, Livvy's older sister, has thrown what we have termed "a fit" when it is time to leave. She cries with her arms outstretched, calling for me, as Jessica is dragging her kicking and screaming out to the car. I want nothing more than to run to her and feel her arms around my neck, comforting her and reassuring her that I love her more than my own life. I naturally bask in this display of affection. It's those moments I live for. Jessica's answer to Rachel's cries for Grandma is generally, "Walk away, Mom; just walk away."

There is no compassion in my children for my grandchildren's need to be with Grandma. I have to remind my grandchildren all the time that although I am their mother's mother, the one thing I cannot do is overrule their mother. Like it or not, agree

8

with it or not, I know my place in the pecking order of my grandchildren's life.

Rachel once asked me if I loved her more than Mommy.

"Your mommy is my daught—" I began, when Rachel interrupted me to clarify her question.

"No," she said, "that's not what I meant. Do you love me more than Mommy loves me?"

In truth, I didn't think anyone loved her as much as I did, but I gave my daughter the benefit of the doubt, "There is no greater love in the world than a mother's love for her child," I replied. "However, my love for you is a very close second."

And I know just how much Rachel loves me, too. She and Livvy were at my house one evening and having some quiet talk time. We were talking about the day and how school had been. We began talking about family members, when Rachel made the comment that she knew that I was her and Livvy's grandma.

"I'll be your Grandma until the day I die," I told her, giving her a warm hug.

"Then you'll just be our dead grandma," Rachel replied.

I could really feel the love.

Grandma's house should be a special, magical place. When one or more of my grandchildren spend the night, for me it's like being young again and having a slumber party. They usually have my undivided attention the entire evening, and I let them choose the activities. Morgan has always had a very vivid imagination, and she has never ceased to amaze me.

One night, Morgan spent the night with my husband and I. At 3 years of age, she was great at pretending. We played dress up and did each other's hair. It was during the hair styling that she began to tell me of her plans for the evening, "I'm going to the Ball to meet the Prince," she said.

"Wow! How exciting!" I responded. I told her to have a great time and reminded her to be home by midnight because of the whole coach/pumpkin thing.

She went to another room and was in there for probably fifteen minutes. She was gone so long, I figured she had lost interest in the game. When Morgan returned, she began to recite her adventures of the evening.

"I danced with the Prince," she said. "He kissed me. He touched my soul."

"He did what?" I asked with just a little bewilderment in my voice.

"He touched my soul," she replied.

"Morgan, you watch way too much TV."

It was during that same evening Morgan and I went outside to enjoy the sultry summer evening weather. Grandpa had already gone to bed, and he was snoring so loudly that we could him hear from outside.

"What's that noise?" Morgan asked me.

"It's Grandpa. He's snoring," I said.

"Snoring? I think Grandpa needs to go pooh-pooh," she replied. She was probably right.

Morgan didn't know all the words to the *Titanic* song by Celine Dion, but she could belt out the chorus just as loud and strong. She stood at the end of our walkway and was near the street with her arms outstretched, singing her little heart out, *"You're here, there's nothing I fear . . ."*

It woke my husband, and he came outside telling me that I shouldn't let Morgan yell and scream so loud because it might wake any neighbors that went to bed as early as he did. With great pride in my voice, I told him that Morgan was not screaming but was in fact singing with the voice of an angel. He gave up, turned around, and went back to bed. You can never argue with a Grandma about the gifts of one of her grandchildren.

Rachel and Livvy spend every Saturday night with Grandpa and I. This weekly sleepover began when Rachel was only 2 years old. We go to church every Sunday morning, but Jessica had to go to work. Rachel is now 9 years old and Livvy is 5. Jessica no longer has to work on Sundays, but the girls still spend the night. On Saturday nights, I try to cook one of their favorite things for dinner, give them dessert, bathe them, and see that they brush their teeth. It is at this point that Livvy always asks for one more chocolate, and I always comply.

Rachel and Livvy do have a bedtime on Saturday night since we all get up early for church on Sunday mornings. At bedtime, we go into their bedroom and begin what Rachel calls "The Jesus Club". We start by telling each other that Jesus loves them. Livvy invariably runs back out to the living room to tell Grandpa that Jesus loves him too. He responds with the same. We then sing a song or two that they have learned at either church or Sunday school. The last part of the club is either telling them a story from the Bible about Jesus' life or explaining something Jesus teaches us. One Saturday night, I decided to provide an explanation to something I had been thinking about all night. It had not been a smooth evening. Rachel and Livvy are typical sisters, and there are episodes of fighting from time to time, so I began talking to them about choices we make — both good and bad. I told them that when we make the wrong choices, it is because we are listening to Satan and not to God. As an example, I got down to Rachel's ear and began whispering, "Come on, Rachel. You know you want to throw a fit. It'll feel so good."

Both girls giggled.

I then told them that the Bible teaches us that if we resist Satan, he will flee from us. "So," I continued, "when you see

11

that you are thinking about making a wrong choice, just say *'Satan, get away from me!'* and the feelings of making the wrong choice will go away."

Rachel asked me if she could say that in her head, because she didn't want her friends at school to think she was weird. I told her that I say it out loud, but if she felt more comfortable saying it in her head, then that was fine. We said our prayers and I kissed both girls goodnight. Several minutes later, I was in the den working on my computer when I heard Rachel say, "Livvy, tell Satan to get away from you! We're supposed to be going to sleep!"

It was a proud moment for me, knowing that at least for the rest of the night they took my little talk to heart.

Each of my grandchildren has their own unique gifts they bring into my life. I love them all the same, but my relationship with each one is slightly different. Rachel and I have made chocolate chip cookies together since she was 3 years old. During football season, we make cookies almost every Sunday afternoon. We have a ritual while preparing to make the cookies. I ask Rachel to tell me the ingredients needed, and she runs through the list while I get each one from the cupboard. There are two rules while making cookies, and Rachel recites these rules as we begin: Clean up as we go along, and taste the chocolate chips when we add them to the cookie dough to make sure they are good. Before we bake the cookies, I get Rachel's stamp of approval that the chocolate chips are indeed good enough to use in our cookies. One afternoon, while eating the first batch of cookies fresh out of the oven, I commented to Rachel that someday she would make the best cookies in the whole world.

"Grandma," she replied, "I already do."

Now it is the three of us on Sunday afternoons: Rachel, Livvy, and I. Livvy has finally made the rite of passage into helping

Grandma bake cookies, too. Although it gets a little crowded and everyone thinks they are the head baker, we manage to make cookies for them to take home for the week.

As a Grandmother, I do more than bake cookies and tell stories to my grandchildren. I also give them lots of hugs and kisses. They are not always in the mood for affection, but the one trick I've learned which almost always works is the 'Pretend cry'. This gets Livvy every time. I can always get a hug and kiss from Livvy with just a few little pretend sobs. In fact, occasionally she will just walk up to me and demand that I cry. When I comply, I get the sweetest hugs of affection.

My son, Jeffrey, has four little girls, Allison, Elaina, Sophia, and Hannah. Allison is the oldest. She and her cousin, Livvy, are the same age, with just two weeks separating them in age. But Allison, Elaina, Sophia, and Hannah live clear across the country in California, so I don't see them on a regular basis, and Allison is not used to my cunning ways. Jeffrey and his family stopped by on their way home from a year in Africa doing mission work last year. My son and daughter-in-law went out for a while to have some alone time together for the first time in a year. I had the privilege of watching my granddaughters while they were gone. During that time, I tried to get a hug from Allison that was not forthcoming, so I used my old standby pretend cry. Allison looked at me and said, "Grandma, calm down."

I was so taken aback by her remark that I didn't know how to react. The pretend cry had always worked before. I didn't know what to say to her, so I thought the best thing to do was to come clean and be truthful. I told her I was calm but just wanted a hug. Again she said no. I asked why she didn't want to give me a hug, and her reply was, "Because you're interesting." I assumed this was a new word in her vocabulary and she was just trying it on for size. She could have tried a different word to describe me, but that one was fine.

"Interesting," I said. "That's not a bad thing; you know." I can live with interesting.

Little boys, I have discovered, are very different. My two grandsons who live near me, Hunter and Christien, are at the age where they don't feel comfortable giving out kisses. They will throw their arms around me and give me bear hugs all day long, but they will turn their cheek to me to avoid the dreaded kiss on the lips. I guess they have discovered that I am a girl and have cooties. I go to their house and walk in to hear screams of "Grandma's here!!!!" They run to me, put their arms around my neck, but turn that cheek. It wasn't that long ago when they gave out slobber kisses. You know the kind, when they have just learned with mouths wide open, spit and slobber running down their face and sometimes meshed with food, and lean over and rub their mouths all over your face. After the kiss, you're left with enough slobber on your face that you need a whole box of Kleenex just to get it all off. But you don't care; your grandchild just gave you a kiss. It is a cherished moment in your life.

I don't remember the exact time they went from being Grandma's little boys to little men, but it happened overnight. I can't even bribe a kiss out of them now. No amount of cookies, chocolate, or ice cream can buy me a kiss on the lips from my grandsons now. The funny thing is, I don't remember ever giving anyone a kiss on the lips except a boyfriend and eventually my husband.

As a mother of four, I had a severe shortage of time and patience. I didn't spend enough time enjoying the little things in life with my children. I always seemed to be in reactive mode. Looking back now, that is one of the main things I would change about myself. I wish I had spent more time playing, talking, and just having fun with my kids. But as it always does, time flew by so quickly, and it felt as if my children grew up before their first birthday had a chance to roll around.

When I was expecting my second child Joey, my obstetrician told me to enjoy my children while they were young. He said that they would grow up before I could blink an eye. He had five children of his own, and, being a doctor, he wasn't home as much as he would like. He said that his children were teenagers now, and they barely knew him. They didn't even look up or greet him when he walked in the front door after working such long hours. I felt so bad for him at the time and have often wondered since if it ever changed for him.

Being a mother was hard. You had to be tough to teach them. You had to be strict to protect them. You had to make them brush their teeth, do their homework, and eat their vegetables. My children loved me and hated me. I often questioned if I was doing the right thing or if I was a good mother. I had spent sleepless nights with sick children, fought with them over their clothes, curfews, music, money, and haircuts,. I was exhausted. After they were grown and became parents themselves, I discovered the joy of Grandmotherhood. I adore my grandchildren. If they are at my house right after school, I take the time to sit down and help them with their homework. I give them their spelling words and correct their math problems. I tell them stories and let them help me cook. I let them play with water at the sink in their attempt to help wash the dishes. I put clean towels in the dryer while they take their baths, so when they get out, they can wrap themselves up in a warm towel. We listen to music, play games, take turns reading books to each other, and I share with them my faith in God and Jesus.

Recently, Rachel was at my house on a Monday holiday. She had a project due at school the following day which she had not even started yet. I gave Rachel ideas of what kind of project she could do and provided all the necessary materials for her to complete it. Rachel worked all morning on the project while I sat at the kitchen table talking with her. When she finished at 1:30, I took her to McDonalds as a treat for all her hard work. At the end of the day, when she met up with her mother, she gave me a hug and told me she'd had a really good day. I will never forget how much that meant to me. I'd had a really good day, too.

I truly did love being a mother, but I found that my grandchildren gave me a second chance at enjoyment of these precious little gifts. I thank God every day for blessing me with four wonderful children and all my precious little grandchildren. I truly have the best job in the whole wide world, forever and ever.

Liar, Liar, Pants on Fire

Maybe it's a natural part of growing up that makes a child lie when they are faced with confessing something they did wrong but are afraid of the consequences. My parents thought that telling a lie was about the worst thing a person could do. Telling a lie to *them* was akin to writing your own death sentence. Being not quite old enough to fully understand that, one night I did tell my parents a lie. I received a dollhouse one year for Christmas, and it was awesome. It was a two-story colonial and came with a swimming pool on the patio. The night I told my parents that lie, I was playing with my dollhouse, specifically, the swimming pool, on our hardwood floors in the hallway. I filled the swimming pool with water and fantasized about all the kids who would come over to swim. When the swimming pool no longer held my attention and I became bored, I put it away, but not before spilling some water on the floor. I didn't realize I had spilled any water at the time.

Later, we *ALL* found out about it. My father came upon the water on the floor and immediately asked which one of us five kids had spilled it. Each of us denied knowing anything about it. This blanket denial only fueled my father's anger. He began to threaten us that if someone didn't confess, we would all be spanked. He wanted to make sure the evil child was punished.

17

This threat, which I knew was very real, just made each of us more frightened, especially me, since I *was* that evil child. It became a personal witch-hunt to my father. He asked us each again who spilled the water. Again, we each denied knowledge of the incident. Consequently, we were all spanked, just to make sure that the guilty one received what was due. After the initial pain wore off, I felt so sorry that my brothers and sisters had been punished for something I had done. I must have been a little lightheaded from the spanking, because I went to my beloved mother to confess my sins. This woman, my wonderful, loving mother, ratted me out to my father like a snitch looking to make a quick buck. Her betrayal of me was swift and held deadly consequences. Needless to say, my father didn't hesitate to make sure that my punishment was significantly enhanced over what my siblings had received. Did I learn my lesson? Probably not. But it did teach me to be more careful around my father and never confess my sins to my mother if I didn't want her to tell my dad.

When my own children were young, I used to go on witch-hunts all the time. I often wondered if my kids were brain damaged or something. I would ask a simple question. Nothing to get excited over, just a question. But I would get lied to EVERY TIME. I discovered that I was just like my dad. I got so infuriated with them. Nothing upset me more than my kids lying to me about something totally insignificant. And, what's more, it was always about the same thing every time — the milk. Who left the milk out? I really do think that they were trying to drive me insane, because it happened all the time. I would waltz into the kitchen without a care in the world. My children would be quietly watching TV in the adjoining family room. I would look on the counter — and there was the milk.

"Who left the milk out?" I would ask so innocently, almost to myself.

Every time I asked this question, it was as if I had never seen the milk left out before. I always just assumed it was an oversight on someone's part. The reply from ALL four of my children was ALWAYS the same, "Not me." I sometimes wondered if I had an invisible child. Apparently, this invisible child was the one who left the milk out on the counter all the time. I wondered if I could claim him on my taxes at the end of the year. I was certainly feeding him. If I had asked my kids about this invisible child, they would probably have lied to me about that, too. I went on the assumption that I didn't have an invisible child, and thus began the inquest. I think it was at that point where they tuned me out. I begged them, "Just say 'It was me' and I will say to you 'Next time, please remember to put it away,' and it could be just as simple as that."

I tried so hard to reason with them. But NO! I still got "It wasn't me." I began my tirade by pointing out to them that they could lie to me now, but sometime in the future their lies would catch up with them, and that I would eventually find out who wasn't being truthful. I told them that mothers had God-given super powers, a magic eye that could read the hearts of all children. With this magic eye, I would find out who the liar was. Sooner or later, the truth would be known. I really thought that if I didn't spank all of them but instead tried to reason, threaten, or plead with them about how wrong it was to lie, maybe it would cease. It never did. I never knew who left the milk out.

Looking back, I am so amused and can't help but chuckle at my attempts to get at the truth. I can just see me approaching my son, Joey, now and saying to him, "Remember on June 16, 1988 at 7:48 P.M., you left the milk out on the counter and lied to me about it. Remember! You're grounded, mister! You can't go to work, have dinner with your wife, or play with your children!

19

See what you get when you lie to me? I told you that sooner or later I would find out! Didn't I?"

As much as I love my grandchildren and believe them to be above such things, they are not exempt from lying. One Saturday morning, Rachel and Livvy were over at our house while their mommy was at work. The girls helped me dust the furniture as only small children can do. We began to tackle cleaning the bathroom when they lost all interest in helping with the chores. Both girls decided that it would be more fun to draw pictures and color in the den. I was in the middle of scrubbing the sink when Rachel came running into the bathroom saying that Livvy had written on the wall in the den with a pencil. Livvy was a few steps behind Rachel already denying the accusation. No, I don't really have super powers or a magic eye, so I had difficulty trying to determine who was lying and who was telling the truth. I suspected Livvy was lying, because Rachel was 7 years old and would never write on the walls at that age. I was much older then and didn't do the tirade thing anymore, either. So I sat both girls down and began talking to them about being truthful and lying. I took it to a higher level and explained to them that when we lie, it doesn't make God happy. Looking intently into their sweet little eyes, I went on to tell them that someday we will have to give God an account of what we have done with our lives. We will have to answer to Him about the things we have done. They hung on every word out of my mouth.

Rachel was the first to speak, "Grandma, it was me. I wrote on the wall."

I was shocked and speechless for a moment. I had been speaking almost directly to Livvy and had barely acknowledged Rachel's presence. Wow! I turned slowly to Rachel with a stunned and bewildered look on my face and asked, "Rachel, why would you blame Livvy for something you did?"

"Because I didn't want to get into trouble," she replied.

"First, "I said, "you need to apologize to Livvy for blaming her for something you did. Second, you need to apologize to me for lying. Third, you have to clean the pencil marks off the wall."

I was ecstatic and elated! I couldn't believe it had been that simple. I actually got through to someone and helped her see that lying was wrong, and she owned up to it. Man! I was getting good at this stuff in my old age. Why hadn't I used this approach with my own kids years ago? I patted myself on the back all day.

About a month later, again Rachel and Livvy were over on a Saturday night. It wasn't long before Rachel came to me about something Livvy had done. Livvy was just a step behind Rachel again and in total denial. It was starting to get ugly.

"Yes, you did!"

"No, I didn't!"

I remembered the little speech from the previous encounter and began again. I spoke to them of God, answering to Him, and being accountable for our actions, etc. This time, no one confessed. What had gone wrong? Was it the eye contact I was lacking? Was I putting the emphasis on the wrong words? Did I not sound sincere? I droned on and on for what seemed like an eternity, but to no avail. They probably forgot why they were even listening to me in the first place. Small children don't have a very long attention span.

I gave up the lecture and my attempt to get at the truth. I made a few meaningless threats and let the girls go back to playing. Maybe my little speech from the previous month was just a one hit wonder. I pray that my words are still somewhere in their little minds and that someday they will draw on them when they really need them. In the meantime, I'm going to have to come up with a new approach, something I've never used on them before. Let's see… I wonder if they've heard the one about the invisible child I keep on retainer who reports to me daily about every move they make?

LET THE GAMES BEGIN

There's nothing like a little competition between kids to see who is the fastest runner in the neighborhood. I have no idea why this is important. What kind of distinction is it to be the fastest? Is it so you can boast that you can outrun a robber, or maybe your older siblings, or even your parents? When I was a young child, my father used to get as many kids in the neighborhood as possible together, line us up in the street, and say those famous little words: *On your mark — Get set — Go!* We ran down the hill, around the corner, back up a hill on another street, around the block, and, eventually, back to where we had all started. The first one back naturally won. I don't know what was won, but you had bragging rights that you were a "Winner". It was a long run, and my dad made us do this as often as he could get us all together at the same time. By the time we got to the top of the hill on the next street, most of us were pooped out and ready to take it at a walking pace. Sooner or later, though, you had to pick up speed, because you certainly didn't want to be known as the slowest kid in the neighborhood. The slowest kid in the neighborhood had to listen to a lecture from my dad about laziness and physical fitness.

My dad loved competition, and running was his favorite. The reason, I guess, was because you didn't need any special equipment. At that time, no one owned a pair of running shoes. No one even knew what they were. We weren't sophisticated enough to know that we needed special shoes to run. We all wore the same $1.00 pair of white or black tennis shoes you got from the local store at the corner.

Both of my older brothers went on to be track and cross-country stars in high school. They attended different high schools, but each made a name for himself in his respective school. I mention this only because once, and only once, during the races my father made us do, I beat both of my brothers. I was fast.

When I was fifteen years old, we started attending a new church. During the first couple of weeks there, I got to know Weldon. He told me he attended West High School.

"My brother just graduated from there," I told him. "He ran track."

"What's his name?" Weldon asked.

"Steve Smith," I replied.

"*The* Steve Smith?" he asked in awe.

"I guess," I replied questioningly.

I had no idea my brother had a "*The*" in front of his name. Had he been that modest or was I just not paying attention? It was probably the latter. As a young teenager, I wasn't interested in much outside my own social circle. Was I supposed to start calling him "*The* Steve" when I wanted to speak to him? I wasn't sure.

My son Joey had the body of a runner. He was lean and had long legs. Joey was really fast on his feet. While camping one summer when Joey was 9 years old, I challenged him to a race around the campground. He was fast, but I had also been fast when I was his age. I still had it, I thought. After all, he was just a kid, and I was still pretty young.

Joey began lightheartedly making fun of me, saying how he'd beat me with no trouble at all. He could beat me walking backwards. Joey accepted the challenge and the race began. We hadn't run fifty yards when he was about twenty-five yards ahead of me. He stopped and waited for me to catch up.

"I'm just trying to build your confidence," I said, completely out of breath.

When I caught up to him, he took off running again, but it wasn't long before he was so far ahead of me that I could barely see him on the horizon. He let me catch up and even let me run past him before he started to run again. How fair was that? He got to take a long break and catch his breath, while I was about to drop dead of a coronary trying, at this point, just to make it around the campground. By this time, I had given up any hope of victory. This was not a tale of the tortoise and the hare. I went down completely defeated and humiliated. I never challenged any of my children to a race again, and I never told my father about my defeat. At the age of 28, I didn't want to listen to the lecture on laziness and physical fitness.

Even if I was out of shape, I still loved sports. While I was growing up, as I remember, there was not much interest in professional football around my house. It wasn't until I was at my best friend Terri's house, one Sunday afternoon, that I discovered football. Terri's father had a football game on TV, and I watched Roman Gabriel of the Los Angeles Rams play quarterback and instantly fell in love with the sport. I became a football junkie.

When I had kids of my own, their father and I instilled this love of football in them. During football season, we were glued to the TV on Sunday afternoon. Everyone had their own team blanket that we wrapped ourselves up in, and we cheered our team to victory each week. We just couldn't get enough. We considered ourselves blessed when there was a Sunday night game. Thursday night games were a cause for celebration. My kids developed their love of the sport during the 80s, the golden years of the San Francisco 49ers and Joe Montana. We lived in San Jose, about forty miles south of San Francisco, and the 49ers were our team. When football season ended, we were left with an emptiness we had difficulty filling.

"What did we do before football season started?" I asked my husband that first week.

"That was so long ago, I don't remember," he replied. "Maybe we could get all the kids together, walk down to the school, and play a game of football."

During the spring, all my children played Little League Baseball. We started slow at first. Joey played minor league the first year. We had a great time going to the games and cheering him on. The following year, my husband became president of the local Little League, and all four of our children played. Having four kids playing a sport at the same time took a lot of organization. Each child had one practice and one or two games each week. There was always one day when I read the schedule wrong or didn't get home in time from work.

"Mom! My game is at 5:30, not 6:00! I'm going to be late!" Joey shouted impatiently at me.

"We're five minutes from the field; you'll be there on time," I assured him.

"Mom! Where's my uniform? I told you I needed it today!" Jeffrey asked while beginning to panic.

"It's neatly folded on your bed, if you'd just open your eyes," I responded with more than a little agitation in my voice. Sometimes they could be so blind.

We literally lived at the ball field and ate hot dogs for dinner six nights a week. In hindsight, we should have just camped out on the Little League field and rented out our house, as little as we were there. At least we could have made a little money. During our tenure in Little League, I was, at various times, team mother and official scorekeeper. It was tough keeping the schedule straight, but I was able to watch at least some of each child's game. Often, this meant going to different fields on the same day and at the same time. I also did this while working full-time. It was a crazy, frenzied time, but we enjoyed it so much that we didn't seem to mind the craziness. I guess we were all just crazy.

Jessica was the only girl on her T-Ball team her first year. She wore her hair in a ponytail tucked in her cap. The only way you could really tell she was a girl was by the butterflies on her blue jeans. She could hit, catch a ball, and run as well as any boy her age. Joey wasn't a power hitter, but he could run fast. He got that from my side of the family. I often thought Jeffrey's head wasn't entirely in the game and that he played just to please his father and me. Jeffrey, however, went on to play baseball the longest, all the way through high school. Jennifer played on an all-girl softball team. Those girls had so much fun, and they were fun to watch. We were so wrapped up in baseball that eventually the only friends we had were from Little League.

We soon discovered that we could only communicate in baseball-eese; for instance, a woman friend of mine once asked, "Did you see that new single dad whose son plays on Joe's team? He an all-star in my book."

I was talking to my husband one day about a mutual friend, "Betty said her marriage to Jim is on the rocks. She said it's the bottom of the ninth, with two outs, bases loaded, and a full count on the batter."

"Wow!" my husband responded, "If he doesn't keep his eye on the ball, he's outta here," and he motioned with his thumb.

We were so busy with baseball, we didn't have time for any other socialization. I think at that point we had lost all our social skills anyway.

On the Monday after the last game of the year, my husband came home from work to find me sitting at the kitchen table sobbing.

"What happened? What's wrong? Are the kids okay?" he inquired with great concern in his voice.

I looked up at him, tears streaming down my face, and replied, "I don't remember how to cook. What are some of the things I used to make?" I asked, trying to keep my voice from quivering. "Did you like my cooking before? Was I any good at it?"

A tender smile lit his face. "Let's start off slow. No one can expect you to just magically jump back into the routine of making dinner every night after eating at the ball field for four months," he said reassuringly. "How about scrambling some eggs or making hamburgers. Anything but hotdogs."

My children have passed down their love of sports to their own kids, too. Three of my grandchildren play competitive sports. They have played soccer, baseball, softball, and flag football. I watch every game I can. I tell my grandkids, "The only reason for me not to be at a game is because I'm working."

Otherwise, I am always there. I have watched them from their first games ever, grow to become a team player, develop their skills, and to eventually be really good at their sport.

Christien is the youngest one to play. He began playing when he was 5 years old, and, for him, this is a time of great fun. The joy on his face while playing his game is priceless. I have seen him raise both arms over his head, indicating a successful goal has been made FOR THE OTHER TEAM! Christien is happy for any player who kicks a goal, whether it is one of his teammates or one of his opponents. I get so tickled watching him on the soccer field "skipping" after the ball. During a Friday night game, as he was doing just that, the full moon caught his attention, and he stopped dead in his tracks, mesmerized by it's beauty. He looked as if he was in a trance. All the parents on the sidelines turned their heads to see what Christien was so fixated on when the other team scored a goal.

Christien's first year in T-Ball was pretty much the same. He played in the grass, chased butterflies, and played all the positions at the same time. He went wherever the ball went. He carried his bat while running to tag each base when he had been called out at first. He did this all with the biggest grin on his face. He was the epitome of "playing for the fun of it" and "not having a clue" at the same time. Christien didn't care or probably didn't even know if he was any good at the sport. He just loved getting to play.

"Grandma, did you see me hit a home run?" Christien asked me with so much pride in his voice.

"I sure did! Christien, you are such an awesome player, and I am so very proud of you," I told him with joy in my heart for him.

Christien's sister and brother, Morgan and Hunter, play to compete and take any sport they play very seriously. One game was exceedingly difficult for Hunter's team during his first year in soccer. Hunter was only 4 years old but was already competitive. Their opponents were scoring goals left and right. Every time someone from the other team was able to get control of the ball, they scored a goal. Hunter finally gained control of the ball at one point but was kicking the ball toward the wrong goal.

Everyone started shouting, "You're going the wrong way! Our goal is the other way! Kick it the other way!"

E. A. ALEXANDER

But Hunter kicked the ball into the opponents net. After the goal was scored, Jennifer asked him if he had heard everyone shouting at him to go the other way.

His reply was, "The other team was scoring all the goals, so I didn't want to be on my team anymore. I wanted to be on the winning team."

A couple of years ago, Morgan played on a soccer team that was so awesome. All the girls played as "one" and they won every game. Most games were as if the other team never showed up to play. There was one game that Morgan scored nine goals herself and was taken out at halftime just to give the other team a chance to score. At the end of the season, after winning all their games easily, a coach from one of the boy's team commented on how well the girls played together. He challenged their team to a game. The game meant nothing. The season was over. It was just an exhibition game for the fun of it — boys against girls. The girls were so excited and they were pumped. They knew they had it in them to beat the boys. The game was one of the most exciting games ever played in soccer history. It ended in a tie and went into overtime. Overtime ended in a tie, so they went to what is known as "penalty kicks" where each child takes turns at kicking the ball into the goal that is defended by the opponent's goalie. The girls lost during this phase of the game and they were crushed. It didn't matter that for all intents and purposes the game had ended in a tie or that the girls proved they were formidable opponents. They all left the field crying. Morgan was inconsolable for three days.

But it's not just their own sport they take seriously. They take all sports seriously. Hunter and the son of a famous Tampa Bay Buccaneer played on the same soccer team together one year. During one Friday night game, Morgan saw the Buccaneer on the sidelines watching his son play.

30

"Mommy, what's he doing here?" Morgan asked nervously.

"He's watching his son play soccer," Jennifer replied.

"But, Mommy," Morgan countered, as panic began to rise in her voice, "he should be with his team. Aren't they supposed to be on a plane right now to New York?"

"Morgan, he does have a life outside of professional football. I'm sure he'll be on the first plane out tonight after this game," Jennifer explained, trying to calm her.

"But Sunday is a big game. We've already lost our first three games this year. He needs to be with his team!" Morgan argued, clearly upset.

Sunday afternoon came, and the Tampa Bay Buccaneers lost to the New York Giants. I guess Morgan could talk to the Bucs' head coach and see about getting a fine imposed for taking time out to be a father.

I believe sports are an important part of growing up. It helps to teach children how to work together as a team. Even players who may not be as endowed with athletic ability as the others on the team are important contributors to the overall team. Team sports foster a sense of self-confidence. It helps a child recognize that they are a part of a team, whether they're a strong player or a weaker one. However, this is only true if the parents and coaches encourage and promote this philosophy and atmosphere in the games. We've all been to a game when either a parent or a coach has made a child feel bad about themselves. This is a very sad reality of sports, but when parents and coaches understand that they are teaching children the fundamentals of the game and how to play as part of a team, it can be like magic. Besides, what grandmother doesn't glow with pride while watching on the sidelines as her young grandchild is "skipping" after a soccer ball?

AND THE THUNDER ROLLS

Thunderstorms in Los Angeles are a rarity. While growing up, I could probably count on one hand how many thunderstorms I saw. When a thunderstorm did happen to come our way, it was as exciting as going to the movies or watching a fireworks display. Everyone grabbed a chair, pulled it up to our picture window in the living room, and watched in awe at the light show. Sometimes we would lose power and my mother would scramble through the house looking for candles to light. She was never very organized, so coming up with enough candles to light at least one room was a feat for her. I remember needing to use the restroom once during a power outage and asked one of my sisters to come with me because I was scared to go by myself in the dark. Those were the times bad things happened according to the scary movies we watched. We would take one candle with us to the bathroom and try to scare each other even more. I loved thunderstorms when I was a child and love them even more now.

When my children were little, it was pretty much the same, except I never had a big picture window in my living room to watch from. Our annual vacations were taken generally in August each year. We camped at a little-known, little-traveled place just outside the south entrance to Yosemite. We loved it there because it was secluded and there was a creek that ran through the middle of it where we played, fished, and raced boats we carved from fallen branches. We would stay in that campground our entire vacation with one day spent in Yosemite Valley, hiking, shopping, and viewing all the magnificent waterfalls.

One summer, while camping there, each night just before bedtime there was a thunderstorm. They were brief, lasting only about ten minutes, but they were spectacular. Initially the night air was cool, but all of a sudden you could feel the air get really warm. It was kind of spooky the way the air changed so quickly. Moments later the light show started. I kept telling my children how wonderful these thunderstorms were. They were a little on the nervous side because the lightning was so bright, the thunder so loud, and we were out in the open with no place to hide. But I loved the storms and did my best to encourage my children to appreciate them as much as I did.

A few days after the thunderstorms started, it was the day for our annual trip into Yosemite Valley and the Village. We drove the mile to the park entrance where we were turned away.

"What's the problem?" my husband inquired of the Ranger.

"Lightning strikes have ignited some trees, and there is now a forest fire burning out of control near the Valley," the Ranger informed us.

My kids turned on me, ready to mutiny.

"You said the storms were cool! You said they were great! Look what they did!" they cried as if it was entirely my fault.

For them, Yosemite was burning down, and I was being held responsible as if I had encouraged the thunder and lightning to come each night. In truth, I did feel somewhat guilty.

We went to Yosemite the following spring, just for the day. We hiked around the area that had been on fire the previous summer, and we all cried at the loss of the beautiful trees. Yosemite is the most beautiful place on earth, and there was a huge area on the side of a mountain that was now barren and full of burned trees. I tried explaining to my children that it was nature's way of cleaning house, but they didn't care. There was too much loss. Every once in a while, one of my children will bring up that summer and the thunderstorms, and they will all turn on me again as if I was the mastermind behind that natural disaster.

My husband and I are very sound sleepers. We have slept through 6.0 earthquakes, children sneaking into our room to snatch the car keys out of my purse, and once we slept through a powerful thunderstorm. One night in particular, there was probably the most fantastic thunderstorm ever seen in human existence. I only know about it because there was an unbelievable color picture on the front page of the newspaper the next morning taken from the foothills by our house of three full-blown lightning strikes hitting simultaneously. The picture was incredible, and I stared at it with awe. I couldn't believe that I had slept through the whole thing. I didn't even know it was supposed to rain.

I guess it is only appropriate that I now live in the lightning capital of the world. There are more than 1,000,000 lightning strikes each year in the state of Florida with most occurring in the summer months. I cannot get my mother to leave California and visit me during this time of year. She believes that all Floridians have an alligator in their backyard and hurricanes hit the state every week.

"Mom," I try to reason with her, "I have only seen alligators at the zoo, and in the seventeen years that I have lived here, we have not taken a direct hit by a hurricane. Besides, if a hurricane were to come this way, we always have plenty of notice to get out of the way. In California, you never know when an earthquake is going to hit."

She's not afraid of earthquakes, but hurricanes terrify her. It's true! When you live in California, you don't think about earthquakes. I never did. When I go back to visit now though, they are always on my mind, and I ask God to wait until I leave if the "Big One" is coming.

I love the thunderstorms that come almost every day during the summer months. The storms usually come across the Tampa Bay and make their way toward the west coast of Florida. The anticipation while watching the storms move across the bay toward us is exciting. The air is dead still, and, all of a sudden, a cool breeze kicks up and you know you have only a few short seconds before the heavens open and it begins to pour. The storms in Florida are strange though. Jessica lived in Pinellas Park, a small city just north of St. Petersburg. She lived just three miles from my house. Jessica would often call me during a storm, commenting on the lightning and amount of rain falling. There were many times I felt cheated.

"I can see the lightening and hear the thunder, but it's hasn't rained a drop," I would complain.

I began to protest that there must be some kind of force field around my house keeping the rain away. I could be at the grocery store just a couple of blocks from my house, and it would be raining cats and dogs, but not a drop of rain would fall at my house. It became a running joke between Jessica and I. One afternoon, Jessica was at the local Wal-Mart, and it was raining so hard she was soaked to the core. Wal-Mart is also just a couple of blocks from my house, so Jessica thought she would test my theory. She drove by my house, and, sure enough, it wasn't raining.

Jessica loves to tell anyone visiting from another state the story of "The Year of the Flood" as she calls it. Jessica's husband was driving Jessica home from work. They had just picked Rachel up from day care when the rain began to pour down in buckets. Trying to avoid the typical street flooding that occurs during these storms, Jessica's husband decided to drive down back streets the remainder of the way home. Not being as familiar with the back streets, he plowed through an intersection with standing water and the car stalled out.

Jessica called me on her cell phone, "Mom, my car is stuck in water. It's raining so hard, and the water is already halfway up my car door! What do I do?" she cried.

"You need to get out of your car and push it to higher ground. Do you see anywhere around you where the ground isn't flooded?" I inquired.

"There's a church across the street where I can see the parking lot," she replied.

I told her to try and get her car there. She couldn't open her car door because the water was so high, so she climbed out the window. By this time, the water was up to the door handle, and she was terrified that her car would be submerged in a matter of minutes. As her husband steered the car, Jessica pushed it to the church parking lot. Eventually the rain stopped; the water subsided; the car started, and they made it home.

Once they were home and Rachel was taken out of the car seat in the back, Jessica was able to inspect the inside of the car more thoroughly. Jessica called me again, "Mom, do you have a wet/dry vac?" she asked very calmly.

"Sure. Did you get water in your car?" I asked.

"The water in my car was up to the car seats. Most of it came out when I opened the car door, but I have to get the rest of it out," Jessica explained.

She spent the rest of the evening and most of the night trying to dry her car out. The next day was hot as all summer days are in Florida, so when Jessica got to work, she left the windows down in her car to expedite the drying process. I called her later that afternoon, and we got lost in the conversation of the thunderstorm currently ripping through the area when Jessica screamed, "Mom, I have to go! The windows are down in my car!"

She called back a few minutes later, "Mom, can I keep the wet/dry vac for another night?"

My granddaughter, Rachel, is terrified of thunderstorms. When she is at my house and a storm hits in the early evening, she will be fine as long as I am with her to provide comfort. When a storm comes in the middle of the night, I am grateful that she sleeps like the dead. She is like her mother who is like me; we are all very sound sleepers. When one hits before she goes to sleep, I usually have to hold her and comfort her until it passes. During one storm, I asked Rachel why she didn't like thunderstorms.

"It's not that I don't like the thunder," she explained. "It's just that I like the thunder that doesn't make any noise."

When I tell people that I am originally from California, they all ask me the same question, "Which state do you like more?"

"There are things I like about both," is generally my reply.

California has gorgeous mountains and beautiful highways that go up and down the coast. The weather is fabulous. They have Yosemite. There's a little Mexican deli in downtown San Jose on 10th and Empire that has the best *chili verde burritos* in the world. There's a See's candy store in every mall. But Florida has the thunderstorms.

WHAT WE HAVE HERE IS A FAILURE TO COMMUNICATE

Communicating with your kids is never easy. Most times, you feel like you're talking to a brick wall. On rare occasions, you think you were really effective only to discover that what you said went in one ear and out the other. My parents communicated with me differently than I communicated with my children. And my children communicate differently with their children than I communicated with them. And so it goes. Each generation works to hone their skills to be more effective communicators than the previous generation.

When I was a child, my parents had the philosophy that children were to be seen and not heard. So when we had a question, we were usually dismissed without any real explanation. It is no wonder to me that I grew up very naïve and uninformed. There were many reasons my parents didn't communicate with us. The main one I think was that their parents didn't communicate with them, so they didn't know how.

There are so many ways to communicate with children: by example, yelling, talking, threatening, sarcasm, lecturing, and the list goes on. I've used them all. But one of my biggest objections to parent/child communication is that parents often think that children are too young to understand complex issues.

It leaves the child to draw their own conclusion to a problem, question, or issue that may not be accurate.

Our next-door neighbor, Jackie, was a wonderful woman. She and her husband never had any children of their own, so, consequently, she loved all the children in our neighborhood. We all loved her, too. When I was about 7 years old, Jackie had a mental breakdown. My parents just told us that Jackie was sick and in the hospital. They didn't specify what kind of sick. I'm sure they thought we were too young to understand the illnesses of the mind. Since we were only told that she was in a hospital, I assumed she was just physically ill and probably had an operation. I knew of no other kind of illness. I only knew that she was gone a long time, and when she came home, she gave my mother pillows she had knitted while in the hospital. I thought the hospital she went to must have been really cool to teach you how to knit stuff. I remember thinking that if I ever got sick and had to go to the hospital, I wanted to go to the one she went to so they could teach me how to knit too.

Jackie wasn't home long before she took a shotgun, and, while lying on her bed, she pulled the trigger with her toe and died. I only knew these details by adult conversations I had overheard. Again, my parents didn't explain to us about taking one's own life, so, for a long time, I believed it had been an accident.

My mother took us to the mortuary for Jackie's viewing and to say good-bye to her. I was seven years old, and it was the first time I had ever seen a dead person. I was a little scared, but I touched her hand anyway. Gosh! Was she cold! After saying our good-byes, we turned away from the casket. Jackie's mother immediately approached my mother and asked if Jackie had said anything to her. I was horrified, and I wondered, *Was she crazy? How could she think that Jackie could talk to my mother when she was lying dead in her casket?*

Her question terrified me to the core of my being. I'd heard rumors from various adults that Jackie had been crazy. Her mother sounded pretty crazy to me, too. It wasn't until I was a grown woman and reflected on the incident that I realized what Jackie's mother had meant.

But my parents never really talked to us about Jackie, her illness, and death. As a child, it was hard to understand what had happened and why she had done it. I came to my own conclusion, right or wrong, that she was playing with the gun and wanted to see if she could really pull the trigger with her toe. And she could.

Mental illness and dying were not the only subjects which were taboo for my parents. When I was growing up, the "hot" subjects were pretty much the same as they are today: drugs and sex. But there are several venues to obtain that information which weren't available when I was growing up: radio, TV, and the Internet. Television and radio were around, but it wasn't the same as it is today. My grandparents would die of a heart attack if they watched television today. I am often offended by what I see on, of all things, commercials! Of course, not all commercials are offensive. We see ads on television every day that really try to help: "Talk to your kids about drugs. Talk to your kids about smoking. Talk to your kids about sex." In the '60s, parents didn't ever communicate with their children about any of these things. My mother, to this day, whispers as she spells the word S-E-X to me as if I am still a little girl.

"Mom, you can say the word. I won't turn into a pillar of salt. I've heard the word before, and I even know what it is. Mom, I *am* the mother of four children, for goodness sake."

The first time I heard the word "marijuana" was the summer between my fifth and sixth grade year of school. The news was on the TV, and my mother was in the kitchen cooking dinner. There had been an arrest, and someone was going to jail because of marijuana. I went into the kitchen and asked my mother what marijuana was.

"It's an illegal drug. Now go and play," she responded.

I left the kitchen still wanting to know what marijuana was. The only drugs I knew were medicine. What did she mean when she said it is an illegal drug? How could medicine be illegal? Did it somehow break the law? What crime did it commit? I think my mother was as unsure of what marijuana was as I. I believe now that she had told me all that she knew. She lived a very sheltered life.

Communicating with my own children was a little different. When I wasn't sure of an answer, I just made one up.

"Mommy, why is the sky blue?" Jennifer asked one day.

"Because it is the prettiest color," I replied as one with complete scientific knowledge on the subject.

I found that other family members also made stories up to explain things they didn't understand. One Easter night, my sister, Mary, was at our house. Joey asked his Aunt Mary where the Easter Bunny lived. He knew Santa lived at the North Pole, but no one had ever told him where the Easter Bunny goes when it isn't Easter.

Mary took both Jennifer and Joey outside and pointed up into the sky. "See the moon up there?" she asked them. "The Easter Bunny lives on the moon, looking down on you all year long, just waiting for Easter to come so he can give all the little children candy, toys, and eggs."

My kids were full of wonder and amazement. They had no idea the Easter Bunny had been watching them their whole lives. To this day, my children talk to their children about the Easter Bunny living on the moon. And the legend continues.

But as I said, communicating with children can be accomplished in many ways. Communicating truthfully with your children is not always the best way to go. It can be hurtful. Jessica learned to speak at a very early age, and from the moment of her first word, she continued to talk nonstop. She would follow me around the house while I was cleaning and tell me anything and everything that popped into her little head. At the dinner table, she dominated the conversation. It was constant. No one else could get a word in. I hate to admit it, but when I had things weighing heavily on my mind occasionally while we were in the car, I turned the radio up so I wouldn't have to listen to her. Sometimes I just needed to hear my own thoughts. We got into the car one day to go to the store, and before I could get the radio volume turned up, she asked, "Mommy, do I talk too much?"

Oh, how I wanted to tell her, "Yes you do, all the time. It drives me crazy." But I wouldn't hurt her for anything. So what I said was, "No, honey, you just have a lot to say."

Then there's communication through sarcasm, one of my favorites. When Jessica was in a bad mood, watch out! The whole world knew it. One Saturday morning when Jessica was about 9 years old, she was in one of her moods — as I called them. She was being rude to just about everyone in the house, and no one knew why. Joey and Jeffrey were in the family room watching TV when Jessica came in and began her tirade. The boys just looked at me as Jessica walked out of the room.

"What's wrong with her?" Joey asked no one in particular.

"Oh, don't pay any attention to her. She's just on her period," I stated matter-of-factly.

Both boys dropped their jaw and looked at me, eyes wide open.

"Really?" Jeffrey asked.

"No, I'm just kidding," I laughed. "Geez! She's only 9 years old!"

Jessica, however, had overheard my comment and didn't find it the least bit amusing. In fact, I don't think I have ever seen her as angry at me as she was at that moment. Sometimes my kids just didn't have a sense of humor.

As my children got older, they started making up stories to me.

"Where have you been?" I would ask one of them when they were late getting home from school.

"Oh, just taking the long way home," they would reply.

And the bad thing was, I believed them as much as they believed me when they were small. When Jennifer was in the 8th grade, we had an interesting conversation over the dinner dishes one night. I had asked about her day, and she went on to tell me the most incredibly fantastic story. I stood there, stunned, holding a plate in midair under the faucet as she relayed a chain of freak accidents that had befallen her classmates that day. The graphic details of these accidents were vivid and bizarre. Just as she finished her story, Joey walked in the kitchen and caught the tail end of her recital.

"Ask Joey," she said. "He was there."

Joey began to chuckle.

"She's just pulling your chain, Mom," Joey responded. "She made the whole thing up."

They both burst into laughter at my expense. I felt so violated. She had sucked me into her extraordinary story, and I had hung on her every word. Jennifer has always been a great storyteller, and I should have known better.

Communicating authority to my children was always a challenge. There is a fine line between instilling fear and teaching respect. All four of my children had the responsibility of washing the dishes one day a week. The other three days were mine. Jeffrey struggled each day it was his turn to wash the dishes. I don't know why he complained so much. We had a dishwasher. All he had to do was empty the dishwasher, put the dirty ones in, and wipe down the counters. But each week it was a hassle. He always acted as if everyone in the house sat around making a mess while he had the sole responsibility of cleaning it everyday. One afternoon, he was complaining so much I just told him to get out of the house and I'd do the dishes myself. It was a beautiful spring day and all the windows were open, letting in the fresh, clean air. Jeffrey stepped outside, and not realizing the windows were opened, he called me a name under his breath but loud enough for me to hear. I ran to the front door and almost tore it off its hinges. Jeffrey saw me and took off running. I yelled at him to come back, but he just kept on going. I didn't run after him. Experience told me I would never catch him. I figured he'd come home before too long. A couple of hours later, I received a phone call from his best friend's mother.

"Jeffrey is at my house and wants to come home, but he is afraid to," she said to me with the lightness in her voice that told me she perfectly understood what had happened.

"Tell him it's okay. I'm coming to pick him up," I replied.

I hung up the phone and reflected on a couple of things. First, Jeffrey's best friend Greg lived in another city a good 5 miles from our house. *Had he walked all that way by himself?* I was concerned about that. *He could have been hit by a car or grabbed by a child molester.* Second, my son was afraid to come home. I was glad he understood that what he had done was wrong, but I felt terrible that he was afraid to come home. I picked Jeffrey up at Greg's, and we talked all the way home about respect and his responsibility to wash the dishes one day each week. I also told him how sorry I was that he felt afraid to come home. We both agreed to work on correcting these issues.

My grandchildren have the same curiosity about what they don't understand. The older they get, the tougher the questions become. Children are much more sophisticated now than when I was young, and the ideas and thoughts that go through their heads are more complicated. I spent the evening with Jennifer's family several years ago. It was Morgan's bedtime, and I went into her room and laid with her on her bed. We talked about school and her friends.

She turned to me with a question weighing heavy on her mind, "Grandma, what happens when you die?" she asked.

I started with the old standby, "You go to Heaven."

But she stopped me, "No. What really happens to your body?" rephrasing her question.

"Do you mean *physically*?" I asked.

"I want to know what happens to your body. Where do they put it? What do they do with it? What happens to it?" she clarified.

I was a little taken aback by the morbid question this 6 year old was asking me, but I would give it the old college try. I went on to explain about morgues, mortuaries, embalming, fixing the hair and make-up, funerals, cemeteries, and even cremation. Morgan seemed satisfied with my answers.

When I told Jennifer about our conversation, she was aghast, "You didn't really tell her all that stuff, did you?" Jennifer pleaded.

"What was I supposed to tell her?" I asked. "Just make something up?"

Jennifer immediately cut me to the quick, "That's what you did whenever we asked you something."

"Yeah," I countered, "but I knew the answer to this one."

Now that Jennifer's kids are a little older, she explains everything to them. She doesn't pull any punches. They are the most well-informed children I know. Morgan, who is 13 years old, is a D.A.R.E. (Drug Abuse Resistance Education) graduate. She knows more about drugs than I ever did. Jennifer has taught them all about sex offenders and child predators, what to watch for, and what to do if someone they don't know approaches them. There isn't a question they can't ask her that she will not give them an honest and thorough answer. This can have consequences you're not fully prepared for, like times they try to educate their peers or other family members on subjects where they have become experts.

One day, Jessica was taking Rachel and Hunter, who were both 7 years old at the time, to Busch Gardens for the afternoon. While on their way, Hunter innocently asked Rachel a simple question, "Rachel, do you know what abortion is? If you don't, I can tell you."

"Whoa! Whoa! Whoa!" Jessica interjected quickly. "Let's talk about the rides we're going to go on when we get to Busch Gardens."

Rachel is not as inquisitive as Hunter, and Jessica is not as direct as Jennifer.

Explaining our own childhood and events from our past often seems barbaric and medieval to my grandchildren. Morgan was listening to the radio one afternoon a couple of years ago when a song by Madonna came on. Morgan knew the song and was singing along when she came across a word, the meaning of which she didn't know.

"Mommy," Morgan asked, "what's a record?"

Jennifer proceeded to explain that when she was younger there were no CDs. Music was recorded on a record — a large, thin, black disk that required a needle and turntable. Morgan was in awe of this description, and Jennifer went on to tell her that this was a long time ago, before people had computers and the Internet. Morgan became thoroughly confused.

"Mommy, if there weren't any computers, how did people get their e-mails?"

She was just too young to understand.

Communicating an upcoming event can also be a challenge. Small children take you at your word and don't understand that sometimes things come up and plans change. Allison was 3 ½ years old when her younger sister, Sophia, was born. To include Allison in the upcoming event, during the last month of her pregnancy, my daughter-in-law, Kristine, made a paper chain to count down the days until Sophia was due. Each day, Kristine and Allison tore a link off the chain and would count how many days were left. Allison was so excited, watching as the day got closer and closer. But Sophia had her own timetable. Sophia was due to arrive on the 18th of the month, but Kristine went into labor on the morning of the 15th. Allison woke up that morning as Jeffrey and Kristine were preparing to leave for the hospital. Kristine told Allison that it was time for Sophia to be born and that she was going to the hospital to have her new baby sister. That statement was very unsettling to Allison. She ran into the kitchen to retrieve the chain.

"But, Mommy, there's still three links left on the chain! You can't have Sophia now; it's not time yet! You have to wait three more days!"

I went to visit my son, Jeffrey, his wife Kristine, and my granddaughters Allison, Elaina, and brand-new Sophia. While Kristine fed Sophia in the bedroom, Jeffrey bathed Allison and Elaina. I hung out with my son and granddaughters in the bathroom. My own children's father had never given any of my children a bath, so I was in complete awe that my son took on the responsibility of bath time. Jeffrey dressed his girls after their bath, and they went back into the bathroom to brush their teeth.

"Kristine," Jeffrey called, "is there some new toothpaste? The one in their cup is all gone."

You could hear it in Kristine's voice, "Jeffrey... if the toothpaste in the cup is all gone, then Allison needs a spanking. I just bought that tube of toothpaste. It's the kind that doesn't have fluoride in it, so it's really expensive. Allison was warned several times not to eat it."

I had to smile. I never knew a child who loved toothpaste as, apparently, Allison did. Jeffrey began to fill me in on the toothpaste problem with Allison. Evidently, eating toothpaste was a favorite pastime of Allison's, and she didn't seem to understand the concept of "Don't eat the toothpaste." During his explanation, Jeffrey handed Allison a brush to brush her hair.

When she was finished with her hair, Allison gave herself one more look in the mirror and turned to her father, "Daddy, I'm ready for my spanking now."

There wasn't an ounce of fear or trepidation in her voice. She could just as easily have said, "Daddy, I'm ready for my tea party now."

Jeffrey looked at me with an expression of defeat on his face and managed a smile. He walked Allison into her room and came back out a minute later.

"She laughed at me! She's three years old — and she laughed at me. I guess I'm going to have to use a new approach. I don't think she fully understands the concept of a spanking as a means of punishment."

Allison is the daughter of two engineers, so it is only natural for her to think in a logical and methodical way. One evening when Jeffrey came home from work, Kristine told Jeffrey of her day, specifically of their four-year-old Allison, "You need to talk to her, Jeff. Allison was very rude to me today. She is starting to talk back to me, too. We need to put on a united front and nip this in the bud now."

Jeffrey called Allison into the room and began reprimanding her, "Allison, you will not talk back to Mommy. She is your mother, and you will show her respect at all times whether or not you like or agree with what she is saying. She is not only your mother, but she is my wife, and I don't ever want to hear about you talking back to my wife again. Do you understand me?"

Allison thought very carefully for a moment before answering, "Daddy, maybe you should get a different wife."

Yeah, Allison is an extremely logical little girl. That solution made perfect sense — to her anyway.

Then there are those moments in time that you wish you could freeze, moments of total communication between two hearts. Before Christien was born, Jennifer became pregnant with another baby. When she was about thirteen weeks along in the pregnancy, she miscarried. By that time, we had all come to love that precious, unborn baby. The loss devastated all of us. Morgan had prayed that Jennifer would give her a baby sister, so Morgan asked if she could name the baby that was lost. Not knowing the baby's gender, Morgan named her Katie, and that unborn baby has been Katie to us ever since. We speak of Katie from time to time, and she holds a special place in all our hearts. One evening, Hunter was sitting with his father, Manuel, and they were just sharing some quality time with each other. Hunter looked up into Manuel's eyes and asked out of the clear blue, "Would Katie have liked me?"

Manuel was so touched by Hunter's question that tears immediately filled his eyes as he answered, "She would have *loved* you."

THE CURSE OF THE MOMMY

Most mothers put a curse on their children that goes something like this: *"I hope that when you grow up you have kids just as rotten as you are."* I know that my mother said that to me many times, and I passed the curse on down to my own kids. And it works! I argued with my mother and talked back to her disrespectfully many times. Each time, she would utter that curse back to me as if she were making a cross with her fingers out in front of her to ward off the evil I was perpetrating. I didn't put that curse on my children out loud or to their face, but I did think it really hard, as if by telepathy I could send the message and the curse would get through somehow. My children exasperated me endlessly. I wished, hoped, and prayed that when they became parents they would fully come to know the meaning of the word "parent", and, to my joy, it happened one night.

Jennifer's husband Manuel works from home, so he is usually there to relieve her when the kids have pushed her to "that" point. However, one night Manuel was out of town on business. This left Jennifer to take care of the kids all by herself without a break or any kind of relief. She called me on the phone that night. She didn't respond to my "hello" but went straight to her reason for calling, "I have just one question for you," she began. "How did you keep from killing us when we were small?"

The tone of her voice said it all. She couldn't see it, but I had a huge, satisfied grin on my face as I replied, "It wasn't easy."

The curse doesn't kick in for a while after you become a parent. Babies are sweet, innocent creatures who warm your heart. It isn't until your children start their own fight for independence that the curse begins. When my children became parents themselves for the first time, I watched them with their own children, and a sense of pride and awe overtook me. I completely forgot about the curse — for a while.

Although Hunter and Christien were born in Florida and I was present at each of their births, Morgan, the oldest, was born in California. Jennifer moved to England shortly after her birth, and I didn't see Morgan for the first time until she was 9 months old. I flew to England just to see her. I would have gone anywhere in the world to hold her in my arms. After all, Morgan was the one who had made me a Grandmother. Jennifer met me at the airport in England, and I immediately whisked Morgan from Jennifer's arms, barely acknowledging Jennifer. Morgan, who wasn't keen on strangers, began to cry and turned to Jennifer with her arms outstretched. I watched as Jennifer gently calmed her.

Later, I was mesmerized as I watched Jennifer feed, bathe, rock, and cuddle my new granddaughter. When did this immature, rebellious, irresponsible young teenager become a grown woman? Wasn't she the one who had argued with me constantly? Didn't we butt heads over everything? I stared at her in wonder and delight. She was an adult, a mother. Life was no longer about her. Jennifer's life now revolved around Morgan, and it was beautiful to behold.

I went to Oregon to see my oldest son Joey, his wife Karen, and their first newborn Jordan. I watched as my little boy who was 32 years old make his own son smile and coo by asking Jordan in a high-pitched baby voice, "What's your name?" I watched him sing *The Star Spangled Banner* to Jordan, a song he used to sing for our amusement and enjoyment in a deep adult voice at home when he was just a little boy. It was overwhelming to me. I was filled with such joy and amazement that this man, my son, who had stretched my patience to the limit, who had tested my resolve at every turn, who had gotten into more trouble than the other three put together, had truly become a sweet, loving, and tender father. This was a man who had struggled with his own demons and had come out on top. The pride in my heart that I feel for him is immeasurable.

Some of the first pictures Jeffrey sent to me via e-mail of his first newborn Allison were taken right in the delivery room. Kristine was covered in sweat, and her hair was slicked back from it, a consequence of being in labor for nearly thirty-six hours. But she was smiling, with her face all aglow, as she held Allison in her arms for the first time. It was the picture of Jeffrey, though, that caught my eye. My son, the man who since the age of 4 years old knew exactly what he wanted out of life and remained true and focused on those goals, had tears flowing down his cheeks.

It reminded me of the day he and Kristine married. As Kristine walked down the aisle, and every eye was on her, my husband whispered in my ear, "Look at your son." My eyes left Kristine and I looked at Jeffrey, so handsome in his tux. There he stood, barely able to contain himself, crying his eyes out at the beauty of his soon-to-be wife and the momentous occasion that had brought us all together that day. As I stared at the picture Jeffrey sent of his new family, I realized that he was now a father, a parent himself. I knew in my heart that Allison was a lucky little girl and that she would have her daddy wrapped around her little finger in no time at all.

At times, Jessica could be somewhat moody as a child. She really radiated motherhood, though, in every sense of the word, on the day Rachel was born.

Jessica had been having contractions all weekend long and didn't know it. She still had a couple of months to go in her pregnancy, and the doctor kept telling her it was her uterus stretching. Never once did he feel compelled to check her out just to make sure. When Jessica could no longer handle the pain, she went to the hospital just to get a shot to help relieve it. After a brief exam, she was told that she was dilated to seven and in active labor. Rachel was born about an hour and a half later, nine weeks early. It was such a scary night, and hundreds of prayers went up to God for Rachel's safety and strength for Jessica to deal with whatever came over the next several weeks.

We were all told by the doctor to expect the worst, but Rachel came out screaming. Although she was so tiny, her medical problems were not life threatening. My little girl, my baby, stayed right by Rachel's side, in charge, in control, being strong, and taking each day at a time. All our prayers were answered, and Jessica just couldn't wait for the day Rachel would be released from the hospital so she could begin her own journey as a new mother. Jessica was so amazing through it all.

My grandchildren are getting older now, and The *Curse of the Mommy* has begun to show. Bill Cosby did a stand up years ago and talked about this very thing. He mentioned how when he had children of his own, his parents would come over and just sit on the couch with smiles on their faces at the pandemonium going on around them. This has happened with my children as well, and I can't help but do the same thing. Children try their parents each and every day. It is a miracle that as parents we survive it all. We do survive, though, just so we can watch the very children who wreaked havoc in our homes and lives go through the same things with their own children.

My sister, Dianne, and her husband Doyle came to visit us one year when Morgan was about 5 years old. We all went to the park to watch Morgan, Hunter, and Rachel play. Hunter and Rachel were about a year and a half old and were not yet at *that* age. When it was time to leave, Morgan refused to go. She was not ready to leave the park and the fun she was enjoying. Jennifer pleaded and then threatened Morgan, but she still wouldn't come. We all began to walk away toward the car, thinking that Morgan wouldn't want to stay at the park alone and would decide to follow us, but she stood her ground. Jennifer finally turned around and headed for Morgan with fury in her eyes. My brother-in-law, Doyle, God bless him, couldn't resist the opportunity, "Morgan, RUN!" he shouted.

Although Jennifer didn't think her Uncle Doyle was the least bit amusing, Dianne and I almost fell to the ground while laughing hysterically. We had both been there before. We have all had a child who at some point in time had been stubborn and obstinate, a child who couldn't be reasoned with, a child who you just knew had to be brain dead. Dianne and I thought it was just incredibly wonderful to watch that same child who had been difficult and stubborn when she was a little girl grow up and have one of her own who was just as stubborn and obstinate. I'm telling you; the curse works!

TIMING IS EVERYTHING

When you think about it, timing is everything, for buying low, selling high, getting in on the ground floor, deciding the appropriate time to have a baby, getting married, retiring, and the list goes on. These are life-altering decisions. There are other moments, though, when timing counts as well. There are times we say the wrong thing at the worst possible time.

We lived on a family-friendly street where everyone knew everyone. Our houses were small and pretty close together, so, consequently, if you were a fighting couple, chances were the whole neighborhood knew about it. Jackie and Earl, our next-door neighbors, were such a couple. My two sisters and I shared a bedroom together. Dianne, who was the oldest, had a twin bed on the wall shared with the living room. Mary and I slept in a full-size bed that was under the window opposite Jackie and Earl's kitchen. Los Angeles was generally warm, so we usually kept that window open at night. Jackie and Earl fought just about every night, and this exchange ALWAYS took place in their kitchen. I remember very few specifics about their fights, probably because I was too young to understand, but I do remember their loud, angry voices. My sisters and I almost looked forward to their fights each night. We would laugh at their arguments and just the fact that they did it all the time.

They fought so much that they made my parents look like *Ozzie and Harriet.*

After I got home from school one day, I found a note from my mother saying that she was at Jackie's house having coffee. I proceeded to go over to our neighbor's house just to let my mother know I was home. She was getting ready to leave Jackie's house anyway, so I stayed and waited for her. While we were on the porch steps and they were saying their goodbyes, Jackie mentioned something about having an argument with Earl the night before.

I took that opportunity to interject my own experiences about their fights, "I know. I hear you and Earl fighting every night through my bedroom window," I boasted.

My mother turned every shade of red there was. She turned to me in complete embarrassment. "Honey, what are you talking about? You must be dreaming about your father and I fighting. You can't possibly hear what goes on in the house next door," my mother said, trying to find a way out of her embarrassment

"Sure I do. Last night they were fighting about how she burned his dinner. Boy was he mad! I think he even called her the 'B' word," I insisted.

My mother profusely apologized to Jackie for my remarks and hurried me home as fast as she could. My bedroom window was shut and locked after that, never to be opened again.

My own children have certainly done their part to embarrass me. During my son Joey's Sunday School class one Sunday morning, his teacher asked each of the children to name someone who was important to them and who needed prayers. A list was made by the children, and his lovely teacher gave a prayer up to God for all the people on that list. My son was so excited and proud of what he had asked God for that he couldn't wait until class was over. He ran to me after class and told me he'd done something wonderful for me. He told me that he had asked for a prayer for me in Sunday School.

"You did? Thank you, Joey. You're such a wonderful son. What was your prayer request?"

Joey's smile was a mile wide. I couldn't help but be in awe of such a beautiful person as my 10-year-old son was becoming.

"I asked for God to help you quit smoking," he beamed.

I froze. No one at church knew that I smoked. I never wanted to admit to anyone who didn't already know that I was a smoker. I was ashamed of my dirty habit. I went to church, for goodness sake! People who went to church and loved God didn't smoke. A person's body was a temple. I was defiling the temple that God gave me. I hated that I smoked. I hated the thought that anyone at church knew I smoked. I was humiliated. I was afraid to face my son's Sunday School teacher, afraid of what she now thought of me. I avoided her for months at church hoping that as time went on she'd forget which child had the mother who smoked. I thanked my son again from the bottom of my heart. At the time, I hoped that God was listening, because I really did need help. I have since kicked that habit with God's help, and I'm now a non-smoker. But I did smoke cigarettes for many years before I quit.

My grandchildren have had their turns at humiliating their parents, too. It's in those moments I take great delight. Right after Livvy turned 3 years old, we had a potluck luncheon at our church after the morning service. We have the typical fellowship hall with the long tables that can seat about six people to a side. Livvy, Rachel, and Jessica sat across the table from Grandpa and I. Next to me sat a very sweet man. Unfortunately for him, he sat directly across from Livvy. She looked so pretty that day, so innocent and sweet. He smiled at her, which was probably the worst thing he could have done.

"You look like an alien," Livvy said to him matter-of-factly. She wasn't trying to be mean, she was just stating what she thought was a fact.

He spoke so softly that I didn't hear his response. I did hear Jessica "shush" Livvy though.

Apparently Livvy didn't hear her mommy, because she spoke a little louder, "You look like an alien," she said again, as if the people at the next table hadn't quite heard her the first time.

He only smiled, and Jessica was the one who spoke.

"Livvy, don't say that. It's not nice. You need to use your manners."

"But, Mommy," Livvy protested even louder, "he looks like an *alien!*"

She said this as though it was so obvious and we were just too blind to see it. I was so grateful at that moment that Livvy was not my child, but I felt the humiliation for my daughter. It's funny when it's not your own child. I had difficulty containing my laughter. I got up from the table to walk outside. Jessica meekly apologized to the gentleman and followed my lead outside while dragging Livvy behind her. We are trying to keep Livvy away from this humble man until she is 30 years old and learns that she doesn't always have to say what she thinks.

That was not the only incident where Livvy's timing was "perfect" at church. One Saturday I had been really busy. I had been going the entire day. Rachel and Livvy had gone to bed at 9:30. Once I got the girls to bed, I called my mother. We spoke on the phone until 11:00.

"Mom, I have to go. I still have to iron Livvy's dress for church tomorrow, do the dishes, sew up a hole in one of Livvy's stuffed animals, and prepare for my Sunday School class in the morning."

At 11:30 Jennifer called, and we spoke until 12:30. By the time I got to bed, it was 1:30 in the morning and I had to get up at 7:00 A.M.. My husband Dennis woke up at 6:00, got out of bed, and began making his coffee, which woke up the girls. They came into my room to wake me up.

I was so tired, but I got up and was in the shower when I heard Livvy call me, "Grandma, come and find me!" she teased.

I was in no mood for play so early in the morning with so little sleep.

"Livvy!" I shouted over the water running, "I'm in the shower! I can't come! Could you please come here?"

Livvy immediately came into my bathroom.

"Sweetheart, Grandma is taking a shower right now, and I'm a little cranky. I haven't had much sleep. I'm so tired that I will probably fall asleep in church today. When I get out of the shower, I will feel much better, and I'll make you a wonderful breakfast. Okay?"

Livvy was a doll and waited patiently for me to get out of the shower. I made the girls pancakes, scrambled eggs, fresh strawberries, and chocolate milk for breakfast, which is what they usually liked to have on Sunday mornings. I got them dressed, fixed their hair in pigtail braids, and we went to church. After Sunday School, we went into the auditorium for our church service. During the main Morning Prayer, Livvy remembered something I had told her earlier that morning. She always picks the time when there is dead silence in the church to make her announcements. Apparently, she likes an audience and wants to make sure everyone is listening.

In her usual loud voice so everyone could hear she said,

"Grandma, you forgot that you were going to fall asleep in church today!"

I thank God each and every day for my church family. No one mentioned Livvy's little reminder to me.

My grandchildren don't just say the wrong thing at the wrong time *about* me, they also say the wrong thing at the wrong time *to* me. My father told me once that when a person becomes an adult they gain ten pounds every decade of their life for no apparent reason. However unfair that may be, I found it to be somewhat true. For me, it was more like twenty, though. But it didn't come all at once. It was two pounds one year, and then the next year it would be three pounds. I vaguely remember a time when I really was a thin person. Actually, the only reason I can remember that far back is because I have pictures. Four kids and a lot of chocolate changed all that. I love my Pepsi and chocolate. It's my indulgence, my vice.

I have admitted my weaknesses for a reason. Friday night was typically soccer night for my grandsons. I was at one of Hunter's soccer games, and someone's children were really misbehaving.

Jennifer began to question me about her own children, "Do you think my kids behave like that?"

"Jennifer," I replied, laughing a little, "your kids are the most well-mannered children I have ever known. They are so polite and respectful. When you had dinner at my house the other night, I asked Hunter if he'd had enough to eat. He told me, 'Yes, I did. Thank you very much for asking.' You can't get much more polite than that."

I was going on and on about my lovely grandchildren and their manners, when Christien walked up and so innocently asked me, "Grandma, do you have a baby in your tummy?"

If a question like that doesn't scream, "YOU NEED TO DIET," I don't know what does.

Children are so innocent with their remarks sometimes, and that's what makes them funny. If a statement or remark was rehearsed or planned, it wouldn't be funny. In 1995, Jennifer gave birth to Morgan during a previous marriage, and she and her husband divorced shortly after Morgan's first birthday. Morgan's biological father pretty much left her life completely after that. Jennifer and Morgan moved to Florida at that time, and it was then she met Manuel. They were married about a year and a half later. Manuel is a wonderful husband and father, so we were all thrilled when he legally adopted Morgan a couple of years after their marriage. We celebrate this special day each year.

Manuel was born in the Philippines but came to the United States as a very small boy. On the day the adoption became legal, Jennifer and Manuel threw a huge party. Everyone came to join the celebration. It truly was a special day. During the party, Jennifer teased Morgan a little by asking her how she felt now that she was half-White and half-Filipino.

Morgan innocently replied to her mother and all the guests who were present, "Mommy, I was born in California. I'm half Mexican!"

Although Morgan was very serious in her statement, the house roared with laughter. Morgan hadn't lived in California since she was a little baby. No one knew where she came up with a statement like that, but that's what made it so funny.

As life usually does, the tables have now turned, and it is also my own mother who embarrasses me now. I guess she is paying me back for all the times I embarrassed her when I was a child.

She is 80 now and has begun to take her place in life that I will take someday with my own children — that of the mother becoming the child and the child becoming the mother. On one of her last visits to Florida in 2006, she had flown non-stop to Orlando from San Francisco. It was a two-hour, one-way drive for my brother-in-law, Doyle, to take her to San Francisco and a two-hour, one-way drive for me to pick her up in Orlando. But she's getting old and can get overwhelmed and confused easily, so we didn't want her to change planes at a different airport. San Francisco to Orlando was the closest non-stop flight we could find for Sacramento and Tampa.

After meeting her plane at the airport in Orlando, my mother began telling me all about her flight. She said there was a darling child on board the plane who she had made eye contact with. They had smiled and laughed at each other on and off during the entire flight. As we got to the elevator that took us to the parking garage, two women, one pushing a stroller got on the elevator, too. The child my mother had been talking about was in the stroller. My mother began talking to the women and told them how precious the child was.

"Are you the grandmother?" my mother asked of the woman pushing the stroller.

I cringed. Both women looked as if they were 25-30 years old. Why in the world would my mother think one of them could possibly be the child's grandmother? I was a young grandmother, and neither woman looked even remotely close to the same age as I. They would have to be at least my age to be the child's grandmother.

The woman politely told my mother that she was not the child's grandmother. I couldn't contain myself and began to giggle. Then my crazy mother turned to the other woman, "I'm sorry. Are *you* the grandmother?"

I lost it. I laughed hysterically. I apologized to the women for my mother's obvious mistake and thanked God that I would never see either of the women again. When I was able to regain my composure, I turned to my mother, "Mom, NEVER ask a woman if she is the grandmother! If you really must know, always ask if she is the mother. That way you haven't offended her if she is the mother and you have given her a compliment if she is the grandmother."

My mother gave me her standard "Okay", and that was the end of the conversation about the child.

At church that Sunday, I taught Livvy's age group for Sunday School, and my mother helped me with all the 3-year-old children. There was one child in the class who my mother seemed to be particularly fond of. When the child's mother came after class to get the child, my mother told me she had almost asked her if she was the grandmother.

"Mom! What are you doing to me? I told you to never ask a woman if she is the grandmother of a child she is with. Always ask if she's the mother! Why would you want to insult anyone? I know that woman. I see her at church every Sunday. If you had asked her if she was the grandmother, I would have been so embarrassed. To tell you the truth, Mom, I would've had to tell her I picked you up for the day from a mental institution and you were going back right after lunch. Or maybe I would've told her that I didn't know you or that you had cataracts and couldn't see very well. Why do you need to know who people are, anyway? If you're curious about a person, make up a story in your own mind as to whom or what they are. Do you REALLY need to know if a person is a grandmother?"

A couple of years later, while on my nightly call to my mother, she hesitantly confessed something she had done earlier in the day.

"You're going to die laughing when I tell you what I did today," she began. "I was at the beauty salon, waiting to get my hair done, and there was a woman with a couple of small children waiting, too. The children were playing quietly, when I struck up a conversation with the woman. Curiosity overtook me, and I just had to ask, 'Are you their grandmother?' while nodding to the children. The woman looked at me in disbelief. 'No, I'm their mother,' she answered. Why do I do that?"

My mother was right about one thing; I laughed so hard that tears started rolling down my cheeks.

"All I can say is, I'm so glad I wasn't there. I'm so glad I don't know those people. How can you go back there and show you're face? What if that woman goes there on a regular basis? What possesses you to do such a thing? Do you just never listen to advice? Did you think my advice wasn't good or beneficial? Why do you always think that people are older than what they are? Does it make you feel younger to think they are older? Do you not see that you made that woman go home and feel bad about herself for the rest of the day? Do you know she's probably standing in front of her mirror right now contemplating plastic surgery because some old, insensitive woman insulted her? You're so lucky I'm not your mother!" I scolded through my laughter.

Between my mother and my grandchildren, I may have to start wearing a disguise so no one recognizes me.

Everyone has made a faux pas at some point in their life, something we said out loud that we wish we could take back. But the ones children and even our elders make, however embarrassing they may be, are priceless.

GAMES PEOPLE PLAY

Some families have 'Game Night' once a week, where they get together as a family and play cards or a board game. Not my family. We were a family of freaks. We made up our own games. One of our favorites was played with my father. It sounds bizarre and probably a little sadistic, but for some reason we loved it. The seven of us lived in a very small three-bedroom house. My two sisters and I shared the biggest bedroom. My two brothers shared the next biggest room, and my parents had the smallest. Their bedroom was more the size of a large closet. It had two doors, one leading to the hall and the other leading to the kitchen. This layout made it perfect to run all the way around the house. My father would sit on the bed with his belt in his hand. The object of the game was to see if you could run past the bed without getting spanked with the belt. We would run past my father, around the house, and get back in line for our next turn. What psycho person came up with that game? To this day, I have no idea who started that game, but it was fun! We would try to psych my dad out and mix him up so he wouldn't be prepared when we ran by. He got us every time, yet we continued to play it often.

Another game we loved was a game called "Hard or Easy". This, too, was sadistic, but we would beg my dad to play it. We would lie across his lap, and he would ask, "Hard or easy?" Trying to be tough, I would always start with "Hard, Daddy." Then he would spank me hard. Again he would ask, "Hard or easy?" Determined to outlast my brothers and sisters in this sordid game, I would respond, "HARD, Daddy!" That one was usually the one to make me plead in the next round for an "easy" one.

My father used to chase us around the house, trying to scare us by laughing that evil laugh you sometimes hear on TV. My dad could do that better than anyone. He does it for my grandchildren now, and they love it, too. Sometimes the chasing would get out of hand; someone would run for the door, and we would all follow outside into the street. My dad would come running after us with his arms waving above his head, laughing the evil laugh. One time a neighbor heard us all screaming and saw my dad chasing us. She came running outside and yelled at my father to leave us poor kids alone. What a party pooper she was.

Talking with my brothers and sisters now about these insane games we played, we all agree that it's a wonder we all grew up to be relatively normal and well-adjusted adults. I have told my children about these games, and they are horrified.

"What kind of sadistic household did you live in?" my children have asked. "Where was Child Welfare Services?"

"They were games, not torture," I countered. I guess you just had to be there.

I grew into an ordinary adult, and when my children were old enough, we played games, too. Not like the ones I played as a child, though. My husband and I loved, and I mean *loved*, cards. All kinds of card games. It was one thing that we shared together and had a passion for. We played Cribbage, Hearts, Spades, Pinochle, Rook, and every kind of Poker there was. We taught our kids how to play Poker at a very young age. For my children and I, playing Poker was a time for fun, laughing, and relaxation. For my husband, their father, it was very serious.

There wasn't a time we played that he didn't threaten us all with calling it a night.

"I'm gonna walk," was his favorite phrase.

He had others, but that was his favorite. To this day, whenever a deck of cards are shuffled, one of my children will utter those words, sending us all into fits of laughter.

Jessica was 4 years old and wanted to play Poker with us so much. She always had a knack for being able to keep up with her older brothers and sister, regardless of what we did. We explained to her that, if she played, she would have to learn the game and play on her own as the rest of us did. So we taught her to play Blackjack, and we played frequently as my children grew.

I was not prepared and was caught off guard at my very first parent/teacher conference when Jessica was in kindergarten.

"Did you know that Jessica's math skills are far ahead of all the other kids in her class?" her teacher asked me in amazement. "Did you teach her math during the summer before she started school? What technique did you use?" she wondered.

I had to think about it for a minute. I hadn't worked with Jessica at all on anything. *How did she get to be so good at math?* I wondered. Then it hit me.

"Umm… we play cards," I said to her timidly. "We taught Jessica how to play Blackjack and told her that if she wanted to play, she would have to count her own cards. I had no idea we were actually helping to develop her math skills."

Wow! I was actually teaching my child valuable skills and didn't even know it!

Her teacher responded, "I would never have thought about Blackjack as a learning tool, but she performs very well in math. She can add up to four numbers together."

I chuckled, "Yeah, but I'll bet you a quarter she's only accurate to 21."

My grandchildren love games, too. When Morgan was the only grandchild in the family, we made up games with her. Morgan's favorite was "Monster". An adult would go into the bedroom while everyone else stayed in the living room. The "monster" had to make scary sounds, and someone from the living room had to go into the bedroom and conquer the monster. My son, Jeffrey, was visiting once and joined in the game. Jeffrey decided he would be the one to slay the monster and stood up to go into the bedroom. Although Jeffrey had only been in Florida for a day, Morgan had quickly become very attached to him. In almost hysteria, she immediately responded, "Uncle Jeff, no! Don't go! — Mommy, you go."

Jennifer's children are now old enough, and they have Poker night almost every weekend. I had been invited by my grandchildren to come and play Poker with them one Friday night, and I was very impressed by their knowledge of the game. Morgan is an extremely conservative player. Her bets are small, and I once watched her fold with the winning hand on the table. If Morgan raises, you can count on her having the winning hand. Hunter bets on everything. His desire to win and win big is evident by his lack of Poker chips fifteen minutes into the game. He's a lot like me — always betting on "last card". Christien hasn't developed a desire or taste for Poker yet, but he willingly accepts the role as "go for". He will go for a Pepsi out of the fridge for someone and keep us all updated on the score of the Tampa Bay Rays ballgame currently on TV, however wrong the score may be.

"Christien," Jennifer asked during a hand, "what's the score?"

"Zero to zero," Christien quickly informs us.

"But, Christien, I hear people clapping and shouting. What just happened?" Jennifer inquired.

"I don't know," Christien responded.

Jennifer got up and checked the TV. "Christien, Longoria just hit a home run which scored three runs! Sweetheart, we're counting on you to keep us posted. We have given you this very important job because we have faith that you can handle it. There's no one else. It's a big job. Are you up to the task?"

Christien just was not old enough to understand the importance of playing one game while keeping tabs on another. We were a sports/game family, and we took it all very seriously while at the same time having fun. We've always been good at multi-tasking.

As a grandmother, I have put together puzzles, played board games, played card games, and even taught them dominoes. But what my grandchildren seem to love the most from me are stories. They love to hear about when I was a little girl, when their mommies were little, and when they were babies. They can't seem to get enough. They really enjoy the stories about their mommies doing something naughty and getting in trouble. Hunter is the one who generally asks for the stories first. It's great! I have their undivided attention during these stories, and they hang on my every word. When I am finished, Hunter will turn to his mother with an all-knowing look and the teasing begins.

Rachel loves for me to tell "smooky stories". Originally, the name was "spooky", but one day she got her Ps and Ms mixed up, and they have been smooky stories ever since. EVERY TIME Rachel comes over, she asks to hear a smooky story. Now Livvy asks for them, too. I began the ritual of the smooky story as a way to teach them a moral or a lesson. So my stories are usually somewhat on the scary side about a little girl who does something her mommy or daddy told her not to do and the bad consequences of her actions. It could be about talking to strangers, getting into a car with a stranger, going somewhere without asking, playing with matches, and the list goes on. The child always has something bad happen to her because of her decision to disobey her parents. I usually get pretty graphic in my details and occasionally need to tone it down a little.

Livvy likes me to tell stories about when I was really scared. For her, Grandma getting scared is the ultimate horror story. Her favorite is about the time our family moved to Sacramento when her mommy was almost 3 years old. My husband, Don, worked the graveyard shift and was gone our first night in our new house. I woke in the middle of the night to hear water running somewhere in the house. I thought one of the kids must have gotten up to use the restroom, so I got up to check on them. Everyone was out cold, but the water continued to run. I went through the house in search of where it was coming from when I came to the garage. Someone was in my garage using the water! I called Don at work, but he was more than a half an hour away and told me to call the police. I called the police, and they asked me if I had gone out to the garage to check.

"Are you *NUTS?*" I asked incredulously. "Don't you ever watch any scary movies where the woman goes to a door and the entire audience is screaming at her to not open the door? She opens the door and some deranged maniac tortures and kills her? I'm not opening that door!" I flatly told them.

I sat in my living room in the dark waiting for the police to come. It wasn't long before a man with a flashlight shined it into my window. I let out a scream. Lucky for me it was the police. They went into my garage and found that the water running was just the water softener recycling. I didn't know we had a water softener. You'd think someone would have mentioned that to us when we moved in. If they had, it would have saved the nice taxpayers a few bucks. But this is honestly Livvy's favorite story. I tell it to her every Saturday night and have for almost a year. Rachel is bored to tears with it. She is now at a point where she wonders how Grandma could be so dense that she would think someone would actually break into the garage just to use her water. I have no answer for that.

My grandchildren also have their own games they like to play — the make-believe ones. Hunter and Rachel were at my house one afternoon when they were both 4 years old. They were playing in the backyard where I had a birdbath that was full of water from the previous afternoon's thunderstorm. Hunter and Rachel found some sticks, dirt, and dead leaves and proceeded to put these treasures in the birdbath. They used the sticks to stir their magical concoction. They made such a mess and were covered with mud from head to toe. I had to get my camera to take pictures for future embarrassing moments when they got older. They were having such a great time.

Jennifer and I were on the patio talking and keeping an eye on them when the subject of Hunter came up. We both remarked how Hunter was such a *boy*. He loved nothing better than to play with bugs, climb fences, play in water, and be an all-around daredevil. He was fearless, and we concluded that he had a death wish. We began making jokes about it, laughing, and having a great time at Hunter's expense. Rachel and Hunter, in the meantime, were playing the superheroes, The Powerpuff Girls, Rachel's favorite. In mid-sentence, while talking about how Hunter was just a "boy's boy", we heard Hunter shout, "Rachel, call me Buttercup!"

Rarely can anything bring so much joy to me than watching my grandchildren play together. It doesn't matter what game they've made up to play. It's always entertaining — whether it's the role of "go for" or a superhero.

THE MAGIC OF MUSIC

When you really stop and think about it, music really is magical. It can transport a person to a time and place in their long-forgotten past. It lives inside most of us and is deep in our soul. Many times, a song has lifted my spirits, brought tears to my eyes, or made me laugh. Hearing an old song reminds me of old boyfriends, close friends, lost friends, my children, my grandchildren, and precious moments in my life. A song can make me remember an exact time in my past. It comes on the radio and I immediately think, *Summer 1969*. I can't help but go back to that time and the people I was with.

Jessica was working late one afternoon due to an anniversary celebration event at work, and she had asked if Rachel and Livvy could stay with me until she got off. While on my way to Rachel's school to pick her up, I had my radio tuned to "The Best Of The '80s" when "The Promise" came on by the group, When in Rome. I immediately began thinking about Jennifer and how we both had really liked that song. One thought led to another, and I reflected on the events of our lives when that song was popular. Jennifer had just come home from her first trip to England while visiting my sister, Mary. We were a family back then, and there were still moments of great joy. It was before *everything* fell apart and our lives were forever changed by the divorce that would come in a couple of years. Tears filled my eyes as I reminisced about that time, the decisions I made, and how *that* family was forever gone. This led me to the thought of another song. "The Way We Were" popped into my head, and I thought about my favorite lines from that song: *What's too painful to remember, we simply choose to forget. So it's the laughter we will remember, whenever we remember the way we were.* Those lines always seem to help me through moments when I drift off to a time and place that's not always easy to reflect upon. And that's the magic of music.

When I was young, Rock–and-Roll had just taken over the world. Some people referred to it as "The Devil's Music". My father hated Rock–and-Roll, but my mother loved it. My mother was a dancer. Not professionally, but when a beat took her, she just couldn't stay still, she had to dance. If I close my eyes, I can still see her. We all loved the early Beatles. Their early music was great! My oldest brother Steve reminded me of a long-lost memory of a particular morning when we were all listening to our stack of Beatles 45s.

It was a late Saturday morning, and most of my siblings were sitting in the living room listening to some of their records. Being young Rock-and-Rollers, we liked to zone out to the music by playing it loud. Good music had to be played loud. Even though our dad was a bit hard of hearing, his eyesight was perfect. As he entered the living room, he noticed all our heads bobbing up and down in rhythm to the sound coming from the stereo, our eyes glued to it as though it was holding us in some kind of hypnotic trance. As he turned to look at the stereo, he could see and hear the vase on it moving across its top, caused by the vibration of the speakers. That's where he drew the line. We all froze at the sound of his loud thundering voice, as he abruptly opened the lid to the turntable, grabbed the needle, and dragged it across the surface of the record.

"I don't want anymore blankety blank records of these no-good-for-nothing, long-haired, blankety blank blank bugs, or whatever the blank they're called, played in this house again. Do you hear me?"

There seems to be a terrifying, God-given sound put in the voices of all fathers when they are speaking to their children at the times they want to make it stick. Our dad was given this gift more generously than all other dads.

"Yes," we all whimpered, as we watched him open the front door.

He glared once more at everyone in the room with a look in his eyes that would scare the largest, most ferocious grizzly, and then he slammed the door as he left. We all just sat there, motionless, waiting for the dust to settle, when my mother walked over to the stereo, calmly opened the lid, and said with her reassuring voice, "What your father meant was, as long as he's here."

At those words, all of our heads turned in unison toward the big picture window that overlooked the front yard and stretched our necks as far as we could to see if our dad's truck had pulled away from the house. When it did, we nodded our heads to acknowledge he had left. Our mother then hit the "PLAY" button on the stereo, and we returned to our zone. Like I said, my mother was awesome.

In high school, I became engaged to my husband, Don. I'm sure I made all of my friends sick by talking about how wonderful my life was going to be once I was married to him. Each week in our school newspaper, I dedicated a song to my future husband. It went something like, "I, Liz, dedicate 'Never My Love' to Don." Yep, I was quite the romantic. One week,

I opened the school newspaper to the song dedications, and there was one dedicated to Don that I hadn't submitted. I was shocked and embarrassed at what was there. I had a pretty good idea who the culprit was, though. When I got to fourth period Biology, I turned on my friend, "Kathy, did you write this dedication in the school newspaper? It's not funny!" I yelled at her.

"Liz, you've got to learn to take a joke," she replied while laughing at me.

The song dedication from Kathy read, "I, Liz, dedicate 'If You Can't Be With the One You Love, Love the One You're With' to Don." Kathy had a great sense of humor, and after all these years, every time I hear that song on the radio I think of her.

My brother Steve plays the guitar, and he's really good at it, too. When we were teenagers, after my sister Dianne married and I had a bedroom to myself, Steve used to come into my room at night, sit at the foot of my bed, and play his guitar for me until I drifted off to sleep. It was a very peaceful way to fall asleep.

Steve was extremely talented, and he wrote many of the songs he played for me. There was one song in particular that I really loved. Steve couldn't sing, so he only played the music. That one song was just beautiful. I began to refer to it as "My Song" and occasionally would ask him to play it. He always knew the one I was referring to and usually relented and played it for me.

A few years later, after we had left home and were both married, I was in a parking lot at a store when an old Beatles song came on the radio that I had never heard before. I don't know where I'd been when it was popular. It was called "Here, There, and Everywhere". I had just pulled into a parking space when the song started, and I quickly threw the car into park. I sat there stunned! It was *my* song! It was the one that Steve played for me at night on my bed in my room! All those years I thought he had written it, when all the while it was a Beatles song! I felt so betrayed! I went straight to his house and demanded an explanation.

"I thought you knew!" he laughed. "Why would you think I wrote it? I'm good, but not that good."

I was so disillusioned. All those years I thought he had been a brilliant songwriter and had written a song that he would someday publish. All the big names in the business would fight over who would record it. The name of this masterpiece would be "Elizabeth", and he would win the Grammy that year for best song. It would later go on all the lists as one of the all-time greatest songs ever written. My brother would be interviewed by all the talk shows, and he would credit me with the inspiration for writing that song. Poof! Just like that, the dream was gone.

Back before we were both married, though, when I was still at home and Steve was still playing his guitar for me at night, we often fought with my mother over the radio in the car. The car radio didn't belong to my mother, the driver; it belonged to the majority. Although my mother loved rock and roll, she did enjoy other music as well. You could always tell when she had been in the car alone, because someone like The Mills Brothers was playing.

"Mom, change the channel," was probably the majority of communication we had with our mother when we were in the car. One Sunday afternoon on the way home from church, a new song came on the radio that I really liked called "I Got Rhythm". My mother started singing along to the song, and I was taken aback by her knowledge of the lyrics. I had only heard it a couple of times and couldn't figure out how she could possibly know the words already. I looked at her in surprise and asked, "How do you know the words to this song?"

She just smiled and said, "It was popular when I was young."

I obviously was too young to have heard of George and Ira Gershwin at the time.

The same thing happened when my kids were very young teenagers. I was driving my kids to the movie theater one afternoon when the song "Tainted Love" came on the radio. At the end of that song, it changes and the singer goes into an arrangement of The Supremes hit "Where Did Our Love Go?" Although I didn't know the words to "Tainted Love", I certainly knew the words to "Where Did Our Love Go?" and I began singing it. My children were horrified that I could possibly know part of one of *their* songs that they didn't know.

"How do you know this song?" they asked almost accusingly. My children weren't quite as nice as I was when I had been their age.

I just smiled and said, "It was popular when I was young."

The music of the '80s was different than what I had grown up with, but I did like most of it. My son, Joey was more into Hard Rock, which I hated, but Jennifer liked the songs that were showcased on MTV. She and I agreed on most of her music — but it was a rarity that we agreed upon anything else at that time. Music was our common ground while she was in her teens. It was one subject where we could communicate. Jennifer was very passionate about her music. She would rip into her purse looking for her sunglasses to wear every time the song "I Wear My Sunglasses At Night" came on the radio. She had posters of the group The Cure pasted all over her bedroom walls. We both loved U2.

Unlike my mother, though, the owner of my car had control of the radio. I frequently reminded my children that when they paid for their own car, they could listen to whatever they wanted on the radio. In my car, I would change it to their station only after scanning my stations and had found nothing of interest. This served two purposes: I got to listen to what I wanted, and it also exposed them to the music I had grown up with. To this day, my children still love Gary Puckett and the Union Gap, Barry Manilow, and the Beach Boys. I love it when one of my kids calls to tell me to turn on the radio because a song they remember I loved a long time ago is playing.

I find it amusing when you consider how people change sometimes in their old age. My father was visiting our family back in 1983 at the time when "Billy Jean" by Michael Jackson was popular. Jennifer was a big Michael Jackson fan back then, and, at one time, she had posters of him in her room. My father and I were at my kitchen table catching up on each other's lives when Jennifer came home from school.

"Grandpa!" Jennifer greeted him, "Can I play my favorite song for you?"

He smiled at her and nodded his head, so Jennifer put her record on the turntable and placed the needle on "Billie Jean". She began dancing there in the kitchen. I waited for the bomb to drop, for my father to go into his usual tirade about Rock-and-Roll. To my complete surprise, my father, who had hated Rock-and-Roll when I was young, got up and started dancing with his granddaughter! I began to wonder who this man was, and I wanted to know what he had done with my real father, when I realized — that's just the magic of music.

By the time Jessica turned 16, she was heavily into Country Music. Through hard work and diligence, she converted me to Country. I didn't go easily. Nobody likes change. But now I listen to Country most of the time. Sunday morning while we all get ready for church, Rachel prefers watching CMT (Country Music

Television) to cartoons. It has actually become a ritual. We have the TV on in the den, in the living room, and in my bedroom, and they are all tuned to CMT, so, regardless of which room we are in, we can still watch it.

While we all now listen to Country Music, when Hunter was a toddler, he loved Ricky Martin. Jessica came over to my house one Saturday morning when I was watching Morgan and Hunter. She brought in a stack of CDs from her car and began playing them for Morgan. Hunter wasn't quite 2 years old and was quietly playing with Legos on the floor, not paying attention to any of the music going on around him. Jessica asked Morgan if there was any kind of music that Hunter liked. Morgan began to giggle and told Jessica that if she had a Ricky Martin CD that had "Shake Your Bon Bon" on it, Hunter would go crazy. Curious, Jessica played that song just to see if Hunter would go crazy. And he did. The second that song began playing, he stopped what he was doing and began dancing all over the room. It was as if the song held him in a spell that he could not control. As soon as the song ended, he went back to his Legos as if the song had never been played. So we played it again, and again Hunter went crazy, his little legs jumping and dancing to the beat of the music. When the song ended, he went back to his toys. Yeah, we played it a few more times, just for kicks.

Now that Hunter is older, he has begun to take notice of lyrics. He recently heard the song "The Devil Went Down to Georgia" by the Charlie Daniels Band. Although he had heard the song before, he had never really listened to the words. The song had him captivated as if a master story teller were recounting a momentous occasion witnessed by many people, but Hunter had been left off the list of the invited so he had missed the biggest event to happen in his life. He began to ask his mother questions about the Devil and Johnny.

"Mommy, was Johnny scared of the Devil? If it were me, I'd be really scared. Who would want to see the Devil? What do you think the Devil looks like? What's a fiddle? Where did Johnny learn to play it so well? Did his mother teach him? If the Devil has so much power, why couldn't he beat Johnny? If I had superhuman powers, I could beat Johnny. Did the Devil ever challenge Johnny again?"

Hunter was thoroughly fascinated by the song. It was the topic of conversation at the dinner table that night. Hunter even called me on the phone before bed, "Grandma, have you ever heard of a song called 'The Devil Went Down to Georgia'?"

I smiled and told him, "I sure have. I love that song."

Hunter was so excited, "I heard that song today. Boy, Johnny sure plays the fiddle really good. Do you know what a fiddle is? I thought he played better than the Devil, didn't you?"

I love to share with my grandchildren the events, great and small, that excite and stimulate their imagination. Hunter has an extraordinary mind. You never know when something will grab his attention and he'll hold it, look at it, turn it over, ponder it, test it, shake it, and marvel at it.

One of his favorite shows is *American Idol*. A couple of years ago, Carrie Underwood won the season-long talent contest. Her first hit song was "Jesus, Take The Wheel". My grandchildren loved that song so much. The first time I heard it when they were in my car, they almost gave me a heart attack.

"GRANDMA! 'JESUS, TAKE THE WHEEL'!" they screamed in unison.

I thought they were trying to warn me of an impending car accident and they were praying for Jesus to take control of the car. It took me a couple of seconds to realize that they were just excited to hear the song, and they were letting me know in case I hadn't heard it begin on the radio.

"Thanks for telling me. What is it about this song that you guys don't like?" I asked them sarcastically.

Christien especially loved it. He would come over to my house and ask that I play the video for him on CMT's website on my computer. I would play it over and over for him. But all my grandchildren loved that song. I don't know if it was because the name "Jesus" was in the title or because they identified with Carrie Underwood from seeing her on *American Idol*.

Carrie Underwood's next song was sweet and nice, and they liked that one too. But Rachel loved the song that followed: "Before He Cheats". Rachel began watching that video over and over. When it came on TV, she would hurry and change her clothes to try and match what Carrie Underwood was wearing. Rachel began telling me quite often that she looked like Carrie Underwood. Since Rachel thought she looked like Carrie Underwood, Livvy thought she looked like her, too. This seemed to get under Rachel's skin a little.

"Grandma, who looks more like Carrie Underwood, Livvy or me?"

Man! I hated being put in the spot of choosing one grandchild over another.

"You both look like her," I replied, non-committedly.

"Grandma," Rachel began with an impatient, condescending tone, "how can we both look like her? My hair is blonde and straight while Livvy's is brown and curly."

It was hard trying to be Switzerland sometimes. I couldn't answer. Livvy walked away with a satisfied look on her face. Rachel's was full of disappointment. Later, I conceded to Rachel privately that she did look slightly more like Carrie Underwood than Livvy.

I also hate to disappoint my grandchildren. Rachel practiced singing like Carrie Underwood too. I was in the kitchen one afternoon when she accessed CMT's website and played "Jesus Take The Wheel". Rachel didn't know I was listening, and she sang her heart out to that song. I was so impressed at her skill and ability. She nailed Carrie's inflections and notes. Rachel was fantastic!

But it was Livvy who really got me one day. I had picked Livvy up from pre-school one afternoon shortly after her 3rd birthday. She was in her car seat in the back and had been very quiet on the drive to my house. I actually thought she had gone to sleep. "Before He Cheats" came on the radio, and my thoughts immediately turned to Rachel and how much she loved that song. All of a sudden, I heard a voice singing… " *'cause the next time that he cheats, oh… you know it won't be on me."*

I quickly looked around for someone else in my car. There was no one except Livvy and I. I looked at Livvy, puzzled, and asked, "Were you singing that song? Do you know the words?" but I already knew the answer.

Livvy just nodded her head yes. I was a little unsettled that a 3 year old was singing a song about someone cheating. How healthy was that? Then it occurred to me that many songs throughout time have been sung about cheating. Besides, Livvy probably thinks she is singing about cheating at a game.

About a year later on a Sunday morning, while we were listening to CMT and getting ready for church, Carrie Underwood's new song, "So Small" came on. Livvy had a question weighing heavily on her mind, "Grandma, what is she singing about?"

I have come to love this question. Livvy and Rachel ask this question often, usually about a song they really like.

I answered, "She is singing about how people often think they have so many problems, and they let those problems overwhelm them."

It was at this point that Livvy interrupted me with another question, "Problems that make them feel lost inside?" she asked.

I was Livvy's grandmother and naturally thought she was brilliant, but I had a hard time believing that a 4 year old could have that much insight. I didn't know all the words yet to "So Small", but I made a guess that those words were somewhere in the song. Brilliant or not, Livvy just wasn't old enough to be so reflective.

"Yes, Livvy, sometimes people get so overwhelmed with their problems that they feel lost inside. But if they only understood that love is the only thing that matters, the only thing that is truly important, then their problems wouldn't be so big; they would be so small."

Livvy looked at me so seriously, as if she were about to tell me something really profound, "Grandma, I have a lot of problems too, but I don't feel lost inside, because I love you and Mommy and Rachel and Josie and my family."

Wow! Two things hit me like a ton of bricks. First, four-year-old Livvy thinks she has a lot of problems. I let that remark go. It took about every ounce of self-control I had to keep from laughing. Livvy was serious, and she was at that age where laughing at her would have been extremely offensive. Second, she grasped the message of the song and what I had said to her. She realized that it's not just about being loved but about loving others. I told you she was brilliant.

Livvy is also the one who seems to think she is in complete control of the radio in my car. Evidently, she didn't get the memo: The radio in my car belongs to me, and I choose the songs we all listen to.

I constantly flip through the channels looking for a song worthy of my attention, and I am always amazed when I hear

Livvy's voice from the backseat, "Grandma! Turn it back! That's my favorite song!"

There is no "please", just her demand that I turn it back. For only being four years old, she knows way too many songs and has way too many favorites.

Recently, as we were driving to my house, an old Reba McIntyre song came on the radio. It was so old that I had only heard it a couple of times in my whole life. I listened to a half a dozen notes and discovered that I didn't really know the song, so I changed the station.

Livvy immediately snapped at me, "Grandma! Turn it back! That was Reba!"

"How do you know that?" I asked, really wanting to know.

She just shrugged her shoulders. Now, whenever a song comes on the radio and Rachel and I can't immediately identify it, we ask Livvy. Nine times out of ten, she knows the artist.

We were in the car one night, driving to Livvy's house, and she was in the back seat when Rodney Atkins' first song, "If You're Going Through Hell", came on the radio. He had other songs, but I really liked his first song the best. But the beginning of it always reminds me of one of Keith Urban's songs. Initially, Livvy thought it was one of her favorite Keith Urban songs too.

"Oh! It's my favorite song... No it's not... Grandma, it's your song!" Livvy said.

"Livvy, you remembered this was one of my favorites? You have such a good memory."

I so admire that my grandchildren remember which songs I like.

"Grandma, I don't have a memory; I just know," Livvy corrected.

Wow! What's it like to just KNOW?

Rachel is a little different. She is at an age where she is trying to understand the world we live in. We were getting ready for church one Sunday morning, and I had just finished putting on my make-up. With blow dryer and brush in hand and ready to fix my hair, I asked Rachel what video was about to come on CMT before I began.

"Grandma, it's one of your favorites: 'Moments'," Rachel responded.

"Moments" was a powerful song by Emerson Drive, and I loved it. I had a few extra minutes to spare, so Rachel and I sat on my bed to watch the video, my arm around her shoulder.

Rachel then asked *that* question, "Grandma, what's this song about?"

Wow! I sat there for a moment, wondering how to explain a song that contemplates ending one's own life to an 8 year old. I told her that the young man in the video was thinking about jumping off the bridge. Rachel looked at me a little puzzled, not really understanding why anyone would want to do that.

"He doesn't want to live anymore," I explained.

Rachel was shocked. It occurred to me that she might never have considered that anyone wouldn't want to live.

"The old man in the video," I continued, "just knows or maybe feels what the younger man is feeling, and he wants to help. The old man tells him that even though he himself is homeless, he's had moments in his life that were incredible — times when he had been at his best and on top of the world — a time when he had made a difference. The younger man understands what he is saying, and he realizes that he's had moments in his life too when he had it all. He realizes he has made a difference, too. The young man finally understands that his life *did* have meaning."

I told Rachel to listen to the words of the last verse, that maybe it would help her to understand even more. As we both listened to the final words of the song, I choked up and tears filled my eyes.

"Grandma! You're not going to cry, are you?" Rachel almost laughed at me.

"Goobie," (My nickname for her is Goobie.) "have you ever had a time in your life when something touched you so deeply that it just brought tears to your eyes, or are you still too young for that?" I asked her.

"Grandma, when I look at you and see tears in your eyes like now, that's what makes me want to cry," my precious granddaughter replied.

The magic of music can be seen and felt in our lives whenever we listen to it. For me, on any given day, I am reminded of so many different people and events in my life that I hadn't thought about in years. "Everything That Touches You", by the Associations, will always remind me of my old boyfriend, AB. He had a beautiful singing voice, and he sounded just like the lead singer in that song. AB died more than fifteen years ago, and that song keeps him alive for me. "Joanne", by Michael Nesmith, will always remind me of Mike, because it's the only song he ever told me that he liked. "Gentle on My Mind", by Glen Campbell, will always remind me of Rusty, because Rusty liked playing Glen Campbell's songs on his guitar, and I always thought Rusty looked like him in that cowboy-ish sort of way. "Texas Tornado", by Tracy Lawrence, will always remind me of Morgan, because she still blows me away. "Can't Buy Me Love", by the Beatles, will always remind me of my mother, because that was her favorite. "I Wouldn't Have Missed it for the World", by Ronnie Milsap, will always remind me of my brother, Steve, because he sang that song to me once. "Please Release Me", by

Engelbert Humperdinck, will always remind me of my brother, David, because he used to sing the first couple of lines to that song all the time, especially to his ex-wife Jan. "Let's Go Crazy", by Prince, or the Artist formerly known as Prince, or whatever he's calling himself now, will always remind me of my sister, Dianne, because we both liked that song, and it's one of the few songs that can make Dianne dance. "He Ain't Heavy, He's My Brother", by The Hollies, will always remind me of my sister, Mary, because I willingly gave up a job I had held for five years and had truly loved for her, all because she needed me. "Try and Catch the Wind" by Donovan will forever remind my of my Dennis because the words fit perfectly in what I feel. And, of course, "Moments", by Emerson Drive, will always remind me of that Sunday morning Rachel and I sat on my bed listening to that song as she told me that seeing tears in my eyes made her want to cry. My list could go on forever — and that's what makes it so magical.

BREAKING THE LAW AND OTHER MOVING VIOLATIONS

U p until I was in my late twenties, I thought my mother was a really good driver. I can't explain why I thought that. She never scared me though when I was in the car with her. I can't explain that either. She was actually a pretty crazy driver. She braked on the freeway for no apparent reason and was easily distressed long before the term "Road Rage" became a euphemism. She had occasional moments when she drove on the wrong side of a divided street or accelerated from a red light to go through an intersection on a green left turn arrow when she wasn't even in the turn lane.

My mother no longer drives, which makes the roads a much safer place to be, and her children can sleep better at night knowing she is not behind the wheel somewhere. She had a careless accident a few years ago that was completely her fault, and she was lucky no one was hurt. When I spoke to her after the accident, she confided that it was not the first time she'd been careless in her driving, and, in fact, she had almost had the same accident at the same intersection before. She also told me of a time when she recently had driven down a narrow street lined with parked cars on both sides, had side-swiped a few of them, and had even torn a side mirror off a car.

"Did you stop, talk to anyone, leave a note — anything?" I inquired.

"Was I supposed to stop?" my poor, pathetic mother asked.

"Mom! How could you side-swipe a car or tear off a mirror and not even leave a note? I think by law you have to at least leave a note," I scolded.

"Should I go back and leave a note? I'm not sure which street it was," she confessed.

Yeah, it was time for her to retire her driver's license. She gave it up, but not without a fight. It's been four years now, and she's still trying to convince us kids that she needs to be able to drive, "Just wait till you're my age," she retorts.

That's her reply to everything. I asked her once why she always wished bad stuff on me.

"Why do you always say to me, 'Just wait till you're my age' as if you can't wait for me to be miserable or something?" I asked.

Frankly, I looked forward to being her age. I couldn't wait to be cold all the time. I was at an age where I was perpetually hot. Being old and cold sounded pretty good to me at times. I told her once that if I made it to her age, I would consider myself truly blessed; she was getting pretty old.

The last traffic ticket she received was just a couple of years before she stopped driving. She was in her early 70s, and she always had a lead foot. Her last ticket was a speeding ticket. Big surprise there. However, being on a fixed income, she had very little discretionary money. So she chose to perform community service rather than pay the fine. My mother assumed that being a frail old woman, she would be required to sit at a desk and answer phones or something similar. The judge had no mercy. My 4'10", 110 pound, 73-year-old mother was fined three days pulling weeds at the local cemetery.

At the end of her first day of community service, she called me on the phone to tell me how it had gone, "I had to pull weeds on the side of the road at the cemetery. At one point, Dianne drove by on her way to the store," she explained.

"Did Dianne see you?" I asked

"She saw me but didn't acknowledge me. She just drove on by, but as she drove by, I saw her laughing."

I couldn't help it. I fell on the floor laughing.

"You know, Mom, I can't tell my grandkids about this. I could never tell them that their great-grandmother is part of a chain gang! I'll never be able to look at you the same way. My mother — doing hard time!"

My mother drove for close to sixty years. That's a lot of experience. She'd been driving long before I was born. But when I was 17, I considered myself a pretty good driver. I had gotten a perfect score on my written test and a nearly perfect score on my driving test. I found out that you don't learn everything in a book or Driver's Ed. My husband Don and I moved to Santa Cruz on our 1st anniversary in 1972. I got a job working at JCPenney. I parked in the parking lot behind the store everyday, and everyday I would go out to my car to go home only to find someone had put a flyer on my windshield. I never looked at it. I just tossed it in the back seat. After about two weeks, I finally looked at what was being left on my windshield each day. They were all parking tickets! Evidently, I was required to put money in the meter where my car was parked. I had no idea I was supposed to pay to work. Didn't I get some kind of break for being an employee? Didn't we get to park for free? I was working, for goodness sake! JCPenney didn't give me a parking allowance, and I was only making minimum wage, $1.75 an hour. Back in 1972, parking tickets in Santa Cruz were $8 each. I had received three a day for twelve days (There was a two-hour parking limit.). That was more than I made during the same time period! I could have stayed home and done nothing for two weeks and saved some money! Thank goodness I hadn't thrown any of the tickets away. I never told my husband about the tickets until years later.

That certainly wasn't the last time I had a brush with the law. At Christmastime in 1973, Don, Jennifer, and I drove from Santa Cruz to Carson to spend the holiday with my mother. It was Jennifer's first Christmas, and I was anxious to share it with my family. Santa Cruz to Carson was about a 370-mile trip down highway 101. Don had worked the night before and was tired, so he wanted to sleep. That left me to do the driving.

A big change was coming that would effect every driver in America. On January 1, 1974, the national speed limit was going to change from 65 mph to 55 mph. Congress enacted the new law in response to an oil crisis. I was driving at about 68 mph when a police cruiser flashed his lights at me. I couldn't believe he pulled me over for driving 3 mph over the speed limit, especially at Christmas. I tried to wake Don, but he was so tired he slept like the dead and wouldn't wake up. He had on his favorite shirt that he often wore as a lightweight jacket over a tee shirt: his army shirt. Don had been in the military serving in Viet Nam, but his stint ended in 1969. He wore that shirt until it fell apart many years later. The officer took one look at Don, who was still asleep, and said that he understood that the military were grossly underpaid, so he wouldn't cite me since my husband must be in the military and we probably couldn't afford to pay a speeding ticket. I tried to comprehend what the officer was saying to me, but I just couldn't understand. Who was in the military?

I looked at Don and realized the officer's mistake. "Oh, officer, my husband *was* in the military. He no longer is," I corrected.

This is where everyone I tell this story to thinks I am an utter idiot, but the truth is the truth.

"I wasn't going to give you a ticket because I thought your husband was in the military. Since you told the truth, I can hardly give you a ticket now. Next time I won't be so generous," he replied.

The officer reminded me of the impending speed limit change and advised me to slow it down. Then he drove away, looking for another motorist to ticket. On the way home a few days later, Don, wearing his army jacket, drove that part of highway 101 back home.

As time passed and my children grew to become teenagers, I feared and dreaded the day they would get behind the wheel and drive. They seemed so young and irresponsible. How could anyone in their right mind give a teenager a license to drive a moving, working car? I wondered how I would handle their first ticket.

In October, 1989, Don and I had tickets to the World Series: the San Francisco Giants versus the Oakland A's. We had been to many Giant games that year and were lucky enough to go to the play-offs. The World Series was the biggest sporting event that either one of us had ever attended. We went to work that day, got off early, and drove straight to Candlestick Park. Our children were at home watching the event on TV. But on October 17, 1989, at 5:04 P.M., there was a 7.1 earthquake that was centered in the Santa Cruz Mountains, sixty miles south of San Francisco and about twenty miles from San Jose, where we lived. It took Don and I forty-five minutes to get to Candlestick Park earlier that afternoon and four hours to get home that night. I was terrified. If San Francisco was as bad as I could see it was, I feared what San Jose must look like. I worried about my children who I had left all alone. I was worried that they were hurt. I could picture them crying for me. My heart ached. Jennifer was at a friend's house watching the game, so Joey, who was 15 years old, was in charge that night. I just prayed they were all okay and that Joey took care of the younger kids.

When we drove down our street, the first thing that hit me was that everyone still had electricity. I hadn't expected that. The second thing that hit me was that our family station wagon was gone. I hadn't expected that either. I ran into the house and my two youngest children greeted me with a great deal of excitement, "You should have seen it! Everything got knocked over!" they reported.

I ran out to the backyard where we had a pool. There was significant water gone from it.

"Don, there must be a crack in the pool. Too much water is gone," I told him.

"No, Mom! You should have seen it! It was like a tidal wave!" they shouted. "A wall of water came out of the pool. We cleaned everything up. Your room was the worst. Some of your stuff got broken."

I then got to my next question. The one I dreaded asking, "Where's Joey?"

Jeffrey and Jessica looked at each other, and Jeffrey clearly felt bad telling me.

"Joey had some friends over. After the earthquake, everyone sort of freaked out. Joey had the keys to your car, so he drove them home."

He had the keys to my car? How'd he get the keys to my car? The car is a stick shift. How does he know how to drive it? I waited for him on the front porch, praying he wasn't hurt. It wasn't long before he pulled up. The first thing I saw was a big dent in the left front fender. Joey got out of the car, and I immediately went on the attack, "You wrecked my car! Was anyone hurt? You wrecked my car!" I shouted at my son.

Joey just shook his head no and walked into the house, down the hall, into his room, and right out his window. It was all such a smooth fluid movement, like a dance step. I quickly turned around, ran out the front door, and caught up with him on the next block. I grabbed his arm and told him he was coming home with me.

"Don't make me go home, please, Mom. Dad's going to kill me," Joey pleaded.

"Joey, Joey, Joey," I chuckled softly, "your father's not going to kill you. *I'm* going to kill you!"

Once home, I started my inquisition, "Joey, as your mother, did I fail to tell you that it is against the law to drive a motor vehicle without a license? As your mother, did I fail to tell you that in the state of California you must be 16 years old to legally drive a car? As your mother, did I fail to mention the month, day, and year you were born? Can you do the math? Do you realize by what I've just told you that you're not old enough to legally drive a car? And do you also realize that *IF* you ever pull a stunt like this again, you will not live to see that age?"

We found out that Joey had not been in a car accident but had hit a light pole in a parking lot. He was severely punished for his deed, and for days the only thing I would say to him was that he wrecked my car. I never knew how long he'd been driving my car or if he had even taken my keys before that night, but I slept with my car keys after that.

My children eventually grew into responsible adults and are legal, cautious drivers now. They are all law-abiding citizens, but sometimes things just happen. Sometimes breaking the law is unintentional.

Jessica's car broke down on the way home from work one day. She called me from her cell phone to ask me to pick up Livvy and Josie (Josie is her new stepdaughter.) from preschool. I only had one car seat in my car. Livvy was almost 4 years old, and she wasn't small for her age. She was almost big enough for a booster seat. Josie was 2 years old and very petite. Easy decision, Josie would use the car seat. It was a short ride from the preschool to where I dropped the girls off, and I took residential streets to avoid fast moving cars just to be on the safe side. Several weeks later, on a Saturday evening, I was taking Rachel and Livvy to a park after dinner for a little playtime before their bath and bed. Livvy asked if she could ride on the regular seat next to Rachel instead of sitting in her car seat.

"Of course not!" I replied, surprised by her question.

"But, Grandma," Livvy returned, "you let me last time."

Livvy had no concept of time, so I had to stop and think for a few seconds when "last time" was.

"Oh, Livvy, you sat in the regular seat because Josie had to sit in your car seat. You only sat there because you had to sit there."

That reply wasn't good enough for Livvy. "Grandma, you let me last time."

I could see where this was leading.

"Livvy, you are not big enough to ride in the seat next to Rachel yet. If we had gotten into an accident that day, you may have been really hurt," I explained.

"Grandma, you need to take better care of us," Livvy said, advising me and not really trying to be sarcastic.

"Livvy, I do take good care of you, but if I had been pulled over by a policeman, I would have gotten in trouble. It's against the law for you to ride in a regular seat until you're a little bigger."

I thought that would nip the whole conversation in the bud. But was I ever wrong! It opened a whole new can of worms!

"Grandma! You broke the law?"

What... had... I... done?

"Well, I didn't want to, and I didn't really do it on purpose, but I had to," I said, defending myself.

Livvy jumped on it, "Grandma! You broke the law!" Livvy said indignantly.

What could I say?

"Yes I did, and I'm very sorry," I pleaded.

"Grandma! You broke the law!" Livvy wouldn't give up, and each time she made the statement, I felt her disappointment in me grow.

Later that night, as I was putting the girls to bed, Livvy began again, "Grandma! You broke the law!"

I began to ignore her. She was beginning to sound like my conscience, like the little angel on your shoulder reminding you to follow the rules.

Later that night, sometime around midnight, I was still up when Livvy awoke to use the bathroom. She never fully woke up, but I could hear her as she got back in bed and whispered, "Grandma broke the law."

Gosh! It had been such a traumatic revelation to her, she was even dreaming about it!

The following evening I received a call from Jessica, "Mom, Livvy seems to be really upset with you. She keeps telling me that you broke the law. What did you do?"

I just shook my head. The kid was going to rat me out to everyone she came in contact with. I began to get a little nervous. We were flying out to California in a few days, and Rachel and Livvy were flying with us. What if we got on the plane and Livvy started telling the flight attendant that I broke the law?

What if Federal Marshals came and arrested me based solely on Livvy's accusations? What if I was driving and got pulled over for a faulty taillight like in the movie, *And Justice For All*, and Livvy told the police officer I broke the law? Would he listen to her? I didn't want to go to jail in California on some trumped-up charge perpetrated by my granddaughter.

"Jessica, you've got to talk to your daughter. She's going to get me arrested if she doesn't keep her mouth closed." I then explained the whole thing to Jessica.

"Mom! You broke the law!" Jessica exclaimed with the sound of total disappointment in her voice.

I gave up. I might as well just call the police now and give myself up. Thanks to Livvy, they were going to get me sooner or later.

If asked, my children would probably say I have a lead foot. I have had two speeding tickets in the thirty-seven years I've been driving. I didn't get my first one until I was well into my forties. I was driving down a street I had driven down many times. Down the street a ways, I saw someone standing in the middle of the road. By the time I figured out that it was a policeman and he was pointing a radar gun at me, it was too late. He motioned for me to pull over, and I burst into tears. I had never gotten a ticket for speeding before.

"Ma'am, did you know you were going 48 in a 25 mile an hour zone?"

I was stunned.

"Was I really going that fast?" I asked, as if the officer was lying to me.

I was sincere in my question. I was daydreaming and had no idea I was going that fast. But the one ticket wasn't enough. A couple of years later, I received my 2nd ticket. This time I almost fought it, because I initially thought it was entrapment. I was driving Jessica to her obstetrician visit when she was pregnant with Livvy. Rachel was 4 years old and in the car seat in the back. I was on a major city street with a posted speed limit of 45 mph. Okay, so I was going about 50 mph when all of a sudden I noticed a speed limit sign that said 35 mph and a police car was just on the other side of the sign. I hadn't noticed any warning of the impending change in the speed limit. The police cruiser flashed his lights at me, so I pulled into a parking lot and turned the engine off. Rachel immediately unbuckled her car seat and got out of it.

"Rachel! What are you doing? Get back in your car seat before the policeman thinks you weren't in it at all and gives me a ticket for that too," I scolded my granddaughter.

My granddaughter and even my pregnant daughter couldn't get me out of that ticket. On the way home, I went by the same place I had been "trapped" and found that there indeed had been a warning sign that read "Reduced Speed Ahead" that I just never saw. I paid the ticket.

I don't want my grandchildren growing up thinking that breaking the law is something that's okay to do when a person thinks it's necessary or they might not get caught. I want them to respect our laws, even the ones that don't seem fair. They're still the law. I pray that Livvy forgets I broke the law that day. And if not, I pray that she will understand that I am truly sorry for disappointing her. I want her to understand that it's not okay to break the law no matter what the circumstances. But it's taught me to be more aware of the decisions I make and how those decisions can impact my grandchildren and their view of the world and of me. This may be the best job in the whole wide world, forever and ever, but along with it, I've found, comes great responsibility.

FOOD FOR THOUGHT

The Bible seems to put a lot of emphasis on food and eating. Jesus' first recorded miracle was during a wedding feast. Later, he fed the 5000 and the 4000. He ate with the tax collectors and Mary and Martha. He told a parable about the prodigal son, who when he returned to his father, a feast was prepared in his honor. In fact, there were all types of feasts recorded in the Bible.

Eating together as a family is a very important part of our life. We celebrate Thanksgiving each year, which is all about the food, family, and giving thanks. There is Easter dinner, Christmas dinner, and the typical barbeques that are associated with Memorial Day, Fourth of July, and Labor Day. And who could forget the food we consume on Super Bowl Sunday?

Supper in our family was the name given to our evening meal, the time we all sat down at the table together to eat. We had a formal dining room where we ate most nights. There were those occasions, however, when my parents wanted to have a quiet dinner together, so my brothers and sisters and I had our dinner at the kitchen table as if we were the hired help. Those were the times when my mother would cook a steak for my father and we kids had hamburgers. I hated those nights. I wanted steak too. One might think those hamburgers weren't so bad, but I would have to argue that they have never eaten one of my mother's hamburgers. My mother had many wonderful talents. Cooking wasn't one of them. She would take a little ball of hamburger and flatten it out to where it was almost paper-thin. You could just about see through it. She had a real fear of raw meat, so she would fry the hamburger patty in a skillet until it was almost burned on each side. Consequently, it was crispy all the way through. The crusty hamburger was then placed between two pieces of bread, not a hamburger bun. The bread was twice the size of the hamburger. We tried to make the bread a little more like a bun by toasting it, but it all just tasted like crumbled leather on toast. Even at my young age, I knew there wasn't enough money for all of us to have steak. My poor father… while he tried to eat his juicy, mouthwatering steak, we five kids would find our way to their table and beg, literally beg, for a bite of it. He always gave us one. Thank goodness my mother usually bought him a big porterhouse. Otherwise, there wouldn't have been enough to go around. I began to make a mental list of things I would do differently as a parent. If we all couldn't have steak, then no one would have steak. It just wasn't fair.

My mother made fried chicken often, and it was one of my favorites. She always made enough to feed an army, too. Once, when I was an adult and having dinner at her house, I asked her why she always made so much food.

"I worry that there won't be enough," was her reply.

"There are just three of us here for dinner, and you're frying twenty pieces of chicken and mashing ten pounds of potatoes! Are you expecting other guests?" I asked her sarcastically.

You'd think after a few dinners of making so much food and having so much left over, she would realize she had made more than enough each time and adjust her recipes or quantities. She never did. Maybe if she didn't always make so much food there would have been enough money for us all to have a steak once in a while. Making too much chicken was fine by me, though. I loved fried chicken. Next to steak, it was my favorite. My brother David loved fried chicken, too.

For some reason, David and I always seemed to be in competition with each other over everything. Mom's fried chicken was no exception. Everyone would finish eating and leave the table. My mother would clear the dishes. David and I were still at the table trying to see who could eat the most chicken. It wasn't that we wanted it or were still hungry. It was a matter of honor, a matter of principle. We would eventually leave the table in a tie and barely be able to walk. But he never beat me. Sounds like I have issues.

We had an extended family dinner every Christmas Eve, and it was just as exciting to me as Christmas morning. The family get-together was always at my Uncle Jim's house where we had supper and opened presents. All the family came, and it was the single best night for me each year. My uncle was a commercial contractor in Los Angeles and was financially pretty comfortable. I will never forget one Christmas Eve when they served prime rib for supper. I didn't know what it was at first. I had never had anything like it. All I knew was that it was the most wonderful thing I had ever tasted in my life. After that, each year I prayed that prime rib was on the menu.

As I said, I didn't know what prime rib was until I was old enough to start dating. My parents seldom took us kids out to dinner as a family, so our exposure to a large variety of foods didn't exist. Having my dad as a father, we were always very well behaved, so my parents never dreaded taking us out. It was always just a matter of money. When we did go out, it was usually for Mexican food at Arturo's. They had the best tacos in the whole world. At that age, I didn't know any other kind of Mexican food — only tacos. It sounds a little disgusting, but I would burp those tacos all night and re-taste them all over again. It was great.

After my parents divorced, they both remarried. My new stepfather had custody of his three children. Consequently, we had a house full of people. Shortly after their wedding, one Saturday morning he decided to take us all out for breakfast. This was a real treat to us. I was about 11 years old and had never been out to breakfast before. We went to the IHOP for pancakes. The problem was, I never liked pancakes or even waffles. After looking at the menu, I told my new stepfather that fact.

"What do you mean you don't like them? Who doesn't like pancakes?" he asked, not quite believing me.

"I don't," I responded.

He turned to my mother and began interrogating her, "Since when doesn't she like pancakes?"

My poor mother tried to defend me, "She's never liked them."

I felt so bad, but I couldn't help what I liked and what I didn't. Apparently, he had enough money for everyone to have pancakes but nothing more. He felt that if I had bacon and eggs or something like that, it would be unfair to everyone else who might like pancakes but would prefer to have something else.

"That's okay; I'm not hungry. I'll just have a glass of orange juice," I relented.

"Everyone is having milk," he retorted.

"Okay, I'll just have water," I said.

I didn't want to be in this situation. At that point, I just wanted to go home. I appreciated what he was trying to do and I didn't mean to be difficult, but if he had ordered pancakes for me, I wouldn't have eaten them and he would have wasted his money. All I could think about was if he didn't have the money for us to have what we wanted to eat, then he had no business taking us all out. Another item went on my mental list. If you can't afford whatever you want on the menu, then don't go out.

I kept to my list when I became a parent. If I wanted steak, we all had steak. In fact, we had steak more than my kids wanted. I couldn't believe their grumbling.

"What's for dinner?" they would ask.

"Steak!" I replied, excited for suppertime to roll around. I couldn't wait!

"Again?" they moaned.

"What do you mean 'Again'? When I was a kid, I never got steak. I would watch my dad eat a steak, and my mouth just watered until it was so dry I couldn't speak. You kids are just so spoiled!"

My husband used to tease me that I could eat steak everyday. Maybe not everyday but at least once or twice a week. I think it was because I was so deprived as a child. At least that's what I tell myself.

Since Christmas Eve was so special to me when I was a child, I wanted to make it special for my children, too. We no longer lived in the Los Angeles area, and my Uncle Jim had died at a relatively young age from a heart attack. So those special nights for me were gone forever and only the memories remain. I will never forget them.

Our family tradition was to go out on Christmas Eve to a nice restaurant for supper. Everyone could order whatever they wanted from the menu. The sky was the limit. It was an exciting day, anticipating our evening meal. Jennifer always ordered lobster. Joey had prawns or crab legs. Jeffrey initially would order a hamburger until he got older. Then he made the transition to steak. Jessica usually ordered a hamburger, too. My children loved going to a nice place and having special food that they never had any other time of the year, like lobster or prawns. We took them out to supper at other times, but not to places like that.

When my children were young, they ate like birds. I could take them out to dinner and order one child's plate from the menu, split it up between the four of them, and they still wouldn't eat it all. I worried a lot about their nutrition. We used to comment that Joey had a layer of skin over his bones. He was so thin. If by chance a new doctor saw him, he immediately wanted to run tests on him to determine if there was a medical reason that he was so small. Our regular pediatrician assured us that Joey was fine. I think my children ate just enough to stay alive. That all changed once they became teenagers. Then I couldn't keep enough food in the house.

I remember the first day I really noticed the change. I came home from work to find Joey baking brownies. You could smell the brownies baking all through the house. I thought Joey was so sweet to make the family some brownies for dessert that night. When the brownies were done, Joey took them out of the oven, grabbed a fork, and began eating them hot right out of the pan. They were gone in about five minutes.

I stood there in shock. "What are you doing? Since when can you eat more than a crumb of food at a time?" I asked.

"I was hungry," was all he said.

And he has stayed hungry ever since. My grocery bill skyrocketed. We went through two full gallons of milk a day. I bought four gallons at a time and would have bought more, but I didn't have room in the refrigerator with all the other food I bought. It was amazing what those teenagers consumed. Yet, they were all still thin. When I made cookies, there were never any left by the time they were all finished baking. They ate them as I made them. I couldn't keep enough fresh fruit, cookies, milk, or orange juice in the house. I would go grocery shopping, buy two shopping carts full of food, and two days later they would complain that there was nothing to eat.

"You guys are amazing! You should go join a circus or something. They could call you 'The Amazing Bottomless Pit Children'," I suggested.

They needed to get an after-school job to help pay for the groceries. Better yet, they needed to get a job at a fast-food restaurant where they could eat at least one of their meals a day.

We almost always sat down together at the dinner table to eat as a family. But there were nights when I was so busy or working late that I just didn't have time to cook dinner. Sometimes there was just too much going on and I was moving in a million directions at once.

"What's for dinner?" my kids would ask.

"Whatever you can find," was my pat answer on those nights.

Joey would go through the refrigerator and make some type of cooked concoction from various ingredients or leftovers. I generally had some type of fish fillet, such as shark, swordfish, or tuna in the freezer for Jennifer. Jeffrey was the one who always killed me. Jeffrey always poured himself a bowl of cereal. He'd no doubt had a bowl of cereal for breakfast and probably had a bowl of cereal when he got home from school. On these nights, he would turn around and have another bowl of cereal for dinner. I don't know if it was because it was the easiest thing for him to have or he just loved cereal that much. I have spoken to his wife Kristine about this, and she tells me Jeffrey still loves cereal and will have a bowl for breakfast most mornings and then another bowl later for a snack.

My grandparents used to take us out to supper when we spent the night at their house. We always went to Bob's Big Boy for a hamburger and fries. It was such a treat for us. I cherish that memory and have wanted to do the same with my own grandchildren. My husband and I took Hunter and Rachel to The Olive Garden one night for dinner when they were both 6 years old. In all fairness to me, they were about 6 ¾ years old. Hunter is a connoisseur of macaroni and cheese. Jennifer takes her children out to dinner often, and Hunter can tell you who makes good macaroni and cheese and who doesn't. He is an expert in the field, hands down. Rachel and Hunter were so grownup that night. They each ordered their own dinner, macaroni and cheese, and were great conversationalists during the entire evening. For months after, Rachel kept asking me when we would take her and Hunter back to The Olive Garden. She had loved their macaroni and cheese and really wanted to have it again. I kept telling her that as soon as I could get them both together again, we would try to recreate that evening.

Time went on, and it just never happened. After her 7th birthday, my husband and I finally took Rachel and Livvy to The Olive Garden for dinner. Rachel was so excited. She had been anticipating this dinner for several months. Both Rachel and 3-year-old Livvy ordered their own dinner — macaroni and cheese. Rachel was so disappointed when her dinner came. The macaroni used in her dish were small shells, and she didn't really care for it.

"Next time we come," I told her, "we'll order the macaroni and cheese using a different pasta."

She looked at me so coolly. "And when will that be? When I'm eight?"

I looked at Rachel with such surprise.

"Are you being sarcastic?" I asked.

Rachel lowered her head a little and looked at her lap. "Yes," and a little smile appeared on her face.

"Good one!" I told her.

There was nothing like a little sarcasm every once in a while. Just to prove her wrong, though, a few weeks later we took Rachel and Livvy back to The Olive Garden for dinner. Rachel ordered macaroni and cheese using Penne pasta. Livvy declared shortly after arriving that she wanted pasta, not macaroni and cheese. I looked at the children's menu which had Fettuccini Alfredo listed. I ordered this for Livvy with the Alfredo sauce on the side. I wasn't sure how she would eat it. As luck would have it, a large party of fifty people had arrived at the restaurant shortly before we did so the kitchen was backed up. Both girls ate salad while we waited. Rachel asked me what kind of dressing was on the salad.

"Italian," I replied.

"I didn't know I liked Italian Ranch dressing," Rachel said a little puzzled.

For her, all dressing was Ranch. Livvy began getting impatient after a while. I didn't blame her. It did take a really long time. Our server kept coming by and apologizing for the delay.

But Livvy persisted, "Where's my pasta? I want my pasta. When are they bringing my pasta?"

Every couple of minutes, the questions started all over again. I finally asked our server if he could just bring out Livvy's plate of pasta.

"Take your time with the rest of our dinner, but I'm here with a three year old who doesn't understand that fifty people are going to eat before her. Please do what you can to bring her dinner as quickly as possible. There's a big tip in it for you!" I pleaded and bribed.

Our server was wonderful, God bless him. Within a couple of minutes, Livvy had her pasta, and she was as happy as I'd ever seen her. She loved her Fettuccine Alfredo. But that episode set a precedent.

My father always comes to my house for Thanksgiving Dinner each year. Wednesday night before Thanksgiving, we usually cook our own prime rib. My daughters and their families come, and we have a great meal and a great time. That year, Jennifer and her family were in Washington D.C. for the holiday with her in-laws, and Jessica had gone to a concert on that Wednesday night while I watched Rachel and Livvy. Since it was only my father, his wife Betty, my husband Dennis, Rachel, Livvy, and I, we decided to go to Outback Steakhouse for prime rib instead of going to the trouble of making it ourselves. We ordered our dinner, with both girls ordering their own — macaroni and cheese (big surprise).

Our server hadn't walked five feet away from our table after taking our order when Livvy began, "When is my macaroni and cheese coming? Where is my macaroni and cheese?"

The kid had the memory of an elephant! I just smiled, realizing the mistake I had made the last time we took her out.

"Salads first, Livvy. Then we'll talk about your macaroni and cheese."

Thanksgiving has always been my favorite holiday. I guess because it is all about the food and family and not about presents and money which you really didn't have being spent. We have celebrated Thanksgiving dinner at my house for over twenty years. We have the traditional ham, turkey, dressing, mashed potatoes, and all the rest of the fixings. And I always make enough food to feed the whole city of St. Petersburg, a trait I probably inherited from my mother.

Hunter, the macaroni and cheese connoisseur, at the age of

6, liked little else. He had a pretty small palate as far as liking a variety of foods. That year, as we all sat around the table finishing our Thanksgiving dinner and eating way too much, Hunter gave me the ultimate compliment, "Grandma, this was the best dinner I ever ate!"

I looked at my sweet grandson with such joy in my heart, and then I saw his plate. He had only eaten a dinner roll — nothing else. There wasn't a single item on his plate that had been touched. I smiled at his wonderful compliment and thanked him from the bottom of my heart. I guess, for him, it was all about the family being together and not about the food. Being together and eating together, regardless of what was eaten, was the best it had ever been for him. That sentiment touched me deeply. Hunter is always the one who can touch you deep in your soul.

Each of my grandchildren has their favorite thing that I make. Morgan loves my homemade apple pie the most. She has been over to my house many times when I make one, and I'm teaching her the techniques involved in making a perfect pie. My own daughters could care less how to make a pie from scratch. A homemade pie for them consists of a ready-made piecrust, ready-made filling, and top it off with Cool Whip. For me, a good pie is all about the crust. My Grandmother taught my mother; my mother taught me, and now I am teaching it to my grandchildren. For Morgan, it isn't Thanksgiving unless I make an apple pie.

Jennifer and her family were out to dinner one night after Thanksgiving and Morgan wanted apple pie for dessert. When it was brought to her and she took her first bite, she couldn't eat anymore of it.

"This doesn't taste like Grandma's apple pie. What did they do to it? The crust is too heavy; there's not enough cinnamon, and the apples are too sour! Don't they know how to make a pie?"

Jennifer was a little surprised. "Wow! You really know your pie, Morgan. Did Grandma teach you that?"

Morgan was clearly upset, "*Nobody* can make an apple pie as good as Grandma! Don't *ever* let me order another pie from a restaurant. It will *never* be as good as Grandma's!" Morgan stated indignantly.

Morgan is my angel baby! In May of 2008, at the age of 13, Morgan made her first apple pie all by herself, and it was marvelous! Just as good as Grandma's.

Rachel's favorite food that I make is homemade chicken noodle soup. For her, there's nothing I make that tastes better. Rachel has even called me during the week to ask me to make soup for Saturday night when she spends the night.

One week, I bought everything needed to make my soup as Rachel requested. I simmered the chicken in my crock pot all afternoon. My soup was wonderful, and Rachel ate two bowls. She even asked for a bowl of soup as an after-dinner snack later that night instead of the typical ice cream or cookies. After church on Sunday afternoon, I asked both girls if they wanted soup for lunch. It was unanimous — Soup for everyone! As we were eating the soup, Rachel made a comment that was so soft yet it was a wonderful compliment, "Grandma, I love your homemade chicken noodle soup so much." She said it almost in a whisper to herself; it was so soft.

I thanked her for her kind words and we continued eating. All of a sudden, Rachel stopped with her spoon in mid-air full of chicken and noodles and looked at me as if I had betrayed her.

"Grandma! You know… this really isn't homemade chicken noodle soup."

I looked at her bewildered. "What do you mean; it's not homemade?" I asked.

"You didn't make the chicken," she responded.

"What do you mean, I didn't make the chicken? I washed it, seasoned it, cooked it, de-boned it, and tore it into chunks for the soup," I said, defending myself.

"You didn't *make* the chicken," she corrected.

"Okay, I get it. Only God can make a chicken!" I retorted indignantly.

"Right, so that makes your soup only *half* homemade," she theorized.

We dropped it at that. Arguing with Rachel has never gotten me anywhere. She can be relentless. It was better to just drop the subject than trying to reason with my sometimes-precious, 8-year-old granddaughter. I didn't want to even get into the pasta I used in the soup that came from a package. Then it wouldn't even be half-homemade. I'll keep that secret to myself for now.

I know that in the years to come my grandchildren will look back on the meals, pies, cookies, and the dinners out with Grandma and Grandpa with great joy and love, in the same way that I remember how special my Grandmother's cooking was and going out to Bob's Big Boy for dinner was to me. Actually, I think they already do.

JUST WAIT TILL YOUR FATHER GETS HOME

There was nothing more terrifying to me than having to face my father when I had done something wrong. Although I have a healthy relationship with my father now, he wasn't exactly a pushover when I was a child. He had very high expectations for his children, and sometimes it was very hard to live up to them. What was even more terrifying, though, was when I did something wrong and my mother would say, "Just wait till your father gets home." Those words were enough to send any one of us five kids into a panic attack. The sense of dread was overwhelming. Waiting in my bedroom for my father to come home should have been punishment enough. All I could do was pray that my mother would forget about telling my dad (which she did quite often) or pray that one of my brothers or sisters did something worse than I did so their punishment would supersede mine.

When I was 8 years old, my friend Pam and I went bike riding. We were pretty far from home but in familiar territory. We rode down a residential street that dead-ended into a busy 4-lane street. Not being able to cross at the dead-end, we decided to ride our bikes to the traffic light at the corner to cross. Doing so meant we rode our bikes against the traffic for two blocks. We were 8 years old and wanted to cross safely, so we didn't think about how we might be breaking the law. Apparently, it was a slow day for the Torrance Police Department, and they didn't see our safe logic — nor did they care. Pam and I were pulled over, so to speak, and cited for riding our bikes against the traffic. I stood there crying as the officer gave me my ticket. All of our friends who lived on that street were there watching us. At that point, I didn't care that they saw me cry. I didn't care that *everyone* would be talking about me at school the next day. I was much more concerned with what was going to happen when I got home. I wanted to scream at the Police Officer, "Don't you know what's going to happen to me when my father sees this? Have you ever heard of Claud Smith?" Plans started forming in my head about running away from home. I needed clothes and money. I could go home and put a few things in a bag, but who had money? I didn't know anyone who had money to give me. Maybe I could tell my mother and she would pay the ticket and never tell my father. Yeah — that might work.

Children have short memories. I had already forgotten about the dollhouse/swimming pool incident and my mother's betrayal. I guess panic can make you forget all kinds of things. Pam and I rode home being very careful not to ride our bikes against the traffic just in case other Torrance Police Officers were also having a slow day and were bored. We didn't say a single word to each other all the way home. When I got home, I told my mother everything that had happened and gave her the ticket. I will never forget the look of utter pity in her eyes as she looked at me. She knew as well as I did what was going to happen when my father came home. She didn't even have to say those words to me.

"But, Mom," I pleaded, "You don't have to tell Dad. Can't you just pay it and not tell him?"

Tears of resignation began to fall from her eyes. "You know

I can't do that. You know I have to tell your father. But please remember how much I always loved you."

Waiting for my father to come home was sheer torture. I envisioned my own slow, painful death. I knew it wasn't going to be pretty. When he finally did come home, both of my parents went into their bedroom and shut the door. I listened at their door from the kitchen with one hand on the back doorknob. If things went as badly as I thought they would, I would shoot out the back door before anyone could catch me. I heard my mother try to preface the ticket by telling him that something had happened and he needed to remain calm. She told the story, providing every detail I had given her and then handed my father the ticket. I waited for his reaction with bated breath, one foot already out the door, ready to run. To my utter and complete shock, he began to laugh hysterically. It was the funniest story he'd ever heard. He wasn't very kind to the Torrance Police Department, calling them an assortment of colorful names because of the citation, but it was funny to him just the same. He couldn't wait to get to work the next day to tell all his buddies the ludicrous story. Sometimes my father could surprise me. Sometimes he could be a pushover after all. I didn't bank on it ever happening again though.

As a parent, I was the main disciplinarian in our home when my children were young. On occasion, I would relinquish my authority to my husband Don and beg him to "punish the children!" There were times when I got tired of being the "bad guy", the "mean one". And I got really tired of him always being the "good parent", the "fun one". As my children got older, I began the "Just wait till your father gets home" routine. Their father would come home from work, and I would tell him all the sordid details of what the one child had done. Then I would order him to go into their room and spank that child. He would look at me with resignation in his eyes but would go into their room as ordered. I would hear crying and begging coming from my child's room, and guilt would overtake me. *How could he spank them? He doesn't love them as much as I do. How could he work all day only to come home and spank my children? He is so heartless.*

Many years later, when my children were grown adults, we were sitting around a table talking about this very subject when they all began to laugh.

"What's so funny?" I asked them, a little confused.

"When Dad would come into our room to punish us, he said he was going to hit the bed and we were to cry as if he was really spanking us," Jennifer responded through tears of laughter.

"You mean... to tell me... he never... did... spank you? Not... *once*?" I questioned, barely comprehending what they were telling me.

They laughed even harder.

"Nope!"

I couldn't believe all the guilt I had harbored all those years thinking that he had spanked them on my orders! At least I could now take that load of guilt off my shoulders. God knows I had many other things to feel guilty about.

Their father was slow to anger, but once at that point, there was no going back. He was easygoing until he was pushed too far. Then there was no reasoning with him, no words of defense accepted, no excuses. We were on our way to Yosemite one year to go camping. My sister, Dianne, and her family were with us, following behind in their truck and camper. We had pulled over to the side of the road at a picnic area just outside Yosemite National Park to have lunch. The kids had wandered off and had found a creek to play in while waiting for me to get their lunch together. After lunch, they went back to the creek while I cleaned up. All of a sudden fighting erupted, and since I was busy cleaning up and repacking everything, I asked my husband to go and put a stop to it. He called the kids into the camper and told them they had to sit there until we left, and he didn't want to hear another word out of their mouths.

"But, Dad—" Joey began.

"Not another word!" my husband immediately told him.

"But, Dad—" Joey started again.

"Joey, if you say one more word, you will be spanked! Not another word!" his father sternly told him.

Joey didn't say another word until we got to our campsite about thirty-five winding mountain miles later. When we got to the campsite, the fight incident had blown over and everyone was ready to have a great time. Joey got out of the camper with just his socks on his feet.

"Joey, get your shoes on," I told him.

"I don't have any shoes," Joey replied.

"What do you mean, you don't have any shoes? Where are they?" I asked, beginning to get a little irritated.

"We left them at the creek where we stopped for lunch. I kept trying to tell Dad that my shoes were down at the creek, but he wouldn't let me say another word."

I think Joey took a little bit of pleasure in apprising me of the situation. There was a trace of a smile on his face. It was at that moment that I decided it might be better if I handled the discipline from now on. At least with me in that role, we wouldn't lose any more shoes, especially when we were out in the middle of nowhere.

My children don't use the "Just wait till your father comes home" line on their kids. In Jennifer's family, Manuel works from home, so he is always there. Jennifer will call on him to take over when she is overwhelmed, but they share in the discipline pretty equally. When my husband and I watch Jennifer's children at our house, the first question out of her mouth when she picks them up is, "Did they behave?" So you'd think Morgan, Hunter, and Christien would know that if they didn't behave, their parents would find out immediately upon their return.

They have gotten really good at this, though. If there is a problem that I have to correct, they automatically ask me if I'm going to tell their parents. I mull this question over in my mind for quite a while before answering. I want to make sure they get the full effect of my dilemma. I certainly don't want to give them a green light on misbehaving. But they know me pretty well; if it's something really big that their parents should know, then I will tell them. I know that if I don't tell their parents, one of the other ones who wasn't involved will. If it's just the usual fighting stuff, then I keep it between us.

Jessica was a single mother for a few years, so she didn't have anyone to hand the discipline off to. However, whenever I watched the girls, I would, on occasion, use the "Just wait till your Mommy comes to pick you up" line on them. Using this threat typically produced the desired effect. I only used it when everything else I tried failed.

It was my husband Dennis, though, who had us all beat. When watching our grandchildren, he didn't like being the disciplinarian, so that left it all up to me. I really tried to encourage him to take the lead when he felt it was necessary, but he just didn't feel comfortable correcting them. One afternoon while we were watching the girls, Rachel came to me about something Livvy had said to her that she didn't like. I told Rachel that she didn't need to tell me every little thing that Livvy said all the time. She needed to stop tattling on Livvy so much. The tattling got under my skin sometimes. It drove me crazy. I could spend my entire day dealing with the tattling.

I told Rachel she needed to get a little thick-skinned and tolerate Livvy a little more, "Don't let it bother you so much. The only reason she says those things to you is so you'll get upset. If she sees it doesn't bother you, then she'll stop."

Just at that moment, Dennis walked up to me, clearly upset, and tattled, "Livvy said '*no*' to me."

I just looked at that huge man who had been blessed with a strong commanding voice. His presence, his size, and that voice could intimidate a ferocious lion. I couldn't help but chuckle to myself that a little 3-year-old girl had defeated him. I found it amusing that Livvy was actually that brave and had the nerve to tell him 'no'. She evidently didn't let the size difference between them get in the way of her saying whatever she wanted. You had to admire that at least just a little bit.

"What do you want me to do about it?" I asked. "You're a grown man. Don't let her talk to you that way."

He looked at me a little sheepishly and replied, "I want you to tell her to stop it. I told her I was going to tell you what she said and that you would put her in time out."

So I guess the threat is no longer "Just wait till your father comes home." It has now changed to: "Just wait till I tell your Grandma."

BEING SCARED
HALF TO DEATH

eing scared when I was small was both fun and... well... scary. My father scared me; my brothers and sisters scared me at different times, and movies scared me. But I loved getting scared. The first time I ever watched *Abbott and Costello Meets Frankenstein*, Dracula (played by Béla Lugosi) scared me half to death. It was a comedy movie, but his character was still very scary. I watched that movie holding a blanket to cover my head when it got just a little too much for me.

My father liked a program called *Strange Tales of Science Fiction* that we all watched together every Saturday night. There wasn't a week when I watched that program that I didn't hide my head in a blanket at least once.

When I was about 10 years old, I watched the movie *The House of Wax* with Vincent Price. That movie was the scariest movie I had ever seen, and it affected me throughout my teenage years. There is a scene in it where the heroine, who is sharing an apartment with a friend, actress Carolyn Jones, comes home to a dark apartment. The heroine doesn't turn the light on. The evil Vincent Price is there, and he had just killed her roommate. The heroine barely escapes with her own life. That part frightened me more than any other part of the movie. That the woman didn't turn on the light or call out to her friend bothered me so much. Who comes home late at night and doesn't turn on any lights? I could never figure that one out. It just seemed so strange to me; she had to have known something was wrong in the apartment, but she went in anyway. At the time I saw that movie, my older sister Dianne and I shared a room together. Dianne was a morning person. I was, and still am, a night owl. Consequently, Dianne always went to bed before me. She would be sound asleep by the time I went to bed. There was not a single night that I didn't turn on the hall light, open our bedroom door to let the light shine on my sister, and wake her up just a little to make sure she was still alive. I didn't turn on the bedroom light nor did I ever fully awaken her. All she had to do was make some kind of sound so I knew no one had killed her and they weren't waiting for me to be the next victim. I usually just called out her name, and she would turn over in bed or make some kind of grumbling noise at the intrusion of her dreams. Her grunts and groans of annoyance were all I needed to be able to go to sleep at night.

This nightly ritual went on until Dianne got married and left me all alone in that room. From then on, I left the light on in my room all evening long and the door open until I went to bed. My room never saw any darkness until I was ready for sleep.

When I was even younger, at the time I shared a room with both my sisters, we had a rule at night: Last one in bed had to turn the light off. The catch was if your feet touched the floor, the sandman would get you. Although this was just a game we made up, I was terrified at being the last one in bed. Unfortunately, I had my share of being that last one. I would jump from the bed to the chair, climb from the chair to the dresser, and then reach for the light switch. Then, in the dark, I had to find my way back to my bed without touching the floor or, heaven forbid, falling to the floor. I was so scared of the sandman that I wouldn't even let my leg hang out over the side of the bed for fear he would grab it and pull me into the sand. And my kids wonder why I'm so neurotic!

Most Friday nights I slept over at my best friend Georgia's house. She lived next door to us until we moved away when I was eleven years old. Georgia and I used to lie in bed those Friday nights taking turns telling a story. One of us would start the story, and when we got tired, the other would continue with the same story. It eventually would turn into a scary tale of our wild imaginations. We did this every week. One Friday night, before going to sleep, we were sitting on her bed while listening to the radio. The Four Seasons were singing "Dawn", and I was singing along. During the song, Georgia kept saying she heard someone at her bedroom window. I thought she was just trying to scare me, maybe start the bedtime story a little early. I didn't hear anything, but she persisted.

"Okay! I'll look out the window, but if nobody is there, I'm going to be mad," I told her, annoyed at her meager attempt at trying to frighten me.

I pulled the shade back and screamed! There *was* a person at the window! It had scared me half to death! Georgia jumped to the window, looked out, and began to laugh. It was a boy from school we both knew. In my fright at someone actually being at the window, I failed to recognize him. We spent the remainder of the evening out on her front porch with the boy, talking and laughing about the whole thing. Georgia and I didn't tell stories that night when we went to bed. It had all been a little too real for me.

When I got married, my husband, Don, worked the graveyard shift, which meant I spent every night alone in my house. When

I was pregnant with our first baby, Jennifer, I had a terrible time sleeping and I was scared most nights. In an attempt to actually get a good night's sleep, I began to take Don to work at midnight and sleep in the backseat of our car in the parking lot under a light. For some reason, sleeping in a parking lot seemed safer to me than in a locked house. It must have been the hormones.

One rare night, when I was home asleep in our bed, I woke up to what I could have sworn was a voice whispering in my ear, "Phillip... Phillip..." the whispering voice said.

I woke up terrified. It didn't matter that I didn't know a Phillip. For all I knew, it was the name of one of the intruders. The voice whispering in my ear was so real though, that I got up, turned all the lights on in the house, got dressed, and walked down to the police station at the corner. The police station was literally one block from my house, yet that didn't seem to calm my fears. I sat in the police station for four hours until daybreak reading wanted posters. It was the only reading material available. Yeah, that helped me sleep better at night! Don thought I was crazy. He spoke to a friend of his at work on the same shift, and Neil said that his wife Glenda had problems sleeping, too. He suggested that I spend the nights with Glenda and we could keep each other company. This idea worked really great. Talk about a spooky house, though! Neil and Glenda lived on a lagoon, and it was almost like a jungle. Their nearest neighbor wasn't anywhere close to being in earshot should someone scream for help. Glenda slept with a shotgun next to her bed, and I wasn't sure if I felt safe or not.

"Glenda," I asked one night, "do you know how to use that shotgun?"

Glenda smiled, "You bet I do. I've been out to the rifle range practicing, and I can hit a target dead on at 20 yards."

Okay, maybe I did feel safer. Although, in all fairness to

Glenda and I, this was in Santa Cruz during a period of time when the Santa Cruz Police were digging up bodies all over the place. Santa Cruz was the murder capital of the country at that time, so we had a right to be scared. My husband eventually changed shifts to the swing shift, and he got off work at midnight. Waiting for him to come home was better, but I still didn't feel safe. So I walked to where he worked, in the dark on a road with no sidewalks or streetlights, to meet him at midnight when he got off work. For protection, I carried a handgun in my pocket. I decided that if anyone had tried to get me into a car against my will, they'd find a little surprise waiting for them when I pulled the gun out. My father taught me how to use a gun at a very early age, and I was pretty sure I wasn't afraid to use it, so I was ready for anyone who tried to mess with me.

For some strange reason, the fear of sleeping alone in my house changed once I had children. Maybe it was because I was no longer alone, but it wasn't as if my newborn baby could protect me. I have never been able to figure out why the fear went away. Maybe it was because I had children that I needed to protect. If that were true, we were in a lot of trouble, because I wasn't very brave.

When my children got a little older, Friday nights became a special treat for them. That was the night my husband took all the kids to the drive-in for a movie. It was also the night I got to have time alone for me. After I started having children, I missed being alone. Go figure! I looked forward to Friday night every week. On the way home from work, I would stop at the butcher and buy the biggest, thickest New York steak they had, stop at the produce section for a potato to bake, and once VCRs came into existence, I would rent a movie I wanted to watch. Once everyone left, I baked the potato, started the BBQ, and when it was all cooked, I ate my dinner and watched the movie in silence. It was heaven for me each week, and the kids got to have time with just their father and get out of the house for a movie. It was a win/win evening.

In 1982, my husband took our four children to the drive-in to see *ET*. My kids loved that movie so much they begged their father to take them to see it again several Friday nights in a row. I had heard about another Steven Spielberg movie playing at the theaters called *Poltergeist*.

"You should take the kids to see that movie next week. I looked the word 'Poltergeist' up in the dictionary, and it means 'a loud ghost'. If the man who directed *ET* wrote a screenplay about a loud ghost, I'm sure it is a children's movie too," I suggested pretty naïvely.

That Friday night, my husband took our four young children to see *Poltergeist*. I have no idea why he ever listened to me. You'd think after so many years of marriage he would stop listening to my suggestions. What did I know? I never went to the movies! While I was at home eating a thick, juicy steak, that loud ghost was horrifying my children! My husband came home looking for blood.

"Do you know *anything* about that movie?" he demanded.

"Not really," I replied, starting to feel a little uneasy at his tone. I got the feeling I was in big trouble and started to back away from him. "Why?"

He really had to try and regain his composure. "It was not a children's movie! It was actually quite scary! I'll be surprised if Jeffrey ever sleeps again!" he shouted.

Jeffrey had a real problem with nightmares. Even movies that weren't scary but left you on the edge of your seat gave him nightmares. We only allowed him to see children's movies or comedies.

The following morning, Jennifer got up and immediately

started in on me, "Way to go, Mom! Jessica cried all the way home. She's only 3 ½ years old, for goodness sake! I'll probably never get my own room now, because Jessica will be forever scared that her closet has a ghost in it. Good one!"

Okay… maybe I used a little poor judgment on that one. It wasn't the first time, and I knew it wouldn't be the last.

Stephen King has always been one of my favorite authors. I have burned the midnight oil many nights reading his books. Although *The Shining* was not my favorite of his books, it was by far the scariest to me. There is a scene in the book which was not in the movie that scared me so much I closed the book in mid-sentence and went to bed. I was too afraid to even finish the sentence. It was the scene where the little boy was outside playing in the playground and he was in some kind of toy tunnel. He felt a presence all around him, and then a hand touched him, or something like that. I can't remember all the details anymore. It's been too many years since I read it. Stephen King also wrote a novelette called *Children of the Corn* that was made into a movie. One Friday night, while my husband and children were out at the drive-in, I became a little bored at home by myself. There wasn't much on TV that I was interested in, so I decided to go to a theater and see Stephen King's new movie instead. I had read it, so I knew how it ended and knew what to expect. I think I left the theater before the movie ended because I was so scared. I drove home only to find my family hadn't returned yet. What kind of idiot was I? Who goes out to watch a scary movie and return to an empty house? I couldn't go into my house alone. It had been empty for at least a couple of hours, and I had forgotten to leave a light on, so the house was dark. Who knew what might be waiting for me inside? I pulled out of my driveway and just drove around for another hour until I was sure my husband and children were home. I had to stop doing stuff like that.

But I loved Stephen King. Although my favorite book of his is *The Stand*, I enjoyed his books about real life situations like *Cujo* and *Misery*, stories that could conceivably really happen. When *Cujo* came out in theaters, I suggested we all go together to the drive-in to see it. It would be "Family night", a special treat, and Mommy was going to go to the movies, too. It was just a story about a beautiful dog that got bit by a rabid bat and consequently caught rabies himself. It was an edge-of-your-seat movie, but not really scary, I didn't think.

Unfortunately, Jessica thought it was very scary. During the movie, she begged us to leave, "Don't make me watch this! Can we please go home? Please?" she cried.

I certainly didn't want to traumatize her for life, so we left. For years after taking Jessica to see that movie, we couldn't say the name Cujo around her without her bursting into hysteria. Her older brothers and sister actually used that to make her cry on demand whenever she made them mad. Jessica often came crying to me complaining that someone had whispered "Cujo" to her.

One of Jennifer's first jobs as a teenager was at a movie theater in downtown San Jose. On her day off, she could get passes to go see movies at selected theaters in the area. When *Misery* was released, Jennifer took both Jessica and I to see it. Jessica was about 11 years old and big enough to handle these types of movies — I thought. The three of us sat in the theater, watching as Kathy Bates broke James Caan's ankles. We all turned our heads and gasped in horror at that scene. But it was the scene when Kathy Bates brought out a syringe to give James Caan an injection of some type of drug that made Jessica scream. At that moment, the movie theater had been totally silent when Jessica let out her scream, and then the theater erupted into laughter in response. Nothing seemed to bother Jessica throughout the entire movie until the syringe: a car accident, broken bones, blood. She took all these in stride. But she couldn't handle the syringe.

Now that my kids have children of their own, one of them will occasionally remark about the lack of good judgment their father and I showed with our selection of movies they were allowed to see.

"Okay, okay, I guess we should have paid more attention to the movie ratings," I said in my own defense.

"That's what they're there for!" has always been the reply.

The last movie Jennifer and I went to see together in San Jose before moving to Florida was *Silence of the Lambs*. I had worked that day, so we decided to go to the 9:00 P.M. show. By the time the movie had ended, it was really late. The movie was disturbing, to say the least, and we talked about it the entire car ride home.

"Oh, by the way," I had remembered, "I need to stop by the store to get some milk for breakfast in the morning."

"Are you *just* getting milk?" she asked.

"Only milk," I assured her.

"Then I'll just wait for you here in the car… well… maybe not. Maybe I'll just go in with you," she said with just a trace of trepidation in her voice.

I smiled to myself but was grateful for the company.

My grandchildren don't watch scary movies yet, but they are afraid of other things. Livvy is afraid of Zombies. She saw a statue of one once and has not stopped talking about them since. Zombies are everywhere for her.

"Livvy, can you throw your trash away in the kitchen?" I have asked her.

"I can't. There's a zombie in there!" she whines.

If she didn't seem so sincere in her fear, I would think she was using that as an excuse to get out of doing a lot of stuff. But her fear seems to be real.

Rachel and Livvy were in bed for the night when Livvy came into the living room crying, "Grandma, Rachel looks like a Zombie!"

I picked Livvy up and tried to calm her, "Livvy, what are you talking about? Rachel is so beautiful. She doesn't look like a Zombie."

I carried Livvy back into the bedroom, and there was Rachel with the covers pulled up over her head.

"See!" Livvy cried. "She looks like a Zombie!"

At that, she hid her face in my shoulder. I pulled the covers down from Rachel's head.

"See? It's only Rachel. Doesn't she look so sweet laying there asleep?" I asked her.

"Okay, she doesn't look like a Zombie anymore. But if she does that again, I will be scared," Livvy warned.

I have tried everything to make the Zombies go away.

"Livvy, there are no such things as Zombies."

She doesn't buy that for a moment. Have I mentioned that Livvy is also the single most stubborn person on the face of the planet?

"Livvy, Zombies are only in scary movies. They don't live in Florida. They don't like the humidity. They're afraid of alligators. It rains too much here. Thunder scares them. Livvy, there are no Zombies at Grandma's house. I don't let them come here. They're afraid of my cat. They're afraid of Grandma. They're afraid of Grandpa. I would never let anything hurt you.

I wouldn't let a Zombie come anywhere close to you."

I've tried them all, but none of these seem to work. Sometimes I wonder if she is like the little boy from *The Sixth Sense* who sees dead people, but in Livvy's case, she sees Zombies — Zombies no one else can see.

We have a swing set in our backyard under an old oak tree. The kids play on this every time they come over. Because the tree is so old, there are knots on the trunk where low branches have been cut away. One of those knots caught Rachel's attention one day. While swinging and singing, (The girls always sing while they swing.) Rachel stopped her swing, jumped off, and came running into the house crying, "Grandma, there's a face on the tree!"

Livvy naturally had to add her opinion, too, "It's a Zombie!"

I had no idea what she meant, but I ran out to the backyard, afraid of what I might find. Rachel followed me out still crying. I looked at the tree but didn't see what she was talking about.

"There! On the side of the tree! Can't you see it?" Rachel cried.

"It's a Zombie!" Livvy chimed in again.

What Rachel was so afraid of was a knot that had a few bumps on it, and by using your imagination, it could, in some small way, look vaguely like a face. I didn't have the slightest clue how to fix it. Just then, Dennis came out of the house wondering what was going on. I showed him the part of the tree that Rachel was so afraid of that she wouldn't come into the backyard anymore.

Grandpa assessed the tree and weighed his options. He walked back into the house and told Rachel not to worry; he'd take care of it. He went out to the garage, got the chainsaw, and went back out to the tree. Grandpa cut the knot down closer to the trunk of the tree, and, once that was done, he painted the knot brown so it would blend in better with the rest of the tree. I was very moved at what he had done for Rachel. It was all she needed to go back out and swing.

The other day, Jessica's family was over visiting. We were all in the den and the kids were playing on my new desk chair. The chair was like riding on the Mad Tea-Cups at Disney World. My chair can spin and spin, and they love it. The girls began to fight over whose turn it was next on the chair, and Livvy ended up getting into trouble by her mother. Livvy stormed off to the guest bedroom where they sleep on Saturday night and shut the door. I could hear Livvy crying and it broke my heart. Jessica ignored her daughter's cries, and I tried to do the same. After several minutes, I asked Jessica if I could go in to check on Livvy and calm her down a little.

"Go in there if you want to," Jessica said with an amused grin on her face.

Jessica was often amused at my expense where her children were concerned. I opened the door, and Livvy immediately got a look of total fear on her face.

"It was an accident! I didn't mean to!" Livvy pleaded.

I hadn't noticed, but before I opened the door, Livvy had stopped crying. She stopped crying because she had knocked over a small table in the bedroom that was next to the bed. It had a music box and a few pictures on it. Everything was on the floor, and I could that tell Livvy had just begun to pick things up. But Livvy was terrified that she was in trouble for knocking the table over. She kept saying over and over, "It was an accident! I didn't mean to!"

My heart just went out to her. I scooped her up in my arms

and told her not to be afraid. I wasn't mad. Then it hit me like a ton of bricks. Was Livvy actually afraid of me, or was it instinct that she was naturally afraid because she had knocked something over? I wasn't sure, and it really worried me. I held Livvy and rocked her in my arms until she stopped crying.

"Livvy, I would never be mad at you for an accident. I cause accidents sometimes too. Everyone does. Please don't be afraid that I would be mad at you for accidentally knocking something over. If you did it on purpose, I would be upset, but never for an accident," I consoled her.

I put Livvy down and asked her to help me pick all the things up and set the table back the way it was.

Later, I couldn't get it out of my mind that Livvy had been so afraid. I just wasn't sure if it had been a natural instinct or if she had really been afraid of me. I hated to think that she was afraid of me. I didn't think I had ever given her any reason to be afraid. But my own children told me a few years ago that they were often afraid of me when they were small. They all told me that I got a look in my eyes when I was angry that frightened them. They said I had the same look as Michelle Pfeiffer in *Ladyhawke* at the end of the movie when she dropped the tethers into the evil Bishop's hands. The look on her face was unnerving, cold, and contemptuous. I felt terrible when my children told me that, and I prayed that my grandchildren never saw that look in my eyes. I adore my grandchildren and never want them to feel anything but safe when they were with me.

Several weeks later, Livvy was punching holes in a piece of paper with a pencil on the couch. I hadn't been paying attention. When she was finished, Rachel called my attention to the couch and the pencil marks on it.

"Livvy," I began, "look at these pencil marks you made

on the couch."

Livvy immediately cut me off, "Grandma, you said you wouldn't get mad at me for an accident."

Man was she good! I looked at her standing there getting ready to cry.

"Livvy, you are so right. I'm not mad at you. I promised you I would never get mad at you for an accident, and I'm not mad. But, in the future, let's only put holes in paper that's on the table, okay?"

I scooped her up in my arms as I had done the previous time and hugged and kissed her face. I've never known anyone like Livvy.

I am now in my early 50s and still have never learned. A few short years ago, my husband Dennis went to Michigan for a week to visit his daughter and grandsons. I love my husband very much, but I enjoy a few days all to myself every now and then. I took this opportunity to rent some movies that I knew Dennis would not care to watch. I enjoy psychological thrillers very much and rented one called *Identity* with John Cusack. I like John Cusack as an actor and was looking forward to watching the movie. I called Outback Steakhouse on my way home from work and ordered take-out for dinner. I no longer go to the trouble of stopping at the butchers for a steak or baking a potato when it is only me. I sat in my living room with my steak, baked potato, and Pepsi and started the movie, just like old times. An hour into the movie, I turned it off and began berating myself for renting and watching such a scary movie all by myself. I was going to be alone for the next few days for goodness sake! And how was I supposed to go to sleep all alone tonight?

I couldn't believe I had been so crazy as to think I would actually enjoy watching a murder mystery all by myself, so I called Jessica and asked, trying very hard not to sound desperate, "Hey, I know it's a school night, but can the girls spend the night? I'll take them to school in the morning. It'll give you a little extra sleep."

I didn't have much alone time that week. I either spent my time with my daughters or had my grandchildren spending the night with me.

A few weeks later, I told my daughters about renting the movie while Dennis had been gone and they both laughed at me. I'm always an easy target for them. They seem to get a lot of enjoyment from my stupidity.

"Mom, didn't you watch the end?" Jessica asked me.

"If I watched anymore of it than I did, I'd never be able to sleep alone again," I replied.

"So you have no idea how it ended?" she drilled. "You'll have to watch it again all the way through. The end of the movie reveals everything!"

"Are you crazy?" I demanded. "I'm too old to watch those kinds of movies anymore. I used to love them. Now I'll have to live without them."

Being scared is something we all eventually grow out of, or maybe we just find more adult things to be afraid of — that is — if we're mature adults. I know I'm no longer afraid of Dracula... I think. I couldn't tell you for sure about Malachi from *The Children of the Corn* though. I think I'll call Jessica on the phone right now and whisper "Cujo" in her ear just to test my theory.

THE CALL OF THE WILD

My father was the "Great White Hunter". If you could hunt it, kill it, skin it, and eat it — he did. He went deer hunting in Utah each Fall, and we ate venison all Winter. As children, he would take us out to vineyards in the valley, and we would be his spotters for rabbit. All the kids in the neighborhood knew that if you found a snake in your yard, you brought it to my dad. He would take an ax, chop off its head, and skin it. Before I was born, while he was working in Culver City at a studio on a construction site, he came across a bull snake. It was huge! He skinned it, and when I began kindergarten, I took it to Show and Tell. It was about 6-7 feet long and 12-14 inches wide. All the kids in school were in awe of this enormous snakeskin. I always thought my father was the bravest dad in the whole world. He wasn't afraid of anything! Not even snakes!

We used to go camping at Lake Isabella on our family vacations. During our camping trips, my father always took us on long hikes through the foothills where there were no trails. On one trip during our hike, we all heard the unmistakable sound of a rattlesnake ready to strike — all of us but my father that is. My brother Steve was the one who warned my father, and we all stopped dead in our tracks, afraid to move. Steve saw the snake first, at my father's feet and about to strike. My father, who always carried a handgun while camping, pulled it out and shot off the first round, missing the snake completely. What is remarkable about him missing the snake is that my father holds a Master rating in shooting a handgun. He NEVER misses. But he not only missed the first shot, he missed the next four as well. I guess he had been caught completely off guard by the snake and had difficulty regaining his composure. It wasn't until the last bullet that he was able to hit his mark. The snake didn't know how lucky it was that my father was out of bullets. If there had been more bullets in the gun at that point, my father would have gone in for overkill. The snake would have been pulverized. Knowing my father, missing the first five times probably really upset him. My dad carried the dead snake back to camp where he skinned it and had us kids hold it up for a picture he still has. It wasn't a big one, just a couple of feet long, but big enough to make a Master miss his mark.

My brother Steve found a snake in our backyard once, and he convinced my father not to kill it but instead to keep it as a pet. My dad built a huge box out of plywood, and we kept the snake in there. We all loved playing with the snake, and he never bit any of us. While the snake was our family pet, I had older cousins who came out to visit us from Ohio. Judy and Francis loved using the snake to scare my mother. They put the snake down my mother's back once, and she danced around the room trying to get it out while we all laughed hysterically.

Another time they put the snake in my mother's purse. When she opened her purse and saw the snake, she let out a scream, which was what we were all anticipating. My mother took all this abuse from my cousins in stride. She was always good-natured about things like that.

It was my cousin's older sister who led to the snake's demise though. Terry was the oldest of the four girls, and she didn't see the humor in the snake at all. When Terry, Judy, and Francis were all at our house for dinner one evening, Judy and Francis took the snake and just dropped it in Terry's lap. Terry was terrified. She screamed and wouldn't stop screaming until my dad grabbed the snake off her lap. He took the snake out back and chopped off its head. It was too small to skin. I was a young child at the time and thought my cousin Terry crying over a silly little snake was so funny. I spoke to Terry about this incident once when we were older adults, and I chuckled at the memory. Terry still doesn't find the humor in it.

My own family had our share of unusual animals. Our neighbors across the street raised rabbits, and Joey asked us if we could have a rabbit for a pet. It was hard to tell him no. We had a fenced yard, and the rabbit had the run of the place. Shortly after getting the rabbit, it disappeared. We thought it had gotten out of the yard somewhere, and Joey asked for a replacement. He brought the new rabbit home and all was right with the world. The following day, the first rabbit showed up, so now we had two rabbits. I went to the grocery store each day to get scraps from the produce department of lettuce, cabbage, carrots, and whatever else I thought they might eat.

One hectic morning, while I was trying to get all four children their breakfast, make four lunches, and get four kids off to school, Jeffrey asked me if he could take one of the rabbits to school for Show and Tell.

"Whatever," was my reply. I really wasn't paying that close attention. I had children who had lost their homework that I had to help find. I also had to sign a permission slip for something and a fight that I needed to break up. After the kids left for school, I sat down to catch my breath and called my sister, Mary, in England. We talked on the phone for a really long time. This was back in the day before *call waiting*. I had completely forgotten about Jeffrey taking the rabbit to school. In fact, it really didn't even register to me that he had taken the rabbit. While I was still in my pajamas, with breakfast dishes in the sink, and on the phone with my sister, the principal of my children's school came to my door carrying our rabbit. I really can't remember a time when I was more embarrassed.

"I tried calling your house, but the line was busy," was all he said.

I made my apologies and thanked him for bringing the rabbit home. I'm sure he wondered what kind of mother I must be to let a kid bring a rabbit to school and just leave it there. What was the rabbit going to do all day? The box my son had taken the rabbit to school in didn't even have a lid. The rabbit probably kept jumping out and disrupting the classroom. I probably got my name put on some kind of list of ditsy parents.

We had the rabbits for about two weeks when it was time for our annual camping trip to Mt. Madonna, outside of Watsonville, for our Memorial Day Weekend. I was packing up the camper the day before and going through the refrigerator looking for stuff that might spoil before our return. I went out to the backyard to feed the rabbits the remainder of lettuce I had in my refrigerator, when I saw little piles of something all over the yard. Upon inspection, I discovered baby rabbits. I immediately ran across the street to the neighbors who had given us the rabbits to inquire as to what I should do. They told me that most rabbits pull their fur out to make a bed for the babies and to look for fur around the yard. If I saw any, I should gather it up, put it in a secluded spot, and place the babies on the fur.

I went home, gathered up an enormous amount of fur, and went to retrieve the babies. Some of them were already dead. It was just too hot and they were directly in the sun. I gathered up the remaining babies and then the mother rabbit. Once I cleaned up the dead babies, I noticed the other rabbit was pulling fur out. Within minutes, *she* was having babies, too. I couldn't believe our luck. I hadn't known the gender of either rabbit at the time. Apparently, they were both female and had both been pregnant.

When my husband returned home from work, I expressed my concerns to him about the rabbits being left in the backyard all weekend with their tiny, new babies. I was afraid that neighboring cats might hurt, kill, and eat them. I told him I wanted to bring them into the house and keep them in our bathroom. He strenuously objected to this suggestion. Naturally I didn't listen to him, and before we left the following day, I brought both rabbits and all the babies into my bathroom. I left plenty of food and water for them and shut the door.

We had a great time camping, but it had been really hot. We experienced the first heat wave of the year that weekend. San Jose can get pretty warm but not too hot. Most people, including us, didn't even have air conditioning in our homes. It's not really needed except on a few days out of the year when a heat wave comes to town. The temperature topped out at 104 degrees that weekend. When we arrived back home, my husband put the key in the lock, turned the knob, and a sickening smell overwhelmed us as he opened the door. He closed it as fast as he could.

"Did you put those rabbits in our bathroom?" he yelled, demanding an answer from me.

"Um... yes, I did. Cats would have eaten the babies!" I tried defending myself.

"I'm not going into the house and neither are the kids until you clean up whatever is causing that smell!"

I didn't blame them. I certainly didn't want to go in there

either. The smell was so bad that I was ready to just cut my losses, leave all my possessions, move somewhere else, and start all over.

I cracked open the door to my bathroom and was shocked at what I saw! There were a billion flies in my bathroom. I couldn't even fathom where they had all came from. Both of the mother rabbits were dead, a couple of the babies were dead, and there were maggots eating them. I was so disgusted that I ran into the other bathroom to vomit. It took most of the evening to kill all the flies, get everything cleaned up, disinfect the bathroom, and move the remaining live rabbits outside. I have no idea why so many of the rabbits died or what had happened. All I knew was that I had about nine live baby rabbits and no mothers.

The babies thrived and were so cute, but I knew that if I didn't do something quick, I would soon be overrun with rabbits. I sat my children down and told them that the rabbits had to go. On top of everything else, we no longer had grass in our backyard. The rabbits had eaten all of it. The kids were heartbroken, but they seemed to understand. I let them come with me to the animal shelter so they could say goodbye. While waiting our turn at the desk, a man behind us saw that we had rabbits. He began asking how old they were and why we were giving them up. I explained that I was worried about having a hundred rabbits within a couple of months.

In front of my children, the man suggested how we could keep the population down, "Why don't you eat some of them?" he asked.

My children were horrified!

He went on, "They're really good to eat, especially when they're young like this. The meat is so tender."

"Sir!" I exclaimed. "My children love these rabbits! They have been pets! We couldn't possibly eat them! Please don't suggest any such thing in front of my children again!"

He didn't say another word to my children or to me, but, as we left, I did hear him talking to the woman behind the desk about taking the rabbits home with him. I just prayed that my children didn't hear that conversation.

We ran into almost the same problem a few years later. When Jessica was in the fifth grade, her class had a pet hamster. Each weekend, a different child took the hamster home to take care of it, so Jessica brought it home over Thanksgiving weekend. She just loved that hamster and had been diligent in her care of it, so her father and I decided to give her one for Christmas that year. On Christmas Eve morning, I went to the local pet store at the mall to buy one. Evidently, hamsters are a popular gift for young children at Christmas. I was unable to find one anywhere within the San Jose city limits. It being Christmas Eve, and not having the main gift for Jessica, I decided to get her a couple of mice. They were cheap.

The mice were a big hit on Christmas morning, and her father and I thought we had made a good choice in buying them for her. We soon discovered that we had purchased both a male and a female, because babies began to arrive. At first we were all excited. We had them out in the main living area of our house, and the kids' friends all came over to see them. Within two days, all the babies were gone. Only their bones remained. I was horrified that the parents had eaten their babies! I went to the pet store and bought a book about mice. I found out they don't like loud areas, and if they feel their young are being threatened, they will eat them. Yeah, that made a lot of sense!

Two weeks later, a new litter of mice were born. This time we put their cage in the closet so they wouldn't feel threatened. This approach worked well. But mice inbreed. I think they are actually born pregnant. It wasn't long before the cage was full of mice. What's more, we had to keep them in the closet so they wouldn't eat each other. What kind of pet was that? I called the pet store, and they said that they would buy back the babies for 50 cents each. I don't know why I didn't keep the mice in their cage and take them to the pet store that way, but I decided to take them back to the pet store in a paper sack. Jessica held the paper sack full of mice while I drove the car back to the pet store.

We were just a couple of blocks from the mall when Jessica began screaming, "Mommy! They're eating their way out of the bag! I don't know if I can keep them in!" she cried frantically.

Visions of mice all over my car ran through my head. All it would take was for one pregnant mouse to get loose in my car without my being able to find it, and within a couple of weeks, I would have hundreds of mice running free throughout my car. I could just see me driving on the freeway and feel one on my foot. I would collide with another car as I looked down and saw hundreds of mice running up my leg. By the time the paramedics arrived, all of the mice would have eaten me, and the paramedics would be perplexed as to what had actually happened. They would think the car had been abandoned and mice had taken over. My husband would think I had run off to Mexico or some exotic place with the pool man, Juan (We really didn't have a pool man.). My children would think I no longer loved them and that I had abandoned them. They would spend the rest of their lives looking for me, never knowing I had died in my car and had been eaten by mice. I couldn't allow a single mouse to get free!

"Jessica! We're almost there! Do the best you can to keep the holes they're making closed. As soon as I get the car parked, I'll take the bag," I promised her.

I parked the car, grabbed the bag, and ran as fast as I could to the pet store. We made it in time and all mice were accounted for, but some of the mice were too young to sell back to the pet store.

"I don't care. Just take them anyway. You can have them for free. They're my gift to you. Feed them to the snakes. Whatever you want; I just can't take any home with me. They're giving me nightmares!" I told the clerk.

We were doing really well for a while without any rabbits or mice. The following summer, though, after returning home from a ball game, my son, Joey, found a huge black bug in our driveway.

"Mom, come here! You've got to see this!" he said excitedly.

It was the biggest bug I had ever seen. I have no idea what kind it was… it was just huge. Joey ran into the house and grabbed a Styrofoam cup to put the bug in. Once he got the bug into the cup, he brought it around to our back patio. He called me outside to take a closer look at the bug. When he took his hand off the top of the cup, the bug flew out and landed on his back shoulder. Joey began screaming for me to get the bug off him as he ran around in circles trying to reach it with his own hands. I was laughing so hard, and the bug was so big, I just couldn't bring myself to swat it off my son.

"I can't touch it!" I said to him through tears of laughter.

The bug finally fell off his shoulder and landed on the patio. I went back into the house and ever so faintly heard my son tell the bug under his breath that it was about to be torched. I heard the words, but either they didn't register or I just wasn't paying that close attention, or maybe I didn't have any idea what my son had in mind. I just walked back into our house while laughing to myself at the image of my son screaming for me to get the bug off him. I realized later that Joey should have spoken a little louder.

I sat down in the family room to watch TV and didn't pay any attention to what Joey was doing. He went into the garage, brought the gas can out to the patio, and poured gasoline into the Styrofoam cup where the bug sat on death row. Joey continued to pour gas into the cup as the gas ate through it. He finally lit a match and there was an audible *SWOOSH*. Everyone for miles around saw a very large fireball as the gas caught fire. Before I could even get the sliding door opened, Joey had run to our swimming pool and tried to pour water onto the gas fire. We all know what water does in a gas fire; Joey just spread the fire all across our patio. My husband came running out with a fire extinguisher and put out the flames. Joey wasn't hurt, and there was no damage done to any property. He looked at the ashes left from the Styrofoam cup, and I could see the look of satisfaction on his face.

Living in Florida, there is an abundance of wild animals around. I live in the city of St. Petersburg with a population of approximately 250,000 people. This is not a small city. Yet I have lizards, cranes, squirrels, armadillos, and possums in my backyard. And they're not indigenous to only my yard. Everyone has them.

The first time I saw a possum in my backyard, I wasn't sure what it was. They only come out at night, so, initially, I didn't get a good look at it. Sometimes cats come into my yard. and when I see them, I shoo them away. Possums can't be shooed. When it saw me we locked eyes, and it just turned around ever so casually and walked away like it was out for an evening stroll. I was stunned. I called my husband to come take a look.

I described to him what I had seen, and he confirmed what I had suspected; it was a possum. It looked like a huge rat to me. I made the mistake of telling Rachel about the possum, and she wouldn't go into my backyard for weeks. Sometimes, now, she will wait in my enclosed lanai to see if one will show itself to her. If she ever does see one, that will probably be it for her. She'll never play outside again.

There are three things that Florida has more of than any other state, I believe: lizards, mosquitoes, and roaches. On any given summer day, walking down a sidewalk is like walking through an obstacle course just trying to avoid stepping on the lizards. They are everywhere. Occasionally, one will get into my house, and my grandkids always let me know when they see one. I tell them that the lizards are our friends; they eat the mosquitoes.

Everyone here gets roaches in their house, too. You just can't stop them or avoid them. All you can do is have a good pest control person come out to your house once or twice a year. They are not the kind of roach that gets into your food. These are the big kind. The kind you hate to step on because of the crunching noise it makes. And just because you've stepped on them and heard the crunch doesn't mean they're dead either. They like to play possum, too. You see one on its back and you assume it's dead, so when you casually pick it up with a napkin it catches you off guard and take off running. They are the kind with wings that you measure with a ruler. They come in looking for water and can usually be found in the bathroom or close to a point of entry. For me it's my family room. Usually they're dead by the time I see them, thanks to my pest control. When you begin finding live ones in your house, it's time to call the pest control people again.

One time, Livvy found a dead roach behind an ornamental

tree in my family room. Since that time, that tree represents to her the place where roaches are. One Sunday afternoon after church, the girls were playing in the family room and Rachel got a little too close to the tree for Livvy's comfort.

"Rachel, be careful. There might be a roach behind the tree!" Livvy warned.

Rachel immediately scooted away from the tree, but Livvy was determined to make sure there weren't any roaches, just to be on the safe side. She tiptoed to the tree and looked all around. She turned to Rachel, "Rachel, it's okay. There aren't any roaches. You can sit there if you want." Nothing like your little sister watching your back.

There was a lizard once in my shower that stayed there for weeks. Rachel and Livvy named it Lizzy the Lizard. Every morning, I got up and took a shower with Lizzy. The heat of the shower and the soap never seemed to bother it. I was always careful not to step on it or clean it with the shower cleaners I used. I figured it was there to eat any mosquitoes that flew around my shower. Lizzy was my protector against them. Rachel and Livvy went into my bathroom each Saturday night to say hello. Lizzy was like their little friend. I never knew what eventually happened to Lizzy. One day it was just gone. I imagine that someday when I move, I will find its remains under my bed or nightstand.

One of the most frightening animal experiences I had was with a squirrel. Rachel was just a couple of months old at the time. She was born nine weeks premature and was in the hospital for five weeks before Jessica could bring her home. The only real problem she had was that her heartbeat slowed a little too much from time to time. Believe it or not, Rachel was put on caffeine to help stimulate her heart rate. The caffeine consequently caused

Rachel to cry quite a bit. In fact, Rachel cried every second she was awake.

Jessica lived in an apartment complex just down the street from where I worked, so every day at lunch I went to Jessica's to give her a much needed break. On one afternoon, Jennifer had come to visit, too. Rachel had fallen asleep in Jessica's arms, and we were all out on her front patio enjoying the shade and quiet time together. From out of nowhere, a squirrel approached Jessica and jumped on her shoulder. Jessica bolted from her chair and began to run, screaming for us to get the squirrel off her back. The problem was, Jessica was running away from us. Jennifer and I kept yelling at her to be still so we could get the squirrel off. She finally listened, and I grabbed Rachel from her arms and ran into the apartment as Jennifer tried to swat at the squirrel. She was finally able to get the squirrel off Jessica, and they both ran into the apartment. When we were able to relax about the situation, we began to laugh. Jessica reminded us of Shelly Long in the movie *The Money Pit* with Tom Hanks, when a raccoon jumped on her shoulder from a dumbwaiter and she reacted the same way; she just took off running and screaming.

The other most frightening animal experience was with a lemur monkey. Our neighbors across the street had one as a pet. The monkey was a friendly little guy but still a wild animal. The owners used to let the monkey loose out in the front yard from time to time. Occasionally, the lemur would come to our house. I got a knock on the door one time from my UPS driver, asking me if I knew where the monkey lived. Evidently, while he was delivering a package to my house, the monkey had gotten into his truck and wouldn't leave.

Rachel and Livvy spent the night at our house one evening, and the next morning I took them to school. As I was strapping

Livvy into her car seat, the monkey jumped into my car. Rachel became hysterical — and I mean hysterical. Livvy started crying too. But Rachel was just the most hysterical person I had ever seen in my entire life. I tried to shoo the monkey out of my car but couldn't get him out. I was afraid to grab him for fear he would bite me. I opened the driver's side door and started honking my horn. I guess between the horn and the screaming from Rachel, the monkey had enough and jumped out. Even though Livvy wasn't completely strapped in yet, I immediately slammed the car doors shut. I figured I would pull over down the street where it was safe and finish strapping her in. Dennis came running out of the house once he heard the horn.

"What's wrong?" he asked, concerned.

"That monkey! Look at Rachel! She's terrified! You need to go talk to them about their monkey or I'm calling the authorities!" I yelled at my innocent husband.

He was furious that they would allow their monkey to roam free throughout the neighborhood and even more furious that it had terrorized our grandchildren. Dennis did speak to the neighbors, and they promised to keep the monkey caged in the morning, in the evening, or whenever they saw that the girls were at our house. We never really saw the monkey again after that. I heard that they eventually got rid of it and have since moved away. But for a long time after that incident, Rachel looked for the monkey whenever she got in or out of our car.

Through all of this, I have come to learn something about myself: I'm not an animal person. I have had my fill of snakes, rabbits, mice, possums, bugs, and monkeys. You'd think I grew up living at the zoo or a jungle all my life and not in the big city. If I never see another roach, possum, snake, bear, lemur, squirrel, or rabbit in my lifetime, that would be okay with me.

CAN YOU HEAR ME NOW?

The telephone was always a source of conflict when I was growing up. We had one phone in the house and ten people who used it, five of whom were teenage girls. We all had friends who called us, and, naturally, there were the calls from our boyfriends. Someone was always yelling at the one on the phone to get off. There was also never any privacy for our phone conversations. The cord didn't reach very far. That's right — this was back when phones were attached to a cord from the wall! Our phone was centrally located in the dining room and went as far as the living room. The other rooms it reached were the half-bath that someone always wanted to use, the kitchen, where we all congregated if we weren't watching TV, or my mother and stepfather's bedroom where we weren't allowed. There was just no privacy! I had daydreams of having my own phone one day, a phone that I could use whenever and however long I wanted. No one would be interrupting me to get off because they needed to make an important call. The phone would ring and it would always be for me. I could talk all night if I wanted. I held onto that dream until I got married.

The phone became such an issue with my stepfather that he put a lock on it when he wasn't home. He had tried to call home one afternoon and continually received a busy signal. This was way before call waiting. He was furious at the incessant beep… beep… beep… of the busy signal. The little lock went on the phone that night. It went around one of the higher numbers like 9 or 0 and attached to the little finger stop. That's right — not only was it a corded phone, but it was also a rotary phone that you actually dialed instead of pushing buttons. We could receive calls, but we couldn't make them.

That little lock caused a lot of heartburn for us kids. The only way around it was to make sure all our friends had our phone number and they knew they had to call us. Next, my stepfather put a time limit rule on our phone use. We were only allowed fifteen minutes per call.

"You've got to be kidding!" we all cried. "You can barely get a greeting out in fifteen minutes. How can I catch up on all the stuff that's happened since I saw my friends earlier today at school! I'll be going to school tomorrow so uninformed!"

The rule I hated most was that we were not allowed to make two consecutive calls. If I found out some really great news from one friend, I had to wait for my turn to come around again before I could call my best friend and tell her. We could have really used cell phones, text messaging, or e-mail back then. We began bribing each other for the next turn at the phone.

"You can have all my turns at the phone tomorrow night if you let me make a phone call right now," I'd plead.

"You know tomorrow is Friday night and I'll be out with my boyfriend," my stepsister would protest. She was never easy.

"What about Saturday night?" I tried again. I just never had anything to bargain with.

The one thing that bugged my stepfather more than anything about the phone, I suspect, was me talking on the phone with my best friend Terri. We spent almost every evening together. We walked each other halfway home down the street at night, and the minute we both got home, we would be on the phone talking with each other again.

"What can you possibly have to talk about? Didn't you just spend the last couple of hours together? Don't you walk to school with her in the morning, have lunch with her at noon, walk home together in the afternoon, and spend the whole evening together?" he'd ask incredulously.

We had important information to exchange with one another. Men just don't get it.

The phone ringing was cause for your heart to skip a beat in anticipation as to who was being called and who was doing the calling. The phone would ring, and people would jump from every nook and cranny in the house just to be the one to answer the phone. Sometimes the only privacy you got was the fact that you answered the phone, and if it was for you, no one knew who you were talking to.

One afternoon when the phone rang, my sister, Mary, and I dashed for the phone at the same time as if it was a matter of life or death. Running to answer the phone from the same direction, we got caught up in each other's feet and we both went down — hard. I was lucky, no damage done. Mary fell and hit her head on one of the dining room chairs. She received a mild concussion and butterfly stitches. A new rule went into effect before the sun went down that night; we could no longer run to the phone. Big surprise there! The first person to call out "I'll get it" was the only one who could go for the phone.

In my own home, there was not nearly as much drama over the phone when my kids became teenagers. I was lucky; I only had two girls, and there is nearly six years between them. What my kids did with the phone was something else. My children are all under the delusion that they are comedians. Movie quoting is a big pastime in our family. There is seldom a conversation, serious or otherwise, that at some point someone will not throw a line in from a movie. I have been known to throw my share of one-liners in on any given conversation when my kids are nowhere to be seen. Most people outside of my own kids never get my attempt at humor.

I was washing dishes one night after dinner, and Jennifer sat at the breakfast bar doing her homework. The phone rang, and Jennifer, being the closest, picked it up and nonchalantly greeted the caller by stretching out the "Ed" while saying, "E——d Rooney!" The line was from *Ferris Bueller's Day Off*. The call was for me, but I couldn't take it because I was on the floor laughing so hard I couldn't even speak. Okay, so maybe my kids get the idea they are comedians because I laugh at their jokes. I'm their mother. It's part of my job to instill confidence in them.

Jessica did something very similar several years later. The phone rang and she greeted the caller by saying, "Come in — Ray," from *Ghostbusters*. The caller usually never got it either and wondered if they had misdialed. Occasionally the caller would hang up. Most times they just asked, "Huh?" Now that caller ID is on everyone's phone, we usually only say the one-liners to each other. My personal favorite is from *The Princess Bride*, "Hello!" I say in a throaty and slightly Spanish voice. "My name is Indigo Montoya. You killed my father. Prepare to die."

But the main problem we had with the phone in my house was when we bought our first answering machine. We were thrilled to have an answering machine, and I praised the brilliant visionary who had invented it. There had been innumerable times when someone left a message for my husband or myself on our manual machine — which was one of our kids — and we never received the message. When my children took a message, we found that their ability to write became non-existent and their memory became that of an elderly person with dementia.

"Did anyone call for me while I was out?" was a typical question I asked upon returning from the store or another errand.

My husband and I are relatively intelligent people. We really thought that, theoretically, together we could produce a Pulitzer Prize winner or maybe even a Nobel Prize winner. But those dreams were dashed and became fleeting thoughts in my mind when my children answered my question with, "Someone called. I think it was a woman. Not really sure. She didn't say what she wanted, and if it was a woman, she didn't leave a number. I told her I didn't know where you were or when you'd be home."

Later that evening, my mother called to ask why I hadn't called her back.

The answering machine was going to take care of all that. From the moment we hooked up our new phone with the answering machine, I thought ALL the missed calls and missed messages would disappear. I couldn't have been more wrong. What ended up happening was the first one home from school would see the message light flashing, listen to the messages, and not write any of them down. Their defense to this was that they didn't delete the messages. They were there for anyone to hear. The problem was that once the messages were heard, the little flashing light went off so everyone else thought there were no messages. One day, I got home from work a little early, before anyone else. The message light was flashing. I hit the little button that allowed the messages to be heard. The machine went through the new messages first.

"You have two new messages," our machine informed me.

Once those messages were heard, the voice came back on,

saying, "You have thirty-six old messages."

I was flabbergasted. When did we get thirty-six messages? Who's calling us so much when we're not home? We'd only had the machine a few weeks. I listened to each one, deleting them as I went.

One message was from my son's school from two weeks earlier, "Can you please give us a call at your earliest convenience so we can discuss the changes we made to Jeffrey's schedule?"

Whoa! After two weeks, how can I call them now? Do I tell them the truth, that my kids are brain damaged and they have been unable to grasp the concept of relaying important messages to their father and I? Or do I play it cool and tell them this was my earliest convenience?

I hated being like my stepfather, but I had to call a family meeting and establish some rules.

"Effective immediately, NO ONE touches the answering machine but me! I will write down the messages and give them to the appropriate person. Anyone caught touching the message button will have that finger cut off of both hands. Does everyone understand?" Turning to Jeffrey, I asked, "By the way, when and why did you change your schedule at school?"

When my grandchildren were very young, about 1 ½ to 2 years old, they often snatched the phone off the table or wherever it was lying around their house and started pressing buttons. Occasionally, somehow, they would call me. I could hear them breathing like an obscene phone caller. I could also hear my daughter and son-in-law in the background, so I knew it wasn't an obscene phone call after all. I usually listened for a while, trying to yell to get their attention, as if they could really hear me. Other times, I listened just because the topic of conversation between the two of them was interesting, and I thought that after a few minutes they would notice the phone on the floor or the kid walking around with it. Apparently, my grandchildren would make the call and then hide the phone, because no one ever knew I was there listening. Most times I just hung up.

Sometimes when my children call me, my grandchildren have something very important to tell me, "Grandma, Audrey fell off the swing today," Livvy would say.

Audrey and Rosa were her best friends at pre-school. Most of Livvy's conversations revolved around Audrey or Rosa. Or Christien would tell me about Hunter getting into trouble.

Some of my favorite conversations have been with Allison and Elaina in California. Allison always has something to tell me when I call Jeffrey or when Jeffrey calls me. I've told Jeffrey many times that Allison talks to me like I see her all the time. She's quite the conversationalist. I called Jeffrey late one night after the girls had gone to bed. Jeffrey said that Allison had a nightmare and was laying in his bed next to him. I asked to speak to her.

"Pumpkinhead, you had a nightmare?" I asked. "What was it about?"

"I dreamed a dog was chasing me, and he caught me and was biting me," Allison responded, her voice still sounding scared.

"Oh, my babydoll… if I was there, I would hold you in my arms, hug you, and kiss you until you weren't scared anymore," I consoled her.

"Grandma, I know you would," she replied ever so sweetly.

But it was a conversation I had with Elaina that brought me to laughter. Elaina is somewhat shy, and she is younger than Allison, so our conversations usually consist of hello, I love you, goodbye. One night, as I was making my rounds with the girls, it was Elaina's turn on the phone.

"Grandma, Daddy is throwing away all our toys!" Elaina said, sounding extremely distraught.

"Why is he throwing away all your toys?" I asked, deeply concerned that my son was breaking the heart of my precious granddaughter.

"He said we had to pick up all our toys or he would throw them away!"

Elaina was in tears at this point, and my heart was breaking. Clearly, my son was taking this a little too far.

"Oh, my precious pumpkinhead, I'll talk to Daddy. Please don't worry," I tried to comfort her.

Jeffrey got back on the phone. I didn't want to interfere, but I couldn't bear to hear my granddaughter who seldom spoke more than a couple of words to me in the past plead with me to rescue her toys.

"Jeffrey, what's going on with the toys?" I asked him with a light tone in my voice.

"I'm not throwing them away," he began. "I told them they had fifteen minutes to pick up their toys. If they didn't get them all put away by then, I would gather the ones left on the floor and they would have to *earn* them back. I guess Elaina freaked out because I was putting the toys in a trash bag. She kept pleading with me not to throw her toys away, and I kept telling her I wasn't throwing them away. I guess she's either not listening or she's not understanding."

"She's probably so horrified that her toys are going into a trash bag that she has blocked out your voice — the voice of the one throwing her toys away," I laughed.

Cell phones are a whole new game. Morgan now has her own cell phone. Although Jennifer and Manuel are opposed to children having cell phones, there are times now when Morgan has soccer or softball practice and neither Jennifer or Manuel can be there to keep an eye on her. Morgan is only allowed to use the cell phone if she needs to talk to one of her parents. I called Morgan on her cell phone once in an attempt to reach Jennifer. Jennifer misplaces her phone quite often and can't find it before the call goes to her voice mail. That wouldn't be so bad, but Jennifer never checks her messages. I had been trying to reach Jennifer for days, leaving her message after message on her home phone and cell, when Jennifer finally called me and actually asked, "Why haven't you called me?"

I would have laughed, but it was so typical of Jennifer.

"I called you so many times and even left you messages. Didn't you listen to any of them?" I asked.

"Mom, do you know how many messages I would have to listen to just to get to your message?" Jennifer replied.

I no longer leave messages for Jennifer. She can see that I called her on her caller ID. That's all she needs to know. I have applied the guilt to her, which apparently doesn't work either.

"You know, Jennifer, one day something may happen. I may really need to speak to you, and you'll never know about it. You'll see that I called, but you're so busy that you won't call me back. I was probably calling you from the hospital because I needed a kidney transplant, and you are the only living available donor. Neither of your brothers or sister was a match. Because you didn't give me one of your kidneys, I will die. Then, several days later, you'll call and I'll be gone. My funeral will have been the day before, and you'll be so upset that you never got to even say goodbye. Guilt will consume you because you could have saved me. My possessions will have already been divided up between your other siblings, and you won't get the one item you've secretly wanted all these years. My phone will have been disconnected because I receive all my bills online and

Dennis doesn't know how to use the computer. You'll drive by my house and see a 'For Sale' sign up because Dennis has to sell the house. You'll be in such shock at all the changes that have taken place in such a short time, all because you didn't pick up your phone when I called."

Jennifer went on the defense.

"If I'm home, I always answer the phone... unless I can't find it."

So, one day, in my attempt to talk to Jennifer, I called Morgan's cell phone. Morgan didn't answer either. When her voice mail came on, I almost died laughing.

Manuel, Morgan's father, has a great sense of humor. There will come a day when their children will be older teenagers and won't appreciate his humor very much, but right now, they don't mind.

The greeting on Morgan's voice mail was Manuel's voice, "You've reached the voice mail of Morgan. I'm sorry, but Morgan is in the bathroom shaving her back. Please leave a message, and as soon as she's finished, she'll call you back."

Dads can be so humiliating!

The phone has changed drastically since I was a teenager. Now the phones are cordless. I can multi-task all over the house now while on the phone. Before, I was limited to how long my cord was. I can wash dishes, make my bed, sort clothes to wash, iron, start dinner, read my e-mails, and even water my grass all while I talk on the phone. My phone is always fully charged and ready to go. My brother, David, seems to call me when he has very little battery power left on his phone. And, boy — can David talk. Actually, I come from a long line of phone talkers. When David calls, we talk until his battery goes dead.

"David, have you ever thought about getting a new battery

or actually placing your phone on the charger at night before you go to bed?" I have teased.

"I still have a couple of teenagers left at home. They talk on the phone long after I go to bed, and we all know how irresponsible teenagers are. They wouldn't know what a battery charger was unless I paid them to know," he replied.

I had almost forgotten what a busy signal sounded like until my sister, Mary, moved back to California from England. I called her one afternoon soon after she moved home.

"Dennis, I think there's something wrong with our phone. It's making a funny sound when I try to call Mary," I told him, very concerned.

"What kind of sound do you hear?" my husband asked me.

"It sounds like a beep… beep… beep…" I responded.

He started laughing. "That's a busy signal. You remember those, don't you?"

It had been quite a few years since I had heard one. What was wrong with her? Didn't she know how annoying it was for someone to call, not get through, and not even be able to leave a message? Did she expect me to keep trying to call her? Wasn't this the 21st Century? Did she live in the Dark Ages? I hate call waiting as much as the next person, but at least I could see who was calling and make a mental note to call that person when I was finished with my current call. Or that person could have the option of leaving a message.

My mother, on the other hand, will put me on hold every time ANYONE calls her. She'll even put me on hold to tell a telemarketer that she isn't interested in what they're selling. She just can't let a single call get past her. She has caller ID so she knows whose calling, but she has to physically tell them she will call them later. It drives me crazy.

My mother had a seizure a few years ago that was very frightening for all of us, and, since then, I call her everyday. I used to work with a man named Joe. Joe was older than I, and he had been married to the same woman for about thirty-five years. He told me once that his wife's mother lived in Pennsylvania. His wife and mother-in-law talked on the phone all the time and it drove him crazy. He complained about it all the time to his wife. They had many arguments about her being on the phone so much with her mother. Then one day his mother-in-law died. Years later, he told me he would give anything in the world for his wife to be able to talk to her mother now. I remember thinking how beautiful and how sad that statement was. So I talk to my mother everyday. We talk about everything and nothing for usually about an hour or so. I worry about her and want to hear her voice everyday. I want to know that she's okay and feeling good. We always laugh, sometimes cry, but I usually come away inspired.

My husband asked me once, "What can you possibly have to talk about for so long? Don't you call her everyday?"

My mother and I have important information to exchange. Men — they still don't get it.

OH FUDGE!

When my mother cooked her homemade fudge, us five kids were at her side the entire time, waiting in anticipation for the finished prize. "Is it done yet?" we would ask over and over with impatience. If by chance we were in our bedroom when she started making the fudge, the smell permeated throughout the house, and we were there at her side in a heartbeat. My mother always let us use spoons to scrape the pan once the fudge was mixed and poured up onto a buttered plate. Nothing on Earth tasted as good as my mother's fudge. *This is what they must make you to eat in paradise!* I can't help but quote or paraphrase a favorite line from a movie here. Her fudge is that good.

The story goes that my mother and father, while on their honeymoon in 1950, decided to make some fudge, but neither knew how. They went to the store, bought some Hershey's Cocoa, and used the recipe on the box. After experimenting with Hershey's recipe and making a few tweaks and changes to it, they were satisfied with the new and improved recipe they came up with. Believe me, it takes great skill to make great fudge. I have been trying to make it as good as my mother's for close to forty years, and I just can't do it consistently. I have told my mother she can never die, because once she is gone, so is the fudge.

When my mother did make fudge, she always put walnuts in it. My sister, Mary, and I hated nuts. My mother compromised, and just before pouring the nuts in, she would take a little out of the pan for us. If we did have to eat it with nuts, I just sucked all the fudge off from around them. It took longer to eat and there was a nutty aftertaste, but it was better than not having any of her fudge at all.

There are two times a year when I can count on receiving fudge from my mother: my birthday and Christmas. Occasionally, I can convince her I have been a good daughter worthy of her fudge, and she will send some to me. It is the fudge I receive for no apparent reason that counts the most. It is when I receive this fudge that I immediately call my brother, David, to let him know that Mom sent me fudge for no other reason than she must really love me the most. David immediately calls my mother to remind her of a promise she made to him after a near fatal accident he had years before when she promised to make him fudge whenever he wanted if he would just survive the accident. I personally think he's done the accident routine thing to death. But she remembers the promise and sends the fudge to him. We do this to her as often as we can get away with it.

David and I have expressed great concern to each other about our fudge supply chain and what we will do when it is gone. I have vowed that I will somehow master the art of fudge making. I haven't been able to do it yet in forty years, but I have convinced David and myself that I will prevail... eventually. I actually have made it as well as my mother a couple of times. As I said many chapters ago, inconsistency is my forte. Out of every twenty attempts, I might get it right once. That's a lot of sugar, milk, cocoa, and time wasted.

My poor deprived children. They seldom have ever had any of my mother's fudge. I have never learned to share it with anyone, not even with my own children or husband. In fact, I don't think my husband has *ever* had any of it, not even a taste. So whenever I have attempted to make fudge on my own, they think it's great. Of course they do. They don't have anything to compare it to. They've never really had the good stuff. It tastes like hers, but it doesn't have the smooth, creamy texture of my mother's.

I've even had my mother come over to my house and show me step by step exactly what she does and how she makes it. It doesn't help. Since becoming an adult, I lived close to my mother for about eighteen months. One night I began making some fudge. I called my mother just to run through the recipe with her.

"You put in one cup of milk, right?" I asked.

"No! You put in a cup and a half!" my mother replied.

"But I already have it all together, and it's on the stove cooking! What do I do?" I asked, worried that I had just ruined yet another batch of fudge.

"I'll be right over," my mother told me. "Don't worry."

When she came over, the fudge was still cooking on the stove. She added a half-cup of milk to it, right in the middle of it cooking! God must also love the way she makes fudge, because no matter what happens, her fudge always comes out perfect. She finished making my fudge — and it was great! If I had done what she did, no telling what it would have tasted like.

My grandchildren... well, that's another story. I will share the fudge that my mother has made for me with my grandbabies. My kids have asked me why I won't share my fudge with them.

"My mother made this for me. Get your own mother to make you some fudge," I've suggested to them.

"But... you are our own mother!" they've cried.

"Well... I feel sorry for you then, because your own mother doesn't know how to make it right."

I am now trying to teach Morgan and Rachel how to make their great-grandmother's fudge. We've done pretty well so far. Over the past couple of years, I have learned some little tricks to help aid in the never-ending battle of creamy fudge making. My mother never uses a candy thermometer. She tests the fudge by hand in cold water. I have learned that she uses ice-cold water, not room temperature water. That makes all the difference. You'd think that after forty years of trying to make fudge that my mother would have told me that little secret sooner. I wonder what else she hasn't told me . . .

When Morgan and I make fudge, I let her test the fudge for doneness herself. I'm teaching her what to look and feel for. Of course, if I had it down myself, I would be a much better fudge maker. Rachel is a little too young to attempt that step. What they both love to do though is what my mother calls "beating the fudge". This is accomplished by stirring the fudge, drawing it up in the air, and letting it cascade back into the pan. It helps to cool the fudge and set it up for cutting into bite size pieces by allowing the air to reach every part of it. They are always tempted to stick their finger into the cascading fudge for a taste. Hopefully, Morgan and Rachel will be better at this art than I am.

Fudge has become all Rachel wants to make at my house now. One day, when I was talking to Rachel on the phone, she asked about making fudge the coming weekend.

"Rachel, I have so many things to do this weekend that I don't know if I will have the time," I responded.

"Please, Grandma," she begged.

"I'll tell you what... your birthday is coming up in about three weeks. I'll make you some fudge for your birthday instead."

The thought of having her own fudge was something she couldn't resist. She was all for it.

Rachel's birthday came and went, and I had forgotten all about the fudge. In my own defense, I had been in the hospital for nearly a week just a few days prior to her birthday, so fudge was the furthest thing from my mind. A couple of weeks later, on a Friday night, Rachel remembered the promise and reminded me of it.

"I'm so sorry, Rachel. I'll have some made for you by the time you get here tomorrow," I promised.

So, Saturday morning, I got up, walked for a couple of miles, came home, took a shower, and began the fudge making process. I made it just like I always do, but it wouldn't set up. I remembered my mother telling me recently that she'd had the same problem. She'd put the fudge back on the stove and cooked it for another minute or two. It sounded like a reasonable solution, so I put the fudge back on the stove and cooked it for another thirty seconds, hardly long enough to do anything. The fudge almost immediately set up, but it didn't look quite right. After a few hours, I took a little taste of it. It was the worst fudge I had ever eaten in my life! I was out of whole milk and cocoa, so I didn't have the time or ingredients to make any new fudge. I would just have to explain to Rachel what had happened and make her more fudge the following week.

When Rachel came to my house that night, I told her that I had made some fudge but it certainly wasn't my best effort. I told her that if she didn't like it, we could throw it away and I would make her more the following Saturday.

She took a spoon and cut into it. "It's a little hard, Grandma," she said, not really complaining.

But Rachel loved it! There's no accounting for some people's taste. Rachel told me Sunday afternoon after eating another big bite of it that it was the best fudge she'd ever had. What kind of statement was that? She didn't have any real experience with good fudge — only what I'd shared with her in the past. What did she know about good fudge? But I was grateful that she wasn't critical, and whether she really did love it or not didn't matter. Rachel was appreciative of my efforts.

Later that night, when I made my nightly call to my mother, I told her the story of the terrible fudge. "Didn't you say that you put some fudge back on the stove once?" I inquired.

"Yes, honey, but that was the fudge I sent to you last month that you said was terrible and you threw away," she laughed.

Okay, good point to remember: NEVER try to re-cook fudge. It doesn't work!

Rachel loves fudge so much that she refers to her great grandmother as the 'Fudge Lady'. I don't even have to be talking about fudge with Rachel. If I mention anything about my mother, regardless of what it is, Rachel asks, "You mean the Fudge Lady?"

My mother came to Florida and stayed with us for about a month at Christmas last year. She had a long talk with Rachel about who she was and what she would do for her, "If you promise to call me Great Grandma from now on, I will make you your own fudge. Your grandma can't have any of it unless she asks you first. Is that a deal?"

Rachel jumped on that and really horded the fudge over my head.

"Don't I share with you?" I practically begged her.

Rachel grudgingly shared her fudge with me, but not without a few bribes and threats.

"Okay, I'll give you a dollar if you share with me," I began. "Look, if you don't share with me, I won't share with you. The

Fudge Lady is my mother, and I have first rights to all her fudge. If you ever want anymore of this, you'll share what you have with me. Just remember, that's my container the fudge is in, and it doesn't leave this house. I'm bigger than you! I'm telling God!"

I hated to strong-arm her like that, but she seemed to forget just who I was there for a minute. I can see we're going to have to work on learning to share with Grandma. Sounds like a good topic for discussion at The Jesus Club on Saturday night.

During my mother's visit that same Christmas, my brother, David, called to speak to her. It was a little late and she had already gone to bed.

"David," I began, "Mom went to bed already. She's so tired from all the fudge she's been making for me since she got here. As soon as I start to run out, she gets the pan out and makes another batch for me. She's so grateful to be here that she's keeping me in fudge," I teased.

"I guess I need to remind her of her promise one more time," David replied, not bothered by my revelation. "You know, she always tells me she loves me the most."

I chuckled at his obvious lie.

"Yeah, and that's why she makes me all the fudge — for no apparent reason," I retorted.

My mother called one afternoon to tell me that David had sent her a gift in the mail from Time Life.

"You just won't believe what David sent me! He sent me five CDs of all my favorite romantic songs! What a wonderful surprise! He's just so sweet! I'm going to have to make him some fudge!" she declared.

WHAT! Boy, where had I been? I had never thought to use that ploy before. I had to hand it to him — David was good.

"Mom," I began, "do you still have that George Strait CD I made you? Or how about the one with all the church songs on it? You know I made those myself. Anyone can buy a CD, but only a child who truly loves her mother will go through all the trouble of selecting the appropriate CDs, picking out only the best songs, and burning them onto another CD for her mother."

My mother laughed. She knew what was going on. "Didn't I just make you some fudge?" she asked.

Well, who was keeping score, anyway?

"I don't think so, unless you count the fudge that I had to throw out because you made it wrong," I replied, trying to sound deprived.

"Okay, okay. I'll make you some too. But it won't be for another week or so. I have to make David's first."

Now wait a minute.

"What do you mean, you have to make David's first? Didn't I make those CDs for you a few months ago? It seems to me I've been patiently waiting longer for my fudge than David," I reasoned. "And besides, you still owe me for the fudge I had to throw away. I mean, really, Mom, that shouldn't count as you making me fudge, because I couldn't eat it. I hate to say this, but if you don't make me fudge soon, I will have to tell the whole world that you made me fudge that was so bad I had to throw it away. Your reputation will be ruined in the community, and I know you don't want that."

"Okay, okay," she sighed, completely worn out by the exchange that perpetually went on between David, the fudge, and I. He had it coming.

My mother surprised me with some fudge recently at a family reunion. It was the first time in more than twenty-years that we were all together as a family. That Sunday, after church, my mother gave me the fudge. I was so elated! I had no idea that she had even thought about making me fudge, nor had I expected her to. But she made some for David, too. In fact, she told me, "The only reason I made you some was because I felt so guilty that I had made David some."

I looked at her in disbelief, barely able to comprehend what she was saying.

"You were going to make David some fudge in front of me and not make me any?" I inquired, so hurt that I apparently had lost favor in my mother's eyes for some unknown reason.

"No, no, no, it's not like that. I wasn't going to make you any because you just almost had a heart attack, and I didn't want to be the one to contribute to anything bad happening to you."

I couldn't resist this opportunity, "Mom, David *did* have a heart attack. I didn't. I'm also on a diet, exercising everyday, and losing weight. David isn't doing anything. If you're concerned about anyone's health, it's David's you should be concerned about."

I was almost indignant. But if you really looked at it, she surely must love me more since her concern was for my health, and she didn't seem concerned about David's at all.

David hid the fudge my mother made for him at the reunion, determined not to share it with anyone. I, on the other hand, was flying back to Florida the following day and didn't want to take any home with me, so I had mine out to share with everyone. I was on a diet, after all, and eating that much fudge was not a good thing for me. David walked up to me and actually had the nerve to ask me for a piece of my fudge.

"Are you kidding me?" I asked, amazed that he could even toy with the idea of me sharing my fudge with him. "Besides, it's plain. You like nuts in your fudge."

David just smiled. "That's okay. I've never had any plain

fudge before. Can I please have a little taste just to see what it's like without nuts?"

He was relentless, and I eventually gave in. Several minutes later, he asked me for another piece.

"Are you crazy?" I asked, stunned at his boldness. "No, you have your own fudge. Eat that."

David looked at me as if I had taken away his reason for living.

"If I had known that the piece of fudge you gave me was the only piece I was going to get, I would have savored it longer."

I chuckled at his lame, pathetic attempt to have more of my fudge.

"That routine isn't going to fly with me. I always give into you. Everyone always gives into you. What is it about you that makes us all do that?" I asked, really wanting an answer.

No one could answer. No one knew. Yep, I gave David another piece of my fudge.

Later, we were all outside eating lunch on picnic tables and enjoying each other's company. David's 30-year-old son, my nephew, Kevin, sidled up beside me. Kevin looked around to make sure no one was listening, and he leaned over to whisper in my ear, "Rumor has it that you have fudge?"

It was a question more than a statement. I looked at him, smiled, and nodded my head yes.

With Kevin's most pathetic, sad eyes, he looked at me and said, "My sweetest and most favorite Aunt Liz, you know my whole life everyone's been taking my fudge away from me. I never get any. Every time Grandma makes some for me, my dad takes it away. Would it be too much to ask if, just this once, I could have a tiny piece of yours?"

I couldn't help but laugh at him. "You sure are your father's son!"

One evening, while on my nightly call with my mother, she said she had a confession to make. Why is it that whenever my mother has a need to confess it always seems to have something to do with disappointing me? I held my breath and asked what she had to tell me.

"I'm making you some fudge tonight," she said hesitantly.

"Please don't take this the wrong way because I am actually thrilled, but why are you making me fudge? It's not my birthday. What have you done?" I questioned her motives.

"Well... here's the confession. I made fudge for David. I later realized that if I sent him some fudge then he'd probably call you and tell you, so I figured my only way out of this was to make you some too," she divulged.

"You'd better never make David fudge for no reason without making me some too!" I scolded. "You did the right thing, Mom. I'm proud of you that you realized that on your own."

A couple of days later, I got a call from David. I had almost forgotten about my mother sending David fudge too, so I thought the call was just a friendly 'Haven't talked to you in a while' call.

"Guess what I got in the mail today?" David teased.

"Yeah, Mom said you'd call. I've got news for you, though. I hate to rain on your little parade here, but she is sending me some too, so HAH!" I snipped.

"I know that. The reason I know," David went on, "is because I got her fudge today and it's plain fudge with no nuts. I called her and she thinks she must have sent you mine with the nuts in it."

Not meaning to sound ungrateful, but that was getting to be so typical of my mother. I was just a wee bit annoyed that my mother couldn't get this one little thing right. How hard was it to wrap the fudge that had nuts, address it to my brother, check to make sure she had the plain fudge, and address it to me? I was *so* going to have to have a little talk with my mother about this mix-up to make sure it didn't happen again.

"Listen, Lizzy," David continued, "when you get my fudge, send it right to me, and when I get it, I'll send you what's left of yours."

"What do you mean 'what's left of mine'? David, have you started eating my fudge?" I started to panic.

I didn't want him eating my fudge. Once you start eating my mother's fudge, it's like eating potato chips. You can't stop at just one piece. You eat until you're almost sick.

"I haven't started it yet, but as soon as I hang up from talking to you, I was going to have a piece or two or three — maybe four," he replied so matter-of-factly, like it was expected of him.

"I'll tell you what," I anxiously began again. "You send mine to me today as soon as you get off the phone, and as soon as I get yours, I'll send yours to you. I'll even overnight it to you. David, seriously, if you don't send mine to me right away, you might as well keep it. I'm really a little fussy about my fudge. I have made Mom promise that when she makes fudge for me she sends it to me within twenty-four hours. I mean, really, fudge has milk in it, and she doesn't put any preservatives in it, so I just can't eat old fudge. It has to be fresh."

"Well, that explains it," David said with a smirk. "That's why Mom always makes me more fudge than you. I don't put any conditions on her."

"Yeah, but for all you know, you're eating year old fudge she found in the back of her refrigerator," I warned.

David began to laugh. He laughed long and hard.

"Lizzy, I'm only kidding. I didn't get your fudge. It has just been a while since we spoke, and I just missed talking to you,"

David confessed.

I wanted to hit him, but how could I when he could be so sweet sometimes. David is the kind of brother that you love to pieces but drives you crazy at the same time.

David called me earlier this year to give me some shocking news, "Some guy at work brought some fudge in today," David began. "I couldn't believe it, but it was better than Mom's."

I looked around my house as if my mother, who lived 3,000 miles away in California, might actually hear him.

"David," I whispered, "that's blasphemy! How can you even toy with the idea that someone could possibly make better fudge than Mom?" I questioned.

"It was so creamy and literally melted in my mouth. He gave me the recipe, and I made some. It was so easy. I'm going to send some to you, and I want you to tell me what you think," David replied, sounding almost devious.

I was really hesitant. I didn't want to get involved in what might turn out to be a conspiracy against my mother's fudge. I didn't want any part in confirming that anything was better than my dear, sweet mother's fudge.

"Please, just try it," David pleaded.

I would like to shake hands with the person who can tell my brother no. I personally don't know that person.

"Okay," I relented, feeling very guilty.

"I'm sending it overnight delivery, so you'll get it tomorrow. I just need your address. I can't find my address book right now," David said. "Call me tomorrow night after you get it."

The next day, I waited for the package to arrive. I felt like a Judas Betrayer to my mother. She was 78 years old and didn't deserve this. What if I did like David's fudge better? I really didn't want to try it because I really didn't want to know. I loved my mother and her fudge too much.

When the package arrived, I opened it slowly, guilt weighing heavily on my mind. Inside the package, I found three CDs of church songs. What??? Where's the fudge? I didn't understand. Had he sent me the wrong package? There is a three hour difference in time between Florida and California, and it seemed like an eternity before my brother got home from work so I could call him.

"David, where's the fudge? Inside the box you sent me was just some church music CDs," I said with confusion in my voice.

David began to laugh.

"I can't cook! That should have been your first clue right there! I just wanted to send you those CDs and surprise you, but I needed your address. As if anyone could make fudge better than Mom. You should be ashamed of yourself that you gave in and said you'd even try something that might be better than Mom's," David teased.

When David and I hung up the phone, I immediately called my mother, "Mom, I have some very distressing news that you'd be really interested in hearing. It may be pretty hard to take, but I'll tell you if you promise to make me some fudge this week," I began.

"Honey, what is it? Okay, I'll make you some fudge, but I can't believe you've stooped to bribing me now," she replied.

"Mom, do you know what David just said to me? He said that he tasted some fudge at work that was better than yours!" I told her excitedly.

"Honey, I've got to go. I need to call David, and if that's true, then I'm never going to make him fudge again!"

Yeah — That'll teach him!

THE OPPOSITE SEX

The first boy I can remember liking as a boyfriend was when I was in the 2nd grade. I think his name was Mike Ferrell. He was short for his age and blond. We were in the same class, and we passed notes to each other all the time. Our teacher, Mrs. DeBerry, either never saw us passing the notes or she decided passing notes at our age was harmless, because she never said anything. What was funny was that the notes always said the same thing: "I love you. Do you love me?" The reply was also the same too: "Yes, I love you. Do you love me?" Back and forth we passed these notes, never varying the message. I guess we didn't know what else to say. After 2nd grade, I never saw him again.

My first real boyfriend came into my life when I was 13 years old. His name was Rusty. He was 15 years old and attended the same church as my family. Our mother's were close friends. He was also a good friend of my older brother Steve, so it was only natural, I guess, that we became close. He was the first boy I ever kissed. We had gone out on a Saturday afternoon on our "first date" with his family to a rodeo. I had never been to one and had so much fun. His family drove me home after the rodeo, and Rusty walked me into my house to say hello to the rest of my family. We ended up going out to the garage where my brothers' bedroom was, and there, in their room, Rusty kissed me. I was in heaven for weeks after that. I was gone, head over heels, in love. Rusty and I were boyfriend and girlfriend for the whole summer.

One Sunday night after church, all the teenagers in our youth group went bowling. Rusty broke my heart at the Gable House Bowl in Torrance that Sunday night. He was the first boy I ever kissed, the first boy I ever loved, and the first broken heart I ever had. Rusty said words to me that I would later hear again and again from other boys when they broke up with me, "We're too young to be so serious." What did that mean anyway? How do you like someone and not be serious about it? If you like someone, you like them.

I cried for three days straight, non-stop, after Rusty broke my heart. I couldn't even come up for air. I couldn't eat, and I didn't want to see or talk to anyone. I was completely devastated. My mother even cried for me. I pined away for Rusty for nearly a whole year. I prayed every night that God, in His infinite wisdom and mercy, would bring Rusty back to me. During that time, I never looked at another boy. Not a single one. I only wanted Rusty — until I saw AB for the first time 11 ½ months later.

It was straight out of a movie. I was going to Delhi for the wedding of my future brother-in-law (although I didn't know he would be my brother-in-law at the time). Delhi was about 300 miles north of Los Angeles, and we drove up there on a Friday night after everyone got off work. In the car was my future husband Don (didn't know that at the time either), his girlfriend Charlene, and her brother AB, whom I had never met. I was 14 and AB was 17. I wasn't looking forward to going on this trip and had almost backed out. Don convinced me to go. I assumed that since Charlene was so pretty, her brother just had to be boring, probably a geek, a nerd, ugly, and, no doubt, lacking any kind of personality.

My bedroom faced the driveway, and I was just finishing my packing when the three of them pulled up in the car. As I closed my suitcase, my best friend Terri, who was curious about what AB would look like, grabbed my arm and said, "Liz, look!"

I looked out the window, and there was a tall, blond, extremely handsome guy getting out of a '65 Mustang and wearing sunglasses. Gosh! He looked so cool! The sun was setting, and the way the light played on his face took my breath away. I couldn't wait to get going. Man! Was I lucky or what?

AB and I hit it off right away. That weekend in Delhi was one of the most memorable of my life. AB drove me to a park during the wedding reception and we parked under a tree. We spent the next hour just talking and getting to know each other better. He drove me all around Delhi as my personal tour guide. On Sunday night, we stayed out front of my future in-laws' house and talked until the wee hours of the morning. It was the middle of August, and even at that hour, it was still hot outside. After all these years, I still remember it so vividly. We belonged to the same faith, which was a big plus for my parents, but AB lived in Fullerton, a good half-hour or more away from where I lived. His parents didn't like the idea of their son dating anyone quite as young as I was either. AB and I saw each other when we could, wrote letters to each other often, and spoke on the phone, but then I heard those words I would grow to hate," We're getting too serious." Yep, AB also broke my heart. I pined away for almost a year for AB, too.

The following summer, we began attending a different church. I met Mike the second week. My best friend Terri came to church with me most Sundays, but she hadn't come that morning. I begged her to come to church that Sunday night just so she could see Mike. I needed her opinion and approval.

"Just remember though, I saw him first," I warned her. "Don't get any ideas."

Mike was tall, dark, and gorgeous. He took me home from a church youth gathering that night, and we quickly became an item. Mike didn't live very far from me, and we saw each other almost every day. I thought I was falling in love with him when he uttered those mean, nasty words to me, "We're getting too serious." I should have seen it coming. Mike no longer wanted to sit with me in church. He used to pick me up on Sunday mornings and we would drive to church together, but he no longer wanted to do that, either. I assumed there were other girls at church he wanted to date. He really broke my heart, too.

I didn't know what I was supposed to do differently to not be serious. It's not as if I didn't know how to have fun or I didn't know how to laugh. But I didn't know how to like someone and not be serious about it. I couldn't figure it out, and it just didn't make any sense to me. I began to feel there was something "seriously" wrong with me.

Don, on the other hand, was older, in his early 20s, and ready to settle down and get married. He never said the words that broke my heart. What was really funny, though, was when Don and I began dating, Rusty, AB, and Mike all called me again wanting to start over. I didn't trust any one of them and was afraid they were just calling me in-between girlfriends. I just didn't want to be the fallback girl. My mother had been that woman to my father for quite a few years. It was a bad place to be.

I trusted Don, and we started seeing each other seriously when I was 15 ½, and by my 16th birthday, we were engaged. We married that June, and the rest, as they say, is history.

Thank goodness Don and I didn't have to worry about the opposite sex with our own children for a long time. The first encounter we ran into was with Jeffrey, our third born, of all people. Every summer when we went camping, we always took along two extra kids. Jeffrey's best friend Greg was one of them, and we usually let the other kids take turns taking one of their friends. Stacey was both Jessica and Jeffrey's friend. We knew their family well, and Stacey came camping with us often. The first year Stacey went camping with us, she and Jeffrey were about 9 or 10 years old. I knew they both liked each other, and they were cute to watch.

One afternoon, my husband and I were relaxing in chaise lounge chairs soaking in the sun and watching the kids play in the creek. Jeffrey got out of the water first, shivering. He ran to the picnic table for his towel and then sat down in a chair in the sun.

"Jeffrey," Stacey called from the water, "would you please get me my towel?"

Jeffrey ran back to the picnic table, grabbed a towel, and took it to Stacey at the water's edge. Jeffrey returned to his chair.

A moment later, we heard, "Jeffrey, would you please get me my shoes? They're by the camper," Stacey asked.

Jeffrey again got up, went to the camper, and took Stacey's shoes to her. Jeffrey returned once again to his chair.

It was just a matter of seconds when we heard Stacey again, "Jeffrey, would you please bring me a chair down here so I can put my shoes on?"

Without a single word, Jeffrey took Stacey a chair, and then he turned to go back to his chair.

I smiled at my husband and said, "Watch this."

"Jeffrey," I requested, "would you go to the camper and bring me a Pepsi, please?"

"Geez, Mom! I have to do everything around here!" Jeffrey complained.

I knew that was coming, which was why I did it. I laughed out loud at his reply, but it broke my heart just the same. Jeffrey was too young for other girls to be more important than I was. But that was only the beginning.

By the time Jeffrey was 15, he'd developed into quite the romantic. I often wished I had known a boy like him when I was growing up. I have no idea where it came from, because there wasn't a romantic bone in his father's body. He had no mentor, no example. I'm sure there are areas in Jeffrey's personality that could stand some improvement, but he makes up for a lot of it with how attentive he can be to the opposite sex.

Jeffrey met me at the door when I came home from work one afternoon. "Mom," he began, "can you take me to the store to buy some stuff for breakfast?" he asked.

"There's cereal and eggs in the frig," I responded. "What do you need at the store?" I asked.

"Tomorrow is Julie's birthday, and I wanted to go to her house before she gets up in the morning and make her breakfast in bed. I've already talked to her mother about it," Jeffrey explained.

"Jeffrey, you don't know how to cook! I can't even get you to pour your own glass of milk. How are you going to make her breakfast in bed?" I asked, completely taken aback by my son's plans.

Where do boys like this come from? Why had I never met any of them? If I were Julie, I'd never let Jeffrey go. I wouldn't care how young I was. My husband's idea of breakfast in bed was to bring me a chocolate donut and a glass of milk and then leave the room to eat alone.

"Julie's mom is going to help me with the breakfast. Oh, and I need to get her some flowers, too," Jeffrey responded, going through a mental list in his head.

Flowers *too*? I was both proud and jealous. He'd never made me breakfast in bed or given me a single flower in his life. I had given birth to this child after hours of agonizing labor. He weighed 8 ½ pounds when he was born, so giving birth to him was not a walk in the park. I saw the writing on the wall. I was Jeffrey's mother. He loved me, but I was moving into 2nd place, and I would never again be number one in his life.

Jennifer took front and center with boys after the camping episode with Stacey. When she was in 8th grade, she liked a boy named Sam. Jennifer was the first girl born in my family, and my sister, Mary, had become very close to Jennifer when she was a little girl. Mary had moved away to England when she got married, and we all missed her terribly. I had taken my first trip to England to see Mary the year before Jennifer's graduation from middle school. We decided to send Jennifer to England for six weeks to spend with my sister as a graduation present. Mary and her family were going on vacation too and, of course, wanted to see Jennifer, but they also wanted her to help with their infant son at night while they went out. It was a good arrangement. The trip had been planned since the first of the year.

Jennifer's graduation day finally arrived. Her dress was beautiful and fit her like a glove. It was baby-pink satin, and I would have given anything to have had a dress like that at anytime in my life. Jennifer was a vision. After her graduation, there was a school dance that Sam escorted her to. I dropped the two of them off at the school gym, and three hours later went back to get Jennifer. The lights were dimmed a little, and it took awhile for my eyes to adjust. I looked for Jennifer everywhere, but I couldn't find her. I saw one of her friends and asked if she had seen Jennifer.

"She's in the bathroom crying. She's been in there all night. Sam broke up with her," the friend revealed.

I ran in the direction the friend had pointed me and found the bathroom without any problem. There was Jennifer, still crying. I wrapped my arms around her and guided her out to the car. We didn't go straight home but drove around for a while talking. Sam had broken up with her because she was going to England and would be gone for six weeks. I listened as Jennifer poured her heart out to me over the hurt she felt because of the breakup. My heart ached for my daughter. I vividly remember how angry I was at Sam. Why did he wait until the dance to break up with her? Why didn't he break up with her the day before or the week before? He had known she was going to be gone. Why did he wait until the biggest day of her life and in front of all her friends?

As I was driving around, I found that I was also hunting Sam. My eyes were looking everywhere. I wanted him in my scope. I wanted to hurt him as much as he had hurt my daughter. Thank goodness I never did find Sam that night, nor did I ever see him again. But Jennifer was close to the age I had been when I experienced my first broken heart, and I knew what she was going through. We drove around for over an hour, talking, crying, and even laughing. My daughter experienced her first broken heart that night, and I had never felt closer to her.

Years later, I discovered those feelings of protecting your child from hurt or pain never leave you. I spoke to my mother about it once and found that she still harbors those "mother protecting her young" instincts. I always thought that once children were grown and became adults, a mother relinquished all those instincts. I guess, as a mother, all you can do is pray your children are happy, otherwise you will never get any sleep at night.

By the time Jessica reached "that" age, my husband and I thought we were pros at handling our children and the opposite sex. It takes a child to prove a parent wrong every time. Jessica was a wonderful child, full of life. She was friendly, articulate for her years, and often seemed older than her actual age. We speculated that Jessica would someday become an attorney. She was very outgoing, fair, and usually saw both sides of an issue. There wasn't a shy bone in her body, and she was compelled to speak her mind to anyone and everyone around her. When she was 11 years old, she came home from school complaining that her stomach hurt.

"Have something to eat," was my standard reply to most complaints.

"I'm not hungry," Jessica replied.

"Do you have to go to the bathroom?" was usually the next question.

"Mom! No! How gross!" Jessica yelled indignantly.

"Then go lay down," I suggested.

Jessica laid on the couch the remainder of the night. She was quiet and didn't speak, complain, or even sneeze. In fact, I hardly knew she was even there. Jennifer and I watched TV together and talked most of the night when I noticed that it was nearly 10:00 P.M.

"Jessica! What are you still doing up? You need to get to bed."

Jessica slowly got to her feet but was unable to stand straight. She slowly walked toward her room.

"Jessica, why are you walking like that?" I asked.

"My stomach hurts, and I can't stand up straight," she said a little weakly.

"Your stomach still hurts?" I asked. "Come here; lay down and let me look at you," I said.

I helped Jessica to the couch and did my little examination. After pushing and prodding, I decided I needed to take her to the emergency room. Jessica's father wasn't home yet, so I left him a note and we went to the hospital.

Jessica's mood picked up a little once we got to the hospital. Her doctor in the emergency room was young and quite cute.

"I like your tie," Jessica said, obviously flirting with him.

Where did she get stuff like this? She was only 11 years old. I was 35 and would never have said that to a doctor in a million years.

The doctor apparently recognized Jessica's flirtatiousness and responded in kind, "I knew a very special young lady would be coming into my emergency room this evening, so I wore it especially for you," he responded.

This banter continued for the entire length of the examination. He determined Jessica did have appendicitis and would require emergency surgery immediately. The surgery was routine and went well.

The next morning, I went to the mall to buy Jessica something pretty to wear in the hospital for the three days she would be confined. I bought her a purple pair of pajamas with a matching robe. It was really pretty, and she was so excited to have something special to wear instead of the typical hospital garb.

Later that afternoon, her little boyfriend David came to the hospital to see her. David's father had brought him. The whole visit and exchange was so precious. After he left, Jessica told me how happy she had been that I had bought the purple pajamas. She said that although she had just had surgery, the pajamas made her feel better and even made her feel a little pretty when David had come to see her. She was 11 years old, and her appearance around young boys was already serious business.

My grandchildren, for the most part, are too young to notice the opposite sex. That hasn't stopped the opposite sex from noticing them. Rachel and I were at the grocery store one evening buying items for lunch the next day. We were at the deli counter waiting our turn. The customer currently being helped was a father with his two children, a young daughter and a son who I would guess to be about 10 years old. The boy couldn't take his eyes off Rachel. He stared at her and smiled. Unlike her mother, Rachel is extremely shy. She tried to bury herself in my dress. She would have crawled right inside me if she could. I whispered to her that the young boy just thought she was really pretty and that she didn't need to be so shy. She could just smile back. The father finished his business at the deli counter and they left. We got our items for lunch and went to the self-checkout. There, at one of the other self-checkout registers, were the father and his children. The little boy walked up to Rachel and said, "Hello, pretty girl."

How precious was that? Rachel smiled at him and then buried her face in my dress again. They left, and as we walked out to our car together, I asked her if anything like that had ever happened before. She said it hadn't, and I knew that little boy was only the beginning.

Livvy, on the other hand, is more like Jessica: she's outgoing and not nearly as shy as Rachel. Livvy also has an insatiable curiosity about everything. Although Livvy is nearly 4, her vocabulary is growing everyday, and I am continually surprised at the grownup words that come out of her mouth. One day at the beach, Jessica had set their blanket down in the sand near a gentleman basking in the Florida sunshine. Once settled, Livvy went over to the gentleman's blanket and plopped herself down.

"So, what's your name?" Livvy asked the man matter-of-factly.

The gentleman wasn't sure if Livvy was flirting with him, interrogating him, being curious, or just being nosey.

He began to stutter, "I'm... uh… uh… Jim. Who are you?"

Livvy didn't miss a beat, "My name is Olivia Sue Binns." (Livvy always uses her full name.) "What are you doing here?" she continued with her inquiry.

It was at that point Jessica called Livvy away from the gentleman and redirected her toward the sand and the surf.

"I'm so very sorry she bothered you," Jessica told the gentleman. "She's just very curious and friendly."

The gentleman smiled, closed his eyes, and went back to his basking. Yeah, someday Jessica will wish Livvy was as shy as Rachel.

There was a gentleman at church who sat in front of us every Sunday. Each week, Del teased Rachel and Livvy and they both acted very shy around him. In reality, both girls loved his attention. Rachel's shy response, though, was genuine. Livvy, I believe, acted shy because Rachel was shy. They looked forward to seeing Del every Sunday and if, for whatever reason, he was not at church on a particular Sunday, the girls asked about him and wondered where he was.

There was another man in their life at church who they interacted with each week and were heartbroken when he wasn't there, Wyndal. Wyndal greeted us all at the door every Sunday and wished us well when we left. Every Sunday as we walked out of the church building, Rachel and Livvy ran to Wyndal for a goodbye hug. Church just wasn't over until they got that hug. Wyndal was a wonderful and loving man. He bent down to them even when he was speaking to another adult. He never shunned or ignored them. He showed his Christian love for them, and they knew he truly cared for them. Each Sunday, I watched Rachel and Livvy run to him, and, each Sunday, I smiled as Wyndal knelt down to envelop them in his arms.

Morgan, my oldest grandchild, is at an age where she has begun to notice boys. Jennifer and Manuel don't allow her to have a boyfriend yet. But that hasn't stopped Morgan from having a "special friend". Morgan's first special friend was Houston. She is at that wonderful age where you can have a couple of different boyfriends at different times but in the same day. They come and go like the wind. Morgan and Houston were special friends for quite a long time in 12-year-old terms. Eventually, Morgan decided Houston was a jerk and immature, so she broke up with him. They got back together the following day and broke up again the day after that because he had a new girlfriend. Twelve year olds are so fickle. I believe those times are a run through of how we learn and handle our relationships with the opposite sex when we are older.

The boyfriends I had when I was young are very much a part of the person I turned out to be. I still think of them all from time to time, and a smile crosses my face. Rusty and I have kept in touch with each other through the years. I still love him, although not in the same way I loved him when I was 13. Now I love him as a person from my past, my brother in Christ, and a cherished, wonderful, and dear friend I've known most of my life. He and his wife Dianne even lived in Florida for a while, and we saw each other occasionally. Dianne also attended our church when we were young, and she and my brother, David, dated at the same time Rusty and I did. The four of us spent a lot of time together. Those really were easy, carefree days.

AB died of a heart attack more than fifteen years ago. He had given me one of the most memorable weekends of my life, and the day I found out he died was one of the saddest days of my life. His sister, Charlene, and I still keep in touch with each other after all these years.

I saw Mike once at a movie theater in Torrance many, many years ago. He didn't see me though. A few years later I called him, and we met in a parking lot of a restaurant for a few minutes, just to say hello. I haven't seen him since. I still think of him often and wonder if he ever achieved the goals he had back when we dated.

My first husband Don and I have been divorced since 1991. We have a healthy relationship with each other now, and that is important to me as I'm sure it is to him. We didn't have this relationship right after the divorce. Our divorce wasn't a pleasant one. It took time to grow and cultivate our relationship into what it is today. But once children come into the marriage and the marriage ends, that person is in your life forever. There will always be grandchildren, birthdays, weddings, graduations, and special occasions where both parents will be present, even when you live on opposite sides of the country. I am always amazed at how often I actually see Don. But you have to get to a point where you can look at the divorce and say that it is over and it's okay; I'm okay. It is no longer about me but about my children. For my children, I care about their father and he cares about me. At one time in my life, I loved him more than my own life. No matter what happened between us or to us, I can certainly find it in my heart to be kind and forgiving. My children deserve nothing less.

IS THERE A DOCTOR IN THE HOUSE?

With five young children very close in age growing up together, there were many times my brothers, sisters, and I got hurt. We were very physical with each other, too. Dianne, Mary, and I used to pinch each other until we broke the skin. David and I went to blows with each other in a heartbeat. He beat me up every chance he got. Sometimes he would sit on me, pin my arms down, and, with his knuckle, tap my chest. That drove me insane. A lifetime later, his children tease him now about how I, his younger sister, used to beat him up. That's actually a rumor I started many, many years ago, but we are getting older now, so who can say for sure. I don't think I ever really did beat him up, but I enjoy the fun at my brother's expense.

As children, we often played in our backyard. There were low-hanging telephone wires back there, but prior to this one particular day, I can't remember ever noticing them before. My brothers, sisters, and I were playing in our yard with a rope that had a rubber ball attached to one end. We were all fighting over it, so I guess we really weren't playing. Somehow, the rope and ball went flying and got caught up in the telephone wires. Easy remedy. We got a kitchen chair and the five of us scrambled on it, each trying to get at the rope and ball while at the same time pushing everyone else off the chair. Even with the chair, it wasn't high enough to get the rope and ball, so my brothers, the Einstein's that they were, decided to get on each other's shoulders to reach the rope. Although Steve was the older of the two, he was the smaller brother. While standing on David's shoulder's, Steve lost his balance, fell off David's shoulders, and right on top of me. It was at this point in time that my mother came outside to see what we were doing. Now you'd think that she would have come out to see what we were doing when we took the chair out of the kitchen, but she waited until she heard the screaming. Steve had a bloody tongue, apparently from biting it when he fell on top of me. My head hurt so much, but my mother wasn't exactly filled with sympathy at the moment. She was too busy pulling bodies off each other. All the while, David maintained an angelic look on his face as if he had been a bystander offering help. I was sent to my room to cry it off. I laid on my bed crying and holding my left hand to the left side of my head when it occurred to me that my hand felt wet. I immediately stopped crying and looked at it. It was full of blood. There's nothing like seeing your own blood to make a child hysterical. I ran to my mother to show her and prove to her that I was indeed actually hurt, something she didn't believe earlier when she sent me to my room. I felt vindicated.

When my father came home from work soon after the incident in the backyard, my mother broke the news to him that, in her opinion, I just might need stitches. My father was of the mind that you didn't give in to pain; you just sucked it up and any injury would just go away — mind over matter. My mother convinced him that the blood coming from my head was not her imagination, and he relented. I was taken to the hospital emergency room for two stitches. My father thought that for the trip and the money there should have been more.

My own children were not nearly as primitive and savage

as my brothers, my sisters, and I were, but they got hurt so much more. There were times when Joey had a regular check-up with the pediatrician, but I was compelled to cancel it at the last minute due to the many bruises and scratches on him. I had a neighbor once tell me that he was fascinated watching Joey, because he appeared to trip over the air. That became our anthem for Joey: "He trips over the air." To this day, I tease him about that.

Jessica had a couple of freak accidents one summer, and I wasn't present at either of them. But I was the one who took her to the doctor. She was getting stitches removed one afternoon by a pediatrician in my doctor's group, a doctor that my children had never seen before. During a camping trip, Jessica had gotten hurt that was just a freak of nature with the help of her brother and cousin. The pediatrician didn't see anything freaky about it and began questioning her as to how I punish her when she does something wrong and what she did to make me angry. I understood why he asked the questions, but I was furious at the same time. If I had been the cause of any of my children's injuries, since I had so much experience with injuries and stitches, I would have taken the stitches out myself. There was a time when we didn't have very good medical insurance when I did just that. Why pay for a doctor's visit when they weren't sick or hurt? All they needed were stitches removed. I talked to my pediatrician once, and he explained exactly what I needed to do to remove them. All of my children have had stitches more than once. They've probably had stitches more than three or four times. At least I know Joey and Jessica have.

When Jennifer was 7 ½ years old and Jessica was 1 ½ years old, they usually took a bath together. Jessica was feeding herself table food at that age, so she went straight from the dinner table to the bath. One particular evening, Don and I stayed at the dinner table talking while Jennifer took Jessica to the bath with her. There was always a plastic cup in the bath that I used to rinse their shampooed hair. Apparently, it was gone that evening. I remember hearing Jennifer ask for a glass and Joey running into the kitchen and grabbing one out of the cabinet. There has never really been a distinction between a plastic cup and a real glass in my household. Everything is a glass. Even now in Florida, there is too much humidity to use real glasses. They sweat too much. I use insulated plastic cups, but I call them glasses. So I didn't think anything of Jennifer asking for a glass, nor did I check to make sure Joey grabbed a plastic cup. I was just enjoying a few relaxing moments after dinner with my husband. They were relaxing moments until Jennifer started screaming, and I mean screaming bloody murder. Don and I jumped up from the table and ran to the bathroom where Jennifer was running into her bedroom with a huge cut in the top fleshy part of the back of her thigh. She had her fingers digging into the deep, bloody wound. It took all our strength to get her to stop running and get her fingers out of her cut. Jessica wasn't hurt. Jennifer had dropped the glass into the bathtub where it immediately broke. Jennifer was able to stand up and get Jessica out of the tub first, and the moment she put Jessica down out of the tub, she slipped and fell right on the glass.

We took her to the emergency room where she needed thirteen stitches. The doctor debated and called in another doctor for advice on whether the stitches needed to be layered because it was a very deep wound. That cut was in a really tricky place, too. She usually peed on it, and I had to disinfect it after each trip to the bathroom. It healed nicely though.

About 2 ½ years later, Don, the kids, and I walked down to the local elementary school to play a little baseball. It wasn't really baseball. It was more like letting the kids bat the ball around and play catch. Jennifer, Joey, and Jeffrey were along the 2nd to 3rd baseline fielding balls while Don hit little grounders to them. Jessica was too young to be around a hard baseball in action, so she played in the grass alongside of me on the sidelines. It was in the summer and we had walked down to the school after dinner. The sun started setting, and I called to Don that it was time to start back home.

"One more ball!" he shouted.

I knew exactly what he was going to do. I watched him throw the ball into the air and hit that ball as hard as he could. It was intended to be a fly ball out in left field so the kids would have to go and chase it. It wasn't though. It was a line drive. The ball found its mark on Joey's left eyebrow. Don had hit it so hard that the impact knocked Joey down. We ran to Joey as fast as we could. It had split his eyebrow, and to Jeffrey it looked like the ball had knocked Joey's eyeball out of its socket. Jeffrey just ran around in circles with his hands to his mouth muttering, "Oh my gosh! Oh my gosh!" over and over and over. Jessica being about 3 ½ years old and not understanding what had just happened just kept saying, "I hate you, Daddy! I hate you, Daddy!" over and over. Jennifer kept her wits about her and let her father and I attend to Joey while she gathered the ball, the gloves, and the bat together.

Don ran home to get the car, and while on his way home came across his brother Doug who lived just a couple of blocks away from us. Doug had been out jogging but stopped to take all my other children to his house while Don and I raced to the hospital with Joey. Don drove like a maniac. I, on the other hand, so surprised myself. Joey was badly hurt and I knew that, yet I was a tower of strength and calm for my son. Don drove through red lights blaring the horn the entire way. We were so lucky that we made it in one piece to the hospital. I held my

8-year-old son in my arms all the way to the hospital. He looked up at me at one point and asked me whose injury was worse, his new one or the time Jennifer cut her leg in the bathtub. I chuckled at the goofy things that run through a person's mind sometimes. I told him that although Jennifer's was bigger and longer, his was worse because it was on his head and it was deep. He seemed to relish that little bit of information.

When Don got to the hospital, he let me out at the emergency room door. I carried Joey into the emergency room where he was taken from my arms to receive immediate medical attention. The moment they took Joey from my arms, I went weak in the knees and they almost buckled. I started to shake uncontrollably. I realized that once I knew that Joey was in the hands of medical personnel and being looked after, I no longer had to put on such a brave front. I got to be a worried mother for a few minutes. Joey required almost one hundred stitches. The doctor layered the stitches and made them so small since the injury was on his face. They did such a fabulous job on Joey, because if you didn't know the injury had been there, you'd never see the scar. Amazingly, Joey didn't have a concussion.

Don was so guilt-ridden over that injury. He slept with Joey that night, waking him every couple of hours to make sure he hadn't slipped into a coma and was coherent. Joey was 8 ½ years old, and that was about the 4th or 5th time he'd had stitches.

My grandchildren are very civilized compared to when I was a child, and they haven't gotten hurt like my children did, but they have had their moments. Christien, my fourth grandchild, was the first to get stitches. I would have put money on Hunter. Hunter was like Joey — always the daredevil, always tempting fate, and always getting hurt. I would have bet the farm on Hunter. But it was Christien. He was due to be born on Christmas Eve, but he didn't arrive until the day after

Christmas. The following year, somewhere around the first part of December, Christien tripped over the vacuum cleaner. He had been walking for a couple of months, but he hadn't fine-tuned his motor skills to the point where he could maneuver around a moveable object. He went down like a ton of bricks, hitting right between the eyes just at the top of his nose and going down one side. This was Jennifer's first experience as a mother with an injury that involved a medical visit. I believe it was harder on her than it was on Christien. All of Christien's 1st Christmas pictures and 1st birthday pictures depict the fall on the vacuum.

A little over five years later, during one of Morgan's soccer games near the end of the season, Manuel and I watched as Morgan and her team played a formidable opponent. Manuel's cell phone rang and it was Jennifer. Hunter had a soccer game at the same time but on the other side of town. Jennifer hadn't paid attention to the jersey Hunter had grabbed to wear to his game, and it had been the wrong one. Jennifer asked Manuel to stop by their house, collect the right jersey, and bring it to them. I stayed at Morgan's game watching, cheering, and taking pictures.

Jennifer called me on my cell phone during halftime. "What's the score?" she asked.

"No one has scored a goal yet," I replied.

It had been a completely defensive game so far.

"Call me as soon as anyone scores," Jennifer said and hung up.

It was just a couple of minutes later when both teams took the field to start the second half of the game. From the kickoff, Morgan's team took the ball down the field to the goal. Morgan had possession, and I could tell she was going to attempt a goal. She had a clear shot and took it. I had the camera up to my eye, watching the game through the lens. Morgan kicked the ball, and it found it's way into the net for a goal. As soon as she kicked the goal, I laid the camera down and grabbed my cell phone to call Jennifer. I was so proud and couldn't wait to tell Jennifer that Morgan had scored the first goal.

After I dialed, I looked up and noticed Morgan was down. I hadn't notice at first. Jennifer answered the phone on the other end, and I stood up and began slowly walking up the sidelines toward the goal. It's not cool for a parent to go running onto the field if the child isn't really hurt that bad. I told Jennifer that Morgan had scored a goal but that she was down and hadn't gotten up yet. I started a play-by-play for Jennifer, telling her that the coaches had run onto the field. Then I told Jennifer that Morgan's coaches were carrying Morgan off the field and that I would call her back in a minute as soon as I found out the extent of Morgan's injury. I ran, and I mean *ran* like I hadn't run in twenty years over to where Morgan was lying down on the bench. I introduced myself to the coaches as Morgan's grandmother and knelt down to talk to my granddaughter who was crying. She complained of her leg and ankle hurting. I asked the coach about taking Morgan's equipment off so she would be more comfortable. The coach advised that if there was damage done, keeping the equipment on would help minimize the injury.

Manuel got there about ten minutes later, and after speaking to the coach and Jennifer, we all pretty much agreed that it was probably a bad sprain but would require an X-ray to be on the safe side. Jennifer asked me to go with Morgan and Manuel until she got there. Later, at an urgent care clinic, when the equipment, shoes, and socks came off, we all looked at each other, knowing full well that it was not just a sprain. We all knew without the X-ray that her leg and/or ankle had been broken. It didn't look pretty. In fact, it looked pretty bad. The X-ray showed Morgan had broken three bones in her leg, and Jennifer and Manuel were advised to go to All Children's Hospital where Morgan could be better treated because one of the breaks was pretty severe.

Morgan ended up having surgery that evening to place a couple of screws in her leg, and a cast was applied up to the top of her thigh. The following day, when Morgan was able to go home, Jennifer and Manuel looked through the pictures I had taken of the game. Although I had actually missed getting a picture of Morgan kicking the goal, I did capture a picture of how she was standing on her leg a moment after kicking the goal and the opponent goalie clearly falling on her leg.

Morgan survived the broken leg just fine. She spent most of the first month in a wheel chair. After four weeks, a new, shorter cast was applied, and Morgan was able to move around much easier by using crutches. At one point, she even went swimming in the pool at my house. "It's waterproof," she said. I was so amazed.

But it's not only my grandchildren who get hurt and need medical attention. One Saturday night after bath time, I was in the process of getting Rachel and Livvy some homemade chocolate chip cookies and a glass of milk for their evening snack. I backed up into the kitchen table pretty hard for no apparent reason that I can recall only to scrape and roll some skin from my finger. I grabbed my hand and started blowing on it. It really hurt. Both girls were concerned because they knew I was hurt and they wanted to see firsthand what I had done. Immediately upon seeing the skin on my finger, Livvy ran into my bathroom and retrieved the first aid kit. She brought it out to the table, opened it, and chose a bandage of appropriate size with built-in antibiotic cream. She tore off the wrapper and ever so gently applied the bandage like a pro. I looked at her work, thanked her, and told her my finger felt better — and it really did. She'd done a terrific job. She closed the first aid kit, grabbed it in her hand, and as she left to put it away, she said, "Just call me 'Doctor'."

SHOPPING IT'S NOT ALWAYS A PLEASURE

Growing up in the '60s was certainly a different time, place, and world than what it is now. My mother always took all five of us kids grocery shopping with her. What a nightmare! I can't even imagine. However, when it was all five of us, she made us stay in the car and wait while she did the shopping. She knew better than to try and shop while dragging five kids through the aisles. I guess the only thing she really had to worry about by leaving us in the car alone was us killing each other. No predator in his right mind would take on a carload of kids, nor car thief, for that matter, either. Back then, I don't think my mother even knew what a "predator" was. My brothers, sisters, and I usually fought the entire time. It just wasn't in us to behave, sing songs, talk nicely to each other, or play games to pass the time. Put us all together in a confined space, and there would always be a fight. I'm sure shoppers went into the grocery store shaking their heads at the screaming and yelling coming from our family car. Come to think of it... not once did an adult ever come to the car window to inquire if we were all right. For all anyone knew, there could have been actual blood drawn. And it's not like they couldn't hear us.

Heaven knows we always had to have the windows rolled down, what with the body heat we generated and the tempers flaring between us active children. We climbed back and forth from the front seat to the back seat and back to the front again. For some reason, we never seemed to mind being left alone in the car to our own muse and imagination, to the screaming and the fighting. I guess you can say we spent that time bonding.

Then there were those occasions when just one of us got to go with my mother alone to the grocery store. Those were special times. Sharing my mother's time with four brothers and sisters meant very little one-on-one time with her. Throw my father into the mix, and it didn't matter that her mind was on what she needed to purchase from the grocery store and you were along just because there wasn't anyone around to watch you at home. It was special just being in her presence all by yourself.

I remember one time going to the grocery store with my mother alone. My mother was focused on finding the items she came to get. I was focused on a pretty little thing on the shelf. I can't remember what it was, but I remember turning around toward my mother but she was gone. To this day, my brother, David, maintains that she tried to lose me. I frantically looked up and down the aisle, and when I didn't see her, I just froze in that spot and cried my eyes out for my mother. Again, no one bothered to ask me where my mother was. No one tried to comfort me or help me find her. Maybe they thought David was right. After several minutes she reappeared, not seeming to notice my tears. She grabbed my hand and pulled me to the next aisle to look for the last item on her list. I was so elated that she had come back for me, it didn't even bother me that she hadn't noticed my tears. Years later, I spoke to my mother about it.

"You thought you were lost?" she asked. "I'm so sorry, honey; I wouldn't have left the store without you."

That wasn't comforting. I had watched my mother on numerous occasions leave the house without her purse, her glasses, or her lists. I was witness to her forgetting all kinds of things at the grocery store — milk, toilet paper, mustard; you name it. Forgetting she even brought me to the store with her in the first place was not out of her realm of possibility. I could easily imagine her not remembering that I had been with her when she had entered the store and not discovering her error until I didn't show up at the dinner table. Even then, it would take her awhile to remember the last time she had seen me. Yeah, I didn't buy the "I wouldn't have left the store without you" line. I knew better.

I took my children to run errands all the time. And yes, I left them alone in the car the way my mother left us alone. Back then, I didn't know what "predator" meant either. My own children, as I've said before, were a little more civilized than I had been when I was younger — but not by much. They fought, just not as much. I also didn't leave them in the car for long. It was usually only if I was just going to be a few minutes. On one particular trip, I went to the store only to get milk or bread, one item, a really quick trip in and out.

"Stay in the car, and no fighting!" I directed. "I'll be right back in just a minute."

When I got back in the car, I didn't notice it. In fact, I didn't notice it until well after we got home.

"Joey, what's on your face?" I inquired.

"What?" Joey asked, as if he had no idea what I was talking about.

He had an open wound on his cheekbone. It was perfectly round. I had heard about ringworm and thought that must be what this was. I called the doctor and made an appointment for the next afternoon.

After inspecting the wound site, the doctor turned to me almost accusingly, "This isn't ringworm. This is a burn."

"A burn?" I questioned. "I'm with him all the time. It's not a burn. I would know if he was burned. I mean, really, look at it; it's perfectly round. What could cause a burn that's so perfectly round?"

"A cigarette," was his reply.

"A cigarette? What are you trying to say? Someone intentionally put a cigarette out on his face?" I asked incredulously.

"Do you smoke?" he asked.

"If I was going to put a cigarette out on my son's face, why would I bring him to you for treatment? I would already know what it is and know how to take care of it myself," I replied somewhat indignantly.

I left the doctor's office never to return. How *dare* he? What kind of monster did he think I was? How in the world could he ever possibly think I would ever hurt my son like that? Joey tried my patience beyond comprehension, but I would never hurt my son.

During the entire ride home from the doctor, I went over and over that conversation in my head. But I kept coming back to the same thing. It wasn't ringworm. The doctor had said it was a burn. How had he gotten burned, and who had done it? When we got home, I took Joey into his room and sat down with him on his bed.

"Joey," I began, "how did you get the burn on your face? You can tell me. Who did this to you?"

"Mommy," he began with a slight tremor in his voice, "I did it."

"*You* did it?" I could barely understand "How?" I asked. "And why?"

"While you were in the store yesterday, and we were in the car, I saw the silver thing. It turned red, and I put it to my cheek just to see what it felt like."

"What silver thing?" I asked, trying to comprehend.

"I'll show you," Joey suggested.

We walked out to the car and got into the front seat. Joey reached for the cigarette lighter.

"I pushed it down, and it popped up. I pulled it out, and it was red, and then I could feel the hot. I put it to my face just to see if it really was hot," Joey explained.

"Can you go back to the doctor's office with me and tell him that?" I asked, only half kidding.

Vindication! But the doctor never knew the real truth. Like I said, I never went back.

When I went grocery shopping, I usually took whoever wanted to come. Sometimes it was all four of my kids, more if they had friends over, and sometimes it was less. On one occasion, when Jeffrey was 7 or 8, he came grocery shopping with me by himself.

As I went up and down the aisles, he began to get a little restless and asked, "Mommy, can I go to the toy aisle until you get there?"

I felt that Jeffrey was old enough to be left alone only three or four aisles away, so I said okay. We would meet up in front of the toys in several minutes, and, just like clockwork, I showed up and Jeffrey was ready to finish the shopping with me.

After we arrived home and I was putting the groceries away, I noticed Jeffrey playing with a little toy that I didn't recognize.

"Where did you get that toy?" I inquired a little curiously.

"I don't know," was his reply.

When a child doesn't know something he should know, it

usually means they do know but don't want to tell. It's never a good sign.

"What do you mean, you don't know?" I asked impatiently. "You must know where you picked it up from."

"Mommy, don't get mad," Jeffrey pleaded.

Okay, nothing ever starts out good when your child tells you not to get mad.

"I got it at the store."

"The one we just came from? But you didn't have any money. How did you get it?" I asked, already dreading his answer.

"This is the part where you're not supposed to get mad," Jeffrey reminded me. "I took it from the store."

"You took it from the store without paying for it?" I asked, starting to raise my voice. "How could you take something that didn't belong to you? What made you think it was okay to do that?"

"You said you wouldn't get mad. I'm sorry." Jeffrey hung his head in shame.

I sent Jeffrey to his room while I thought about what he had done and the punishment I had to impose. Finding the phone number in the yellow pages, I called the store and spoke to the store manager. I explained to him what Jeffrey had done and told him I would return with my son to pay for the toy, but I asked that he educate my son on the consequences of shoplifting.

I went to Jeffrey's room to tell him we were going back to the store and that *he* would confess to the store manager that he had stolen the toy and apologize to him for taking something that didn't belong to him.

Although I was extremely disappointed that Jeffrey would steal a toy, I was proud of him that he took the responsibility for his actions and confessed to the store manager that he took the toy without paying for it. Jeffrey didn't cry. He didn't beg me not to take him. He did ask me if he really had to, but he didn't beg me not to make him. I was proud of him. I paid for the toy but threw it in the trash when we got home.

As my children got older, shopping became more serious. In 1988, when Jennifer was 15 years old, she was very much into designer clothes. She refused to wear anything that didn't have a designer label. We were shopping in Macy's one Saturday afternoon when Jennifer spotted a *Guess* sweater that she couldn't seem to live without.

"Mom, can you buy this for me? Please?" Jennifer begged.

The sweater was $75.00! I loved my daughter and wanted her to have nice things, but not at the expense of us all not being able to eat for a week.

"Jennifer," I began, "we can't afford to spend so much money on one piece of clothing."

"Please? I promise not to be embarrassed if any of my friends see me with you," Jennifer continued.

Wow! As tempting as that offer was, practicality won me over.

"Jennifer, we can't afford it," I said a little too loudly for Jennifer's taste.

Jennifer looked from side-to-side to see if anyone had heard me. She put her arm around me and led me away to a private area. In a low but calm voice, she said to me, "Mom, tell me I don't need it. Tell me it's the wrong color for me. Tell me it doesn't look good on me. Tell me anything you like, but when we're out shopping in public, please don't say 'We can't afford it'."

I had to admit — she had me there. I had embarrassed her in front of a bunch of total strangers, none of whom she'd ever see again. I didn't know what had gotten into me, talking to my daughter in a normal tone of voice.

A year later, Jennifer went through the whole gothic thing or whatever they called it. She wore black constantly. Every stitch of clothing was black. She dyed her hair an extremely light blonde. She also wore bright-red lipstick and black make-up. She was thin and pale, so the look I guess she was going for was one of starvation and/or death. I hated the way she dressed. I will never forget September 23, 1990, the Saturday Jennifer came to me saying that she wanted to change her look. She wanted regular clothes again. I was ecstatic.

"Anything you want!" I promised quickly. "Let's go to the mall right now!" I said eagerly. I wanted to go before she changed her mind.

I had so much fun shopping with Jennifer that afternoon. I would have bought her everything her heart desired. Anything for her to look normal again. We bought jeans, shirts, tops, skirts, and shoes. I was using my credit card at this point, completely out of money. I didn't care. I was getting my daughter back.

As we were walking out of the mall, with our arms loaded with newly purchased clothes for my lovely daughter, Jennifer turned to me. "Mom," she started, "I can't do this. I thought I could, but I can't."

"Sure you can. You're just not used to this stuff. It's like riding a bike. It'll all come back to you. Just give it a chance. Let's go back to Macy's to see if they still have that sweater you liked so much last year," I pleaded.

Jennifer looked me squarely in the eyes. "I tried," she said, knowing my disappointment.

In an instant, all my hopes and dreams were dashed.

"Let's go take it all back and get our money. I appreciate your effort, Jennifer. I know it wasn't easy," I said with resignation, trying to be supportive but still brokenhearted at the same time.

It took Jennifer another couple of years before she looked like a normal human being again. She has begged me to never show her children the pictures taken of her during that period of her life. I haven't made any promises. I'm holding on to them for the most opportune time.

Shopping with my grandchildren is pretty much the same as it was with my own children, except that I never leave them in the car alone, not even back before you could pay for your gas at the pump and had to go inside to the cashier to pay. I didn't even leave them in the car then.

My son, Joey, and his wife Karen were visiting from Oregon a few years ago, and everyone was at my house to see them. I needed to go to the grocery store for some odd thing and asked who wanted to go with Grandma. Morgan, Hunter, and Rachel wanted to come. Both Jennifer and Jessica asked me if I was sure I wanted to take all three children with me.

"Piece of cake," I assured them. "I used to take all four of you to the store with me all the time."

I soon realized I had been a lot younger then. When we got to the store, they all hung on the side of the grocery cart and rode through the aisles with me pushing. They began to fight over who was going to put what in the basket. I initially told them we would all take turns. That idea became a bust, so I had to put my foot down and proclaim that only I would put anything in the cart. I was probably in the store for about ten minutes, but it felt like an eternity.

When we got to the checkout, I let them help me put the items on the belt for the clerk to scan. One item fell to the ground, and Rachel and Hunter both began to fight over who was going to put the item back on the belt. I nipped it in the bud by picking it up myself. This simple act threw Rachel into a "fit". She began to scream and cry. We've all seen this display — the poor woman who everyone has already judged as a bad parent/grandmother who has the spoiled, rotten kid throwing a fit in the grocery store. Morgan and Hunter just stood there in horror, as Rachel ignored my pleas of composure and continued to sit on the floor crying and screaming.

I hurriedly paid the bill and told Rachel to get up, take my hand, and walk to the car with me. Rachel continued to ignore me, so I had to pick her up screaming and now kicking. Every eye in that store was on me, and I knew they either felt contempt for my parenting skills or felt pity for my humiliation. Morgan and Hunter didn't say a word but just followed me out to the car.

Getting Rachel into her car seat was one of my all-time greatest achievements. Hysterical children have superhuman strength. I lived a few blocks from the store, so it only took a couple of minutes to get home. When we rounded the corner of my street, Rachel suddenly stopped screaming and crying to abruptly apologize.

"Too little, too late," I responded.

I walked in my front door and immediately said to Jessica, "You need to take Rachel home."

Rachel did regain her composure and sincerely apologized for her behavior. Call me crazy, but Rachel goes to the store with me often and is always a big help. She has never thrown a fit like that again. In fact, we recently went to the store and both Rachel and Livvy were so well behaved that I felt compelled to tell them, "You guys were so good at the grocery store. Thank you so much."

"Were we just good?" Rachel wanted to know.

Evidently, she thought they deserved a little more recognition than just being good.

"Okay, you were between very good and excellent," I corrected.

When it comes to Rachel and Livvy, I never seem to get to have the last word.

"Grandma," Livvy replied, "I wasn't even trying to be good. I was just pretending."

She was pretending to be good? I know better than to try and clarify any of Livvy's comments, so I just thanked her for being such a good pretender.

The one thing I really have to psych myself up for is taking Livvy by the shoe department in any store. It doesn't matter if it's Wal-Mart or Macy's. Her reaction to shoes is always the same, "Grandma, these shoes are so pretty. Will you buy them for me?"

"Livvy," I begin, "these shoes aren't even your size."

"But, Grandma," she persists, "I want them anyway."

"Livvy, Livvy, Livvy, if you want these shoes, then we need to get ones that will fit your feet. These won't fit your feet. These are a woman's size 8, and you wear a children's size 9. These would fit your mommy."

On average, Livvy will grab every third shoe on display and think they are so beautiful that she must have them at all cost. She will beg and plead, not caring that they are never a children's shoe or even remotely close to her shoe size. It's a battle that I usually win but not without a few casualties. Livvy is relentless, and I'm a real soft touch where she is concerned.

Probably one of the most unusual and memorable times I've had at the store with my grandchildren was the Saturday morning Rachel, Livvy, and I went to Wal-Mart. It was beginning to feel a lot like winter, and I had gone shopping earlier in the week for church dresses with long sleeves. All their current dresses were sleeveless. Let's face it; in Florida, you seldom need anything warm to cover your arms. But on occasion, in the winter, it can get cold. So I bought them each a long-sleeved dress.

When they came over that morning, I asked them to try on their new dresses to make sure they fit properly. It was supposed to be cold the following morning. Rachel's dress was brown. The dress itself was sleeveless, but it had a short, velvet, long-sleeved jacket. I had never seen a brown dress for an 8-year-old girl before, but it was really pretty. Livvy's dress was long-sleeved black velvet on the top, and the skirt was a sheer white fabric with black polka dots and a thick red ribbon around the waist/hips. The girls tried on their new dresses, and they looked like princesses. They asked me to fix their hair, and when I was done, they each grabbed a toy crown. Yep, they looked like princesses all right. They even brought a crown for me to wear.

"Okay. Let's get the dresses off. I have to go to Wal-Mart this morning," I said, after giving them plenty of time to admire themselves.

"Grandma, can we wear our new dresses to the store? We promise we won't get them dirty. Please?" Rachel started.

"Grandma, we promise to be careful," Livvy chimed in on cue.

I'm such a softy when my grandchildren look so cute and when they're using their manners.

"Okay," I conceded, "but seriously, don't get them dirty. You're wearing those dresses tomorrow for church, and I don't want to have to wash, dry, and iron them before you've even worn them to church."

"Grandma, can we wear our crowns, too?" Livvy asked

"Of course you can. How else will anyone know you're princesses?" I replied.

"Grandma, will you wear your crown, too?" Rachel requested.

"Rachel, I'm a little old to be wearing a crown," I told her.

"But, Grandma, how will anyone know you're the queen if you don't wear your crown?" Rachel responded.

She had a good point. How *would* they know? So Rachel, Livvy, and I went to Wal-Mart all dressed up in our Sunday best and wearing our crowns. You wouldn't believe the people that stopped us to ask if we were going to a party. Rachel just told everyone that Grandma bought them a new dress and that they got to wear them to Wal-Mart.

On the way out, an older gentleman stopped us. He had just purchased a disposable camera and asked if he could take a picture of the girls in their pretty dresses and crowns. He reached into his bag, shuffled everything around looking for the camera, pulled it out, and took a couple of pictures of the girls.

I had a special time with my granddaughters that morning. My little princesses made me feel like a queen. It was a morning I will never forget and hope they will always remember too.

MY HOME IS MY CASTLE

When I was growing up, our house was my father's castle. We all knew it. He ruled with an iron fist, and we were at the mercy of his whims. But he had to fight to keep it that way. Our front door lock was broken in the way that it was perpetually locked. There was no way to unlock it and keep it that way. My father was a carpenter, so you'd think that getting a new doorknob would be a piece of cake for him, but he never fixed it.

By virtue of the fact that there were five precocious children in the house, the locked front door was often used as a means to get back at a sibling. All you had to do was get to the front door first, get the key from under the mat, unlock the door, get the key out of the lock, and get the front door shut before the sibling chasing you caught up. They could pound on the door all day long, but you could be inside laughing at them, and there wasn't anything they could do.

This happened between my brother, David, and my sister, Dianne, one afternoon after school while waiting for my parents to get home from work. David was not always nice to us when we were small. His defense to us now is that my older brother Steve used to beat him up every day. Since he was the next oldest, he, in turn, was mean to my sisters and to me. Lame excuse. However, one day David was teasing Dianne on their way home from school. Dianne began to cry, which only fueled David's meanness. He took off running for home. Dianne realized what he was going to do, so she took off running after him. But she was no match for David. He got into the house first and shut the door before Dianne could even get to the front porch. Dianne kept pounding on the door for someone to open it. I was in the house and went to let Dianne in when David blocked the door, laughing, "What do you think you're doing?" David asked me.

"I'm going to let Dianne in, and you can't stop me!" I yelled.

"You and what army? Do you really think you can overpower me by yourself?" he teased. "I dare you to try. Come on. Try and get the door open."

I may not have been a match for David either, but I was still tough, and I wasn't afraid of him even though he'd beaten me up many times before. I went for it. I jumped on David and started pulling his hair with one hand and grabbing for the doorknob with the other. Dianne continued to pound on the front door and started kicking it so completely frustrated, humiliated, and angry. We all heard it at the same time and stopped in our tracks. The sound we heard didn't sound good. I slid off David, and he gently opened the front door to find Dianne staring at the lower part of the door. David and I looked in the direction Dianne was staring, and we both saw it. Dianne had kicked a hole in the door. Wow! She was going to get it when my dad got home. I was so glad I wasn't her at that moment! You can't wipe up a hole in the door like you could wipe up spilled water on a hardwood floor. I was going to miss her.

David, Dianne, and I made a pact that we would never reveal where the hole came from. Despite our fighting, we really did love each other and didn't really want to see anything bad happen to one another.

My father came home from work first, before my mother. He often came home in an angry mood after fighting the traffic, and that night was no exception. However good or bad his mood was prior to walking up to the front door mattered little. He took one look at the hole in the door, and the first words out of his mouth when he entered his castle was, "Which one of you kids put the hole in the door!?"

We were all in our rooms playing quietly and trying to pretend nothing had happened when our bedroom door flew open and my father's intimidating figure stood in the doorway.

"What happened to the front door?" he roared.

"I don't know," I said. "It was like that when I came home from school."

He basically got the same answer from each of my brothers and sisters. I have often wondered if he just wasn't sure it was one of us or not. Later that night, my father decided to drive down to Redondo Beach pier and get some salt-water taffy, one of his favorites. He asked me if I wanted to go with him. I loved walking on the pier, especially at night, so I said I would go. I just didn't see it coming. We got into his truck and he started the engine.

"What really happened to the front door?" he began, before we even got off our street.

My heart sank. I couldn't believe he had used the pier as a rouse to get me alone and confess. Divide and conquer. He was pretty clever. I had to hand it to him. I guess he thought I must have been the weakest link, the one easiest to crack. I learned at a very early age that I would never do well under torture. I would be the one who would divulge all our country's secrets if captured. So I knew I would end up delivering my sister into my father's hands for punishment sooner or later. He knew it too. In all fairness to me, it did take a promise though.

"You know, if you tell me the truth, I promise I won't spank that person," he vowed.

"You promise?" I asked him so naively.

"I promise," he stated again.

I knew better than to believe that promise. I knew it in my heart, but I gave Dianne up anyway. I knew there was no way out for me or for her. Yeah, Dianne got a spanking for kicking that hole in the door, but until we moved away, the hole was still there. He never fixed it or the lock.

In my castle, everyone pretty much did what I wanted. It was my castle after all. It wasn't until I got a job and started working outside my home, my domain, that things began to fall apart, and I discovered that I had a revolution on my hands. It started so quietly that I didn't realize what was happening at first. I came home early one fall day to my house being 10,000 degrees inside. It felt like I had walked right into an oven. The heat was like a solid mass that hit me square on. My face began to melt right off my head. Apparently, the rule of "No one touches the thermostat" had flown out the window. Someone woke up cold, had turned the heater all the way up, and had forgotten to turn it back down prior to leaving for school.

I sat my children down to reinforce the rules on the heater. No one ever listened to me though. I came home frequently to every window and door in the house open, trying to cool the house down, and my brilliant children never went around closing the doors and windows before I came home. I told them often that if they were going to break the rules, they should at least have the intelligence to be smart about it.

"If you're going to turn the heater up high enough to melt all the plastic in the house, make sure you get home soon enough to clean the mess up before I come home so I don't have to know about it."

They weren't that smart. Leaving the heater on full blast all day while no one was at home was just the tip of the iceberg. My alarm clock went off at 4:30 A.M. every morning. I had to be at work by 6:00. The alarm went off and I struggled out of bed and didn't open my eyes until the water from the shower eventually woke me up. One morning in the shower, with my eyes barely open, my hand reached for the shampoo only to find nothing there. My eyes opened wide, frantically looking through the water while trying to locate the shampoo. It was nowhere to be found. I turned the water off, grabbed a towel, and headed for the other bathroom. There, in my children's shower, was my shampoo and conditioner. I stared in disbelief. I certainly didn't mind them using my shampoo and conditioner if they happened to run out, but they needed to: A. Tell me they were out of their shampoo and conditioner so I could buy more, and B. Put my shampoo and conditioner back in my shower before I know it's missing.

Another family meeting ensued. Once again, I went through the rules. It was like talking to zombies. They all sat there with blank stares on their faces, as if they didn't have a single clue what I was talking about.

A couple of weeks later, after having a successful shower, I opened my vanity drawer to grab my brush and blow-dry my hair, only to discover my brush was gone. Okay, this was starting to feel like an invasion. It's not like I owned the only hairbrush in the house. Everyone, and I mean everyone had their own hairbrush, all kept in the other bathroom. I stomped into their bathroom, opened the drawer, only to find the drawer empty of all brushes — including mine.

Have I mentioned that I'm not a morning person? I went into everyone's room, turned on the light, and woke everyone up at 5:00 A.M.

"Find my brush!" I said sternly.

"What?" was what they each replied.

"What do you mean, 'What?' Find my brush right now before I'm late for work. If you guys aren't smart enough to use my brush and then put it back where you got it, then you don't deserve to sleep. Now find my brush!"

"Hey, I found my brush!" one of them called out as they were looking under their bed.

"Wonderful. Now go put it in the drawer in the bathroom before you lose it, and then get back to looking for mine," I ordered.

"Why do we have to look for your brush?" Jeffrey asked.

The kid was asking for it. You'd think he didn't even know me at all.

"You're looking for my brush because it's not in my drawer, and I'm not the one who lost it," I said through clenched teeth.

On the way home from work, I stopped at the store for five new hairbrushes. I began to keep two brushes in my drawer at all times. So if I got up and there was only one brush in the drawer, I would know that someone had used my brush and hadn't put it back, and I would still have a brush to use for my hair. But like I said, my kids were not that bright. The little "find my brush" exploration at 5:00 A.M. happened quite a few times. I used to reason that when the day came and we moved from that house, we would find a treasure trove of hairbrushes. I never found a single one.

My children are still the masters of their castles. Their children are much too young for the eventual overthrow. But Jennifer's kids are on the verge of mutiny. And I can tell you without a doubt who is the eventual ruler of that kingdom: Hunter.

Jennifer and Manuel rented a four-bedroom house for ten years. They often talked to the owners about buying it, but the owners wanted to hang on to it. Eventually, the owners relented and sold the house to Jennifer and Manuel. For ten years, the owners would never allow Jennifer or Manuel to change anything about the house. Now that they owned it, they couldn't wait to make changes. I must tell you that Manuel is a white-collar worker. He knows very little about fixing things. Technical things, like computers, he can fix with his eyes closed, but for physical labor projects, he has no experience.

Jennifer bought him some tools one year for Christmas a couple of years after they moved into the house. We all got a good laugh at that one. Jennifer had such a sense of humor. I think that all the tools she bought him are still in the original boxes and packages. So it was funny that the very first thing Manuel wanted to tackle in their own home was to fix the drain in the children's bathroom. It had been slow for years. Manuel had spent an enormous amount of money on Drano and Liquid Plumr to no avail. He decided to take the elbow out from under the sink to see what he would find.

Jennifer called me barely able to speak because she was laughing so hard, "Mom, you won't believe what Manuel found when he took the elbow off the drain under the sink. He pulled out a toothbrush, a dinner fork, some loose change, and a full Skittles candy wrapper! No wonder the Drano and Liquid Plumr never worked! Okay, so the kids dropped a toothbrush down the drain," she said. "I can buy that. Maybe they were washing some coins and they went down the drain. I want to know why a fork was in the bathroom and why it was down the drain. But, most of all, you can't get an empty, complete candy wrapper down the drain without forcing it down there. Someone had to deliberately push that candy wrapper down the drain. Mom, what's wrong with my children? Please tell me we used to do stuff like this," Jennifer pleaded.

"There is nothing wrong with my grandchildren," I began with a huge smile on my face.

"But, Mom," Jennifer cut in, "last week Manuel happened to be going into his office when he walked by the bathroom. The bathroom door was open and he happened to glance in. There was Hunter, sitting on the toilet while eating a bowl of macaroni and cheese. Manuel almost had a heart attack. Seriously, what's wrong with my children?"

"They're children. You've got to hand it to them though. They're a little more entertaining than you guys were. Just out of curiosity, what did Hunter say about eating his mac and cheese while on the toilet?"

"He said he didn't want his lunch to get cold," Jennifer replied.

Sounded logical to me. Yeah, he's the one who would be king.

CALGON, TAKE ME AWAY!

My father was seldom able to get a full week off work at a time, so our family vacations usually consisted of going to Kernville and Lake Isabella for a long weekend. We just took little trips when we could and went about three times a year. My father loved getting up in the middle of the night, usually around 3:00 A.M., to reach the campground first thing in the morning. He had a utility truck where he kept all his tools for work. He would clear out the tools from the back of his truck, and my mother would pack all the necessary camping gear in there. Us kids also rode in the back of the truck. In those days, it just seemed natural to put the kids in the back end when there wasn't room in the cab of a truck. As normal kids would, we loved it! It was the best part of the trip. While driving through the winding mountain roads, there was one thing you could always count on: at least one of us would get carsick. Whoever it was would stick their head over the back end of the truck and let it go. Sometimes we made a game of it; who could leave the longest trail on the road.

Camping at Kernville was usually lots of fun for everyone. I said "usually" fun. On one trip, my father planned to leave right after work on a Friday. It was a holiday weekend, and he wanted to leave early enough to get a campsite that night. Even back in those days, traffic in Los Angeles was a nightmare. It took us forever to get out of the city. By the time we arrived in Kernville at the campsite, it was late. My father was in a bad mood from fighting the traffic and from working all day. Most of the other campers were in bed for the night. We were lucky to get the last campsite available. My father pitched the tent, and my mother put us kids to bed. When we had all settled down, my father asked my mother to make him a cup of tea so he could relax and unwind after working all day and fighting the traffic. My mother started the camp stove, put on the water, and made him a cup of tea. I need to say here that when I became an adult and went camping, I always made a list. In fact, I usually had several lists going just to insure nothing would be forgotten. My mother, on the other hand, never made a list. She always packed by the skin of her teeth and shooting from her hip. Consequently, she always forgot to pack something.

This trip was no exception. To everyone's dismay, my mother had forgotten to pack any sugar for the trip. When she handed my father the tea and he discovered that there wasn't any sugar, he didn't hesitate to let the whole campground know my mother had left the sugar at home. He ranted, raved, and carried on for so long, "I can't believe you didn't bring any sugar! What kind of person forgets to bring sugar? Didn't you make a list of food to bring? How are we supposed to get through the weekend without any sugar? Are you sure you didn't bring any sugar? Look again! I can't believe you didn't bring any sugar!"

My father woke a man in the next campsite. The fellow camper evidently got tired of listening to my father carry on like such a maniac. The man got out of his bed, got into his own food supply, and brought my father some sugar. The man told my father to keep the sugar. He'd get more later. Then he ordered him to drink his tea and shut up. There was another thing you could always count on: camping with my father was never boring.

My mother and father divorced when I was 9 years old. Believe it or not, it wasn't about the sugar incident. It's never about the sugar. They had other, more serious problems. But, after their divorce, we never went camping again.

My husband and I started taking our own kids camping when our youngest child, Jessica, was about 4 years old. We had purchased an old beat-up camper a couple of years before with talk and plans of camping every weekend. Our first camping trip was in August. We drove up to the high country in Yosemite. I am afraid of heights, so I had a difficult time just getting there and keeping my psyche intact. My husband was the driver but had no problem pointing out the scenery to me, "Honey, look over there! Isn't that awesome?"

I could barely look where he was pointing. All I could think about was how close we were to the edge of a cliff, and he wasn't even looking at the road but looking off in some other direction. Did he think the truck could drive by itself?

"Yeah, great! Beautiful! Just keep your eyes on the road."

Once we got there safely and had parked our truck, I had a real chance to check out the scenery. I was absolutely awestruck! I couldn't believe what I saw! It was the most beautiful place I had ever seen! The serenity and magnificence of it all was breathtaking! The meadows, the streams, the mountains, it was my own personal "happy place". It was how I envisioned Heaven would look.

As beautiful as the high country was, during the day it was hot, and as soon as the sun went down, it was below freezing. We were so unprepared for the freezing nights. On the way out from the high country, we drove through Yosemite Valley, and that's where I fell head over heels in love.

"This is where I want to die and be buried! This is where I want to spend each and every vacation!" I declared to my family.

The waterfalls and the granite cliffs and rock formations were incredible! From that moment on, Yosemite was our vacation destination. We decided not to camp in Yosemite Village but instead camped in a remote area just outside Yosemite National Park. We spent one day each vacation in the Village hiking to waterfalls and enjoying nature at it's finest. Yosemite is a very special place for my family.

We discovered the remote campground by accident our very first trip. I still kept in touch with my childhood friend, Terri, who had camped in Yosemite the year before. She loved the campground where they stayed, so I thought we'd try it out. But my kids were bored there, and they didn't have much to do. They wanted water to fish and swim in, so we went in search of such a campground. We found one just inside the park's southern entrance. It had a fast-flowing creek running through it, and the kids just loved it there. Unfortunately, we were only there for a couple of days because we were to meet up with my brother and sister's families at Lake Don Pedro for a few days camping. When we got to Lake Don Pedro, we found the lake had very few trees around it. There wasn't much shade, and it was about 10,000 degrees outside in the sun. There was just no way to keep cool. The lake was too warm for swimming, and being out in the sun was just asking for skin cancer. We took a vote and decided we'd all go to Yosemite to the campground my family had just come from.

I failed to mention earlier that not only did we have an old beat-up camper, but we also had an old beat-up truck. We entered Yosemite from the north where there is a very steep grade. Part way up the grade, our truck got vapor lock and stalled. I have no idea what vapor lock is, but that's the story I was told by the men in our group. We believed the men because they seemed to know what they were talking about. I sat in the truck waiting for it to become "unlocked" and muttered to myself how much I hated our truck.

My brother, David, heard my comment, and I was immediately scolded, "You shouldn't hate your truck. It's a good truck," David reassured me.

What did he know? He'd just met the truck. The truck and I had a long history that wasn't very pleasant. He'd see. We got back on our way, and it wasn't long before the truck vapor locked again and stalled.

"I hate this truck! I hate this truck!" I chanted over and over.

David again heard me and repeated what he'd said before, "You shouldn't hate your truck. It's a good truck!"

Yeah, yeah, I heard it all the last time it stalled — remember? Again, we were on the road almost to the top of the grade. Just a few more feet and we'd make it when, yeah — you guessed it — we vapor locked again. This time I got out of the truck and began to cry.

"I hate this truck! I hate this truck!"

David walked up to me and said, "I don't blame you! I'd get rid of that piece of garbage if I were you."

We never did. We kept that old, beat-up truck for years and drove it on every camping trip we went on. We just drove it in the evening after the heat of the day had passed and never had a problem with it vapor locking again.

We made it to the campground late in the afternoon, but there weren't any campsites left. The Ranger said that if we drove down the road a mile or so, made a left, and drove five miles down a narrow, winding, potholed, dirt road, we'd come to another campground that would have space available for us. It was considered an overflow campground. We drove down that dirt road for what seemed like hours but finally came to the campground. It was perfect! No one else was there, and it had a creek flowing right through the middle of it. Every campsite was next to the water.

After everyone set up camp, I looked through my camper to see what I could find that would stay on a hook. Ironically, we had all brought fishing poles, but no one had thought about bringing any bait. All I came up with were miniature marshmallows that I had brought to make Rice Krispies Treats. I cast my line in the creek. It was about knee-deep, and I really didn't expect to catch anything, but I needed to unwind after the terrible road trip. Evidently, trout love marshmallows, because my line wasn't in the water thirty seconds before I caught my first fish. After that, I was hooked myself.

I became known in my family as the master fisherwoman. We loved that campground so much that we decided it was the spot we'd camp at every year. We did camp there every year, and every year we had an eventful vacation.

My husband was the typical Neanderthal — fire was good! He never built just a campfire though; it was more like a bonfire. Each year, he took the kids in search of fallen branches or small logs. They hauled their bounty back to camp where my husband would cut it up into appropriate sizes for burning. When the sun began to dip behind the mountains, he gathered the wood needed for that night, carefully stacking the logs for optimum burning, and lit the match. As it burned, he stood back and sighed with great pride, "Now that's a campfire!" My children all thought he was a brilliant campfire builder too. I have watched them. They build their campfires the same way — with the same fervor.

Every year there were the injuries, too. We all took the injuries in stride and even came to expect them. The only question was who it would be on a particular trip. On our last camping trip, we even took bets. The first year, there was just a minor injury. Jessica was roasting marshmallows on a stick near the bonfire when her marshmallow and the stick caught fire. She blew the fire on her stick so hard that not only did she blow the fire out but the stick whipped back and hit her in the mouth. That was bad enough, but on the end of the stick was a melted marshmallow. The melted marshmallow stuck to her lip and practically melted her lip off as well.

I was off fishing. My favorite time to fish was at dusk. I could hear Jessica screaming all the way down the creek. When I made it back to camp, my husband had everything under control including ice on her lip. That didn't stop him from giving me an earful, "You need to be here when the kids get hurt! I wasn't sure what to do. Didn't you hear her screaming?"

I'd really like to know why it's always a mother's responsibility to take care of an injured child. Can't a father keep it together long enough to just use common sense in dealing with an injury? I assured him that he had done a great job in taking care of Jessica and didn't need my approval or advice on how to treat every bug bite, scratch, scrape, or burn. He did good!

We ran the whole gamut of injuries from the burned lip, to broken bones, to a concussion, and everything in-between. One of my favorite injuries, if you can have a favorite injury, was Joey's hand. I was making dinner one evening and Joey came into the camper and asked me for a paper towel. I had no idea why, but I asked him why he needed one.

"No reason," he responded.

Okay, that answer always peaks a mother's suspicion. I turned and looked at him. He was holding his hand, and it was bloody.

"What happened?" I asked, knowing I wasn't going to like the answer.

"You know the new fillet knife you bought Dad? I just wanted to look at it and pulled it out of its sheath. As I pulled it out, it cut my hand."

Yep — I didn't like the answer.

"Didn't I tell you not to touch the knife because it was really sharp?"

At that point, it didn't really matter. He hadn't listened and now he was cut. I looked at the cut closely. It wasn't deep, but it was in a bad part of his hand. It was near the side of the hand and in the crease where you bend it. I knew it would be difficult to stop the bleeding because of the location of the cut. We initially applied pressure. No success. My sister, Dianne, and her family were camping with us as they often did. Dianne was a pro at cuts. She made butterfly bandages and applied them to the cut. That worked until Joey moved his finger, and the bleeding started again. Next, my husband applied the butterfly bandages but also bound his entire hand so he couldn't bend his fingers. That worked until he hit his hand on something, and it began to bleed again. We decided to try one more thing and if it didn't work, we'd have to take him to a hospital for stitches. Dianne and my husband put butterfly bandages on his hand, bound his fingers together, and then bound his arm to his body. He couldn't move or use the whole upper left side of his body. Success!

We camped outside of Yosemite every summer and camped outside of Watsonville at Mt. Madonna each Memorial Day. My husband's two bothers and their families camped with us each year. Our annual mini-vacation to Mt. Madonna began the year my sister-in-law was late in her pregnancy and didn't want to be too far from home. My sister, Dianne, is also married to my husband's younger brother, Doyle. So even though we camped each year with my husband's two brothers, I camped with my sister.

Our three families camping together was so much fun. The kids were all the same age and played together like brothers and sisters — but better. Each year, my sister-in-law made homemade, fresh strawberry ice cream. I always looked forward to her ice cream. It was the best.

On our first night at Mt. Madonna one year just after dinner, just after washing the dishes, just before the strawberry ice cream, we all heard a scream. Everyone stopped dead in their tracks… waiting to see if it was a play scream or a hurt scream. Jessica caught her breath and let another scream go. The kids were off playing in the trees away from camp. We couldn't see them, but we could hear them. When we heard Jessica's second scream, we turned toward the sound. My nephew, Ben, came running out of the trees and into the campground carrying Jessica in his arms. She was bloody from the chest up. Doyle ran to Ben grabbing Jessica out of his arms. My husband reached Doyle and grabbed Jessica out of his arms. A fleeting thought crossed my mind: they looked like they were running a relay race and Jessica was the baton. My husband laid Jessica on an empty picnic table where he began the search for the injury site. My sister Dianne joined him, and they narrowed it down to the right side of her head.

I called my husband aside and told him, "I don't care if it's a pinhole. She's lost a lot of blood. We need to get her to a hospital."

We left the campsite and headed for town in search of a hospital. It was a little more than a pinhole but not much, just requiring two stitches. She had on a shirt, sweater, and jacket, and her blood had soaked through all three layers of clothing. It was incredible the amount of blood she lost for such a tiny cut.

When we got back to camp, Dianne came running up to us full of excitement. "I've reconstructed the accident!"

She took us into the trees.

"Jessica was standing here between these two trees. Ben and Jeffrey were sword fighting each other with two branches fifty feet away. The boys hit each other's sword really hard; one broke off, hurled through the air, and just by freak accident it hit Jessica in the head. It's just amazing that Jessica got hit so far from where the boys were playing — and she was between two trees!" Dianne said, a little proud of her reconstruction.

"Great detective work, Sherlock!" I replied a little sarcastically.

Dianne may have been a good detective that time, but she almost killed some of us one trip. We camped at a different campground each year at Mt. Madonna. One year, we camped near what could have been called a cliff. The side of the mountain dropped off almost straight down. I couldn't even see the bottom of the cliff. One morning, the kids hiked down that cliff and told tales of their adventures at lunch.

It intrigued Dianne so much that she wanted to hike down the cliff as well. "If the kids can make it, we most certainly can!" Dianne announced.

The thing about my sister, Dianne, was that she was the sensible one, the reasonable one, so you just naturally trusted her judgment. We obviously had a lapse in judgment that day, and we were all sucked into her crazy idea. After lunch we took off, and, almost immediately, Jeffrey lost his footing and slid part way down the mountain until he hit a rock with his foot. My husband was the first one to make it to Jeffrey who was now crying in pain. He carried Jeffrey in his arms up the mountain, with Doyle behind pushing them upward and trying to keep them both upright because of the steep slope. You'd think that would be enough for us to give it up and go back to camp too. But not Dianne! We proceeded down the mountain. All I thought about was the climb back up and the heat of the day. And, of course, no one brought water. We made it down the mountain in one piece and only found the bottom. It was a little anti-climatic.

We finally began the arduous trek back up, and it was really a scorcher of an afternoon! I began having difficulty about ¾ of the way up. I became beet red in the face and had difficulty breathing. I heard Dianne up ahead of me yell to one of the kids who had already reached the top to go back to camp and get water for us. By the time I made it to the top, the water was waiting for me. Dianne poured some on my face first and gasped at the steam that appeared. When we got back to camp, Jeffrey was soaking his foot in a tub of ice. He was able to move his foot okay, so we didn't think it was broken.

A week later, after having a shower, Jeffrey accidentally kicked the couch and crumbled to the floor like a house made of matchsticks blown apart by a breeze. I asked him if his foot had been bothering him prior to the kicking of the couch. He said he had gotten into trouble at school earlier in the week because his foot had hurt so much that he had taken his shoe off in class and couldn't get it back on. I felt like a terrible mother. His foot had probably been broken all along, and I hadn't even had it x-rayed. I took him to the hospital emergency room where it was confirmed: His toes were not broken, but three bones in his foot were. I received the award that year for the world's worst mother.

One of our last trips to Mt. Madonna was a year that the 4th of July fell on a Sunday, providing us all with a three-day weekend. My family decided to spend our holiday at Mt. Madonna since it was only an hour-and-a-half drive from home. That was also the year my oldest son Joey became one of "those" teenagers that adults find difficult to like. We all now refer to that time in our life as "The Dark Years". It was a time of great turmoil in our lives and the beginning of the end of just about everything we all held dear. It certainly wasn't Joey's fault. Joey was never the center of "The Dark Years", just a part of them as we all were.

Fourth of July night, we walked out to a point on the mountain that overlooked a small city below. We thought that if there was a fireworks display, then that would be the spot to see it. There wasn't a moon that particular 4th of July, and it was pitch black in the dark. I had never seen such darkness before. Jeffrey had brought his scooter camping with him, and the kids were all taking turns riding around in the dark on the road leading to the lookout point. We waited for a couple of hours for the fireworks show, but I guess the town was too small for a display.

On the road back to camp, I remember just how dark it was. Joey laid down on the side of the road and grabbed my foot as I passed by just to scare me, and I never saw him. The kids began making scary noises. We were having a great time scaring each other… until Joey got back on the scooter. There was a slight downgrade, barely noticeable, going into the campground from the road we were on, and Joey hunched over the handlebars of the scooter as he rode into the campground going full speed. All of a sudden, we heard a loud thud. We all began calling out Joey's name but heard nothing. Joey had only been about twenty yards ahead of us at the point of impact, but we couldn't see anything. We finally reached what Joey had hit. While we were out on the point, the rangers had suspended a log barricade across the road, chest high, to keep cars from going out to the point where evidently there had been a problem with drinking. We didn't know they had done that, nor could we see the log until we were right on top of it. Joey had hit that log face first, full speed, and had been knocked unconscious. We continued calling for Joey, trying to feel around in the brush for him beside the road, when we finally heard moaning. We found Joey on the side of the road, braces and teeth hanging from his mouth. My husband carried 15-year-old Joey back to our camper and we assessed the damage.

Joey kept saying, "I don't remember anything. What happened? I can't remember. Where am I?"

I jumped on that opportunity as fast as I could, "Joey, you are a straight "A" student. You love school and sports and excel in all you do. You're a wonderful person and a joy to be around."

My other children didn't recognize the opportunity that had fallen in our laps but criticized my attempt at change.

"Mom! What are you doing?"

Disappointed that my other children were not visionaries, I turned to them as calmly as I could. "I'm trying to help your brother! If he can't remember anything, then maybe he can turn his life around a little easier! It's certainly worth a try!"

The bottom line was that he remembered everything up to the point of impact. I drove Joey and my other son Jeffrey down the mountain to the hospital. On the way, Joey asked questions and I provided the answers.

"Where are we going?"

"We're going to the hospital."

"What happened?"

"You ran into a log across the road and probably have a concussion."

"Where are we?"

"Mt. Madonna."

"Is it Memorial Day?"

"No, it's the 4th of July."

"Where are we going?"

"We're going to the hospital."

"What happened?"

"You ran into a log across the road and probably have a concussion."

"Where are we?"

"Mt. Madonna."

"It is Memorial Day?"

"No, it's the 4th of July."

"Where are we going?"

"Ask your brother."

Joey did have a concussion, but he didn't have to stay in the hospital. He slept most of the next couple of days as his brain healed. We just woke him up from time to time to irritate him and ask him questions to make sure he wasn't experiencing any further or lasting brain damage.

"Joey, who's the president? No, not of the Little League, of our country! What's my name? My name's not Mom. What did my parents name me? What school do you attend periodically? Who really killed JFK? Explain the theory of relativity. Who let the dogs out? How would you achieve world peace?"

His answers were vague but coherent enough to satisfy me that he was going to make a full and complete recovery.

We used to say that Joey had a death wish. He was the one who never seemed to have any fear of anything. If there was an obstacle in front of him, he climbed it without hesitation. My husband and I allowed the kids to explore the campground without supervision. They just weren't allowed to wander too far, and we asked that they stay in earshot of us in case anyone got hurt or we wanted them back at camp.

One afternoon, Joey and Jeffrey went exploring along the creek near Yosemite. Joey saw a huge rock face that had his name on it, and it called to him. He couldn't resist. He began climbing the rock face and was about ¼ of the way from the summit when he began to panic. Joey was so high up on the rock face, probably at least fifty feet, when fear seized him for the first time in his life and he froze.

"Jeffrey, go get Dad! I can't move! I'm going to die! I'm going to fall right here and die on those rocks below!"

Jeffrey, who usually tended to overreact in a crisis, remained levelheaded and calmly talked his brother down off the rock face without the help of their father. Once down, Joey boldly debated on whether to try to climb the rock face again, because he didn't make it to the top on the previous try.

"Are you crazy? Are you nuts? Do you really want to die?" Jeffrey yelled at his brother.

Joey didn't try to climb the rock face again, and neither of my sons told me about the incident until they were grown adults.

Yes, there were injuries and near injuries every single year, but they never slowed us down or discouraged us from camping in the wild. The fun we had far outweighed the mishaps. Our biggest and most favorite pastime was fishing. We only fished once a year, and it was there at that campsite just outside Yosemite. We were by no means experts. I'm sure we used the wrong bait, the wrong size hooks, and the wrong size line. We barely knew what we were doing, but we had a great time doing it!

The only one who didn't really have an interest in fishing was Jeffrey. He was just too practical for the sport. He didn't see the great attraction in baiting a hook, throwing it in the water, and sitting around waiting for some hungry fish that might just take the bait without actually getting hooked. He looked at it as a waste of time. Watching my other children catch fish was thrilling and generally funny, or, at the very least, entertaining. We fished at all hours of the day and night, whenever the mood struck us.

One night, after I had come back from fishing, Jennifer grabbed her pole, went up the creek about fifty yards, and threw her line in the water. It wasn't long before one of the kids came back to camp looking for a flashlight.

"What are you looking for?" I inquired of my child.

"Jennifer caught a fish and flung her whole line up out of the water. We heard the fish fall off her line onto the bank, and we need a flashlight to find it."

That was Jennifer. When she caught a fish, she got so excited that she couldn't reel the fish in. Instead, she either took off running inland with her pole in her hand or she flung her line all the way up out of the water. She never lost her fish though, and she was always fun to watch.

I decided to go fishing late one afternoon before dinner. I just wanted to go for a little while before I had to start cooking. I looked at fishing during that time of day like having a cocktail before dinner. It was relaxing and gave me the added energy to finish the day. Plus, fishing was usually my time alone, my time for me. I don't care what anyone says; camping is a ton of work for the mother. On that particular afternoon, Jessica wanted to go with me. She was about 6 years old but already loved to fish. I had previously decided where I wanted to go, and there was only room for one person. But Jessica was my daughter and she wanted to fish with me, so I said she could come.

When we arrived at the spot, I noticed a flat rock just on the side of the bank in about two inches of water and well away from where I wanted to fish. I prepared Jessica's line and told her to attempt to get her line in that direction. She was dead on. Her hook landed right on top on the rock. Perfect! I baited my hook and cast my line right where I wanted it to go too. Jessica and I sat there waiting.

All of a sudden, Jessica broke out singing a Mike and the Mechanics song, *"All I need is a miracle. All I need is you. All I need is a miracle. All I need is you."*

I smiled at her. Gosh! She was so precious! As I was glowing with maternal pride, Jessica began to scream, "I got one! I got one!"

I coached her and she landed a nice rainbow trout from the top of that rock in about two inches of water. I guess she got her miracle. I never got a bite in that spot again.

My favorite place to fish after dinner was just downstream from our campsite and across the creek. I caught fish there every night, every year. We ran low of bait one year after a few mishaps, and I began fishing with cheddar cheese. I just cut it up into little squares, and it stayed on the hook pretty well. The fish seemed to love it, so it became my bait of choice.

One night at my fishing hole, the fish were able to take my bait without getting hooked. The moment my line hit the water, a fish would snag the cheese and swim free. It began to make me crazy. I threw cast after cast into the water and immediately felt a strong tug on my line. I tried to set the hook but just couldn't. After a couple of hours, I gave up and went back to camp empty-handed, which was a rarity.

The next night, I headed back to my spot right after the dinner dishes were done. The same thing happened. Cast after cast, the fish took my bait and swam away as soon as my line hit the water. I was furious. Going back to camp empty-handed the second night in a row, I vowed vengeance upon the fish that kept evading death, "I'm a person; you're a fish! I can outlast you! You're not that lucky!"

I prayed that no one heard me talking to the fish as I walked back to camp.

The following night was our last night camping. It was now or never. I fished there for a couple of hours, going through the same torturous game the fish were playing on me. Cast — take the bait — swim away.

"One more cast and I'm packing it in for another year," I said to the fish.

The fish's luck finally ran out. It took the bait, and I was able to set the hook and land that trout. As I walked back to camp, I looked at that fish, wondering if it was the one that kept getting away or if it was just another dumb, inexperienced fish that got a little too greedy and careless.

My husband's last official duty each night before bed was to clean any fish I had caught that night. We had a dishpan in the camper we used for the chore, and, as he cleaned them, I spoke to him of my struggles to land each fish. The newly cleaned fish went into a Baggie and in the freezer for the annual fish fry later.

The catch that night was just the one fish. It was fat, and I commented that it looked pregnant. A twinge of guilt flooded me as I thought about the baby fish that wouldn't be born because I just *had* to catch one more fish.

Don cut the fish open and began to laugh, "You caught the fish that took all your bait," he said.

"How do you know?" I asked him.

"It's not pregnant. It's full of cheese!"

I peered over his shoulder, and a feeling of total satisfaction flooded over me. The fish was stuffed with cheese! It was incredible! It had cheese throughout its entire body!

"That's right! I'm the master fisherwoman, and you're just a fish! And a dead one at that!"

My satisfaction was complete.

Don and Joey usually went fishing before daybreak. That was just too early for me. They got up before the sun and usually headed downstream. They were back by breakfast and usually empty-handed. Once, Joey said the funniest thing to me after one of those fishing expeditions that still brings a smile to my face whenever I recall the incident. Joey was about 10 or 11 years old and loved to fish as much as I did. Through the years, we hiked all through the area in and around that campground and came to know it like the back of our hand. But that particular fishing expedition was probably only about our third trip, and we hadn't completely explored the area yet. Joey and his father had gotten up while it was still dark and hiked farther downstream than they had ever gone before. I got up at daybreak and fed the rest of the kids breakfast, thinking that Joey and his father would be back to camp soon. Morning began to quickly pass, and I thought they must be catching fish by the bucket load or they would have been back already. I couldn't imagine any other reason they would still be out.

Around 11:00 A.M., they both reached camp empty-handed.

"Where have you been all this time if you weren't catching fish?" I asked, just a little irritated since I had already cleaned up the breakfast dishes.

"Mom, I almost saw a bear!" Joey was so excited.

I couldn't help but explode with laughter, "Joey, how do you *almost* see something? Either you see it or you don't. If you didn't see it, how do you know it was a bear?"

He didn't hesitate, "It sounded like a big animal. I could see color but couldn't make out a shape. It was a bear alright."

I was so happy by his response. Although I thought his statement was funny, I was afraid I might have broken his spirit and enthusiasm by my questions.

Later, I found out the rest of the story and why they had been gone so long. Joey didn't want me to know because he was embarrassed, but his father felt it necessary to tell me.

While downstream, the fish just weren't biting. They continued downstream for a long way looking for that perfect spot. Finally, Joey wanted to begin the trek back toward camp by himself. On his way back to camp, he came upon a fork in the creek that he hadn't seen in the dark on his way down. Even with the sun up, it was hard to see it unless you knew it was there. So when Joey approached the fork, he was unsure of which way to go. Joey chose the wrong fork and continued going in the wrong direction. Don finally decided to get back to camp too but never came across Joey, so he began to worry. He called Joey's name over and over but never heard an answer. He remembered seeing a fork in the creek behind him and decided it was worth a look just in case Joey had gone up the wrong way.

In the meantime, Joey didn't see any familiar landmarks and knew he must be lost, so he stopped where he was, next to the creek, and decided to wait for someone to find him. During his wait was when he "almost" saw a bear. Joey heard noises coming from the bushes, saw flickers of color, and was afraid it was a bear. He got into the creek, thinking that if it were a bear it wouldn't follow him into the icy, cold water which until recently had been snow. He was able to climb onto a huge boulder in the middle of the creek and stay there until his father found him about an hour later. Joey's clothes were still wet and he was frozen, but otherwise he was fine and very excited about the "bear" sighting. He couldn't wait to get back to camp to tell everyone about it.

It was a few years before I confided to Joey that I knew he had gotten lost. I was proud of him for knowing to stay by the creek instead of trying to find the way out himself. It was the smartest thing he could have done. More than twenty years later, though, I still laugh at him for almost seeing a bear, and he still defends his statement.

Jeffrey's best friend Greg always came camping with us. In fact, Greg practically lived with us each summer. I considered him my third son. Everyone in the family, including aunts and uncles, thought of Greg as part of the family, and when he was not present at a family function, everyone wanted to know why he wasn't there. Greg always wanted to catch fish, but most years he was unsuccessful. One year, about the end of our trip, when we had enough fish in the freezer for our annual fish fry, all the boys went out fishing just to make sure we'd have enough. Joey caught a couple of trout, and Greg brought one back to camp as well. The fish were cleaned and put in the freezer with the rest. The following day, we discussed the fish fry and decided to cook our bounty that evening.

Joey came to me that afternoon with a revelation, "Mom, do you know which fish Greg caught?"

I looked at him, puzzled. At first I thought it was a trick question.

"No, do you? Why do you want to know?" I asked.

"Well, Greg didn't really catch that fish. We found it on the bank of the creek. He wanted to bring a fish back to camp so much."

I opened the tiny freezer in the little camper refrigerator and threw all the fish out.

"Mom!" Joey cried, "What are you doing?"

I sighed as I put my hand on his shoulder.

"Fish are only good when properly cleaned after they're caught. I have no idea why that fish died. Maybe it had a disease. How long was it dead? Maybe it had already begun to rot on the inside. More importantly, I have no idea which fish it is. Do you want to take a chance on eating a fish that could make you sick, or possibly worse, kill you? Tell Greg to come here."

I felt so sorry for Greg. All he wanted was to pull his own weight and contribute to the food supply like everyone else. I knew he was embarrassed by what he'd done. He vindicated himself with a brilliant idea that turned out to be the funniest and most entertaining sport my children ever participated in: Fish Hunting.

I have no idea if fish hunting was legal, but the kids only did it on that trip. They got into the creek and reached back and below the bank where all the fish hid, and they caught a ton of them barehanded. It was a real team sport. They all worked together, screaming and helping each other. My husband and I took our lawn chairs down to the creek, sat on the bank to watch the spectacle, and died laughing.

"Joey, it's coming toward you!"

"Did you get it?"

"Where'd it go?"

"I got it! I got it!"

"I dropped it!"

It went on and on. They were screaming at each other a mile a minute. When one of them actually caught a fish, it was thrown up on the bank. Fish hunting made up for all the fish we had to throw away because of Greg's poor judgment, and it was a lot more fun than using a pole.

When we weren't fishing, we were involved in other productive and adventurous activities. One of our favorite competitive sports was boat racing. Each year, usually Jeffrey and Jessica gathered large rocks from the creek and spent a couple of days making a boat course for racing in the creek. In the meantime, all the kids and their father would find a suitable piece of wood and would begin whittling it into a "boat" using a pocketknife. There was only one knife, so everyone had to share. The boats didn't necessarily look like boats, but as long as they floated, it was fine. More than one entry per person in the race was also acceptable. The kids usually named their boats, too. Once everyone had at least one boat, the races began. That was the time when you found out whose boat was the one to beat, if your boat needed serious remodeling, or you needed to start over from scratch. The boat races were so much fun.

We used just that one pocketknife for several years. My husband finally decided that each of the kids were old enough and needed their own knife so they could carve their boats without having to wait in line. It worked out great — for a while.

My husband and I went fishing together one morning. We told the kids we would be fishing upstream and told them the general area where we could be found if needed. Don and I seldom fished together. Usually one of us stayed in camp with the kids "just in case" something happened. We had been gone about an hour when I heard Joey calling me.

"Joey, we're over here. Are you going to fish with us?" I asked.

"Mom! Jeffrey was whittling one his boats when his hand slipped. He cut his ankle really bad. Hurry!" Joey shouted.

Don took off running back to camp and I followed. Jennifer had already taken charge of the situation while waiting for us to return and had applied a pressure bandage to the wound. Don got back first and looked at Jeffrey's ankle.

"Wow!" was his first reaction, which caused a little anxiety for Jeffrey.

When I finally got back to camp, I ran to my injured son and took a look.

"Wow!" was my initial reaction too.

Our dramatic response to Jeffrey's cut caused him to break down and cry. As I tried to soothe my young son, I turned to my husband, "I don't believe we can fix this one with a butterfly bandage. He needs to get to the hospital quickly."

Don immediately volunteered to take Jeffrey to the hospital in Oakhurst, fifteen or twenty miles away.

When they returned, Jeffrey was still a little high on pain relievers. He was fine, but his wound had required several stitches and he was silly from the drugs.

It was at that moment I turned on my husband, "Why did you buy them all their own knives? Aren't they a little young for knives of their own? Look what happened!"

I knew I was being unfair. Heck, I thought it had been a good idea myself and was jealous that I hadn't thought of it first. But my son had been hurt. I had already gathered up all the knives while Jeffrey and my husband were gone.

"That's it for whittling this year. Everyone races with the boats they already have. Your father and I will determine next year if you can have your knives back," I announced.

The problem was, at that particular time in my life, I wasn't exactly the most organized person in the world, and I knew the knives would get misplaced and that we would never find them again. We were going to have to come up with another plan.

Another activity we enjoyed most afternoons was creek walking. During the year when the kids wore out their tennis shoes, I set them aside for creek walking on our vacation. We all used those old worn-out, beat-up tennis shoes for creek walking. There were too many rocks in the creek to walk barefoot, so we wore those shoes to protect our feet. And we walked in the creek because there wasn't any other way to get downstream. After a while, the path gave way to the creek and there were cliffs on both sides. There was no other way to go except through the creek.

My sister, Dianne, her husband Doyle, and my nephews, Johnny and Ben, usually met us each year at our campsite outside of Yosemite for a couple of days. On one particular hike while they were camping with us, Doyle took the lead. We hiked downstream through the creek for such a long way. We passed the fork in the creek that Joey had missed on a previous trip when he had gotten lost, and we began to hike through unfamiliar territory. When everyone was ready to start the long hike back to camp, Doyle decided it would be more interesting to take a different route back. He thought it would be cool to climb the cliff next to the creek and hike back along the rim following it. Like sheep to the slaughter, we blindly followed Doyle up that cliff. We literally had to slowly crawl our way up because the cliff was so steep. It was even steeper than the cliff we had hiked down at Mt. Madonna a couple of years before. I couldn't even stand up while climbing. We all got so dirty, and it was really hard work getting all the way to the top, but we made it. I don't think any of us was very happy to be there either. It was the middle of the afternoon and in the heat of the day. And, as was typical of us all, we had failed to bring any water with us. Once to the top of the cliff, the brush was so thick that we couldn't get through it. We all turned on Doyle.

"What now? What other bright ideas do you have?"

We did the only thing we could do — we crawled back down to the creek. As soon as we got back down the cliff, we put it to a vote. It was unanimous — Doyle was ousted from ever being the lead in a creek walk again. To this day, we still tease Doyle about that hike and laugh with the memories of that hot afternoon and crawling up the cliff without a single protest.

Joey and I went hiking upstream one year farther than any of us had ever gone. We came across one small waterfall after another. At each waterfall we came to, Joey just had to see what was above it, and, each time, he called down to me saying that I just had to see it! The climb up the waterfalls got a little treacherous at times, but we were both able to manipulate the boulders and reach the summit of each one. The following morning, we took our entire family to show them the wonders Joey and I had discovered the previous day.

When we ended our hike upstream and decided to go back to camp, my husband suggested that we go back a different way. He and his brother were so much alike! Don wanted to once again climb the cliffs and go back to camp along the rim of the stream. I guess none of us had learned anything from that hike downstream. Yep, we followed him to the top only to find dense brush that we couldn't get through, just like downstream. And, once again, we had to crawl back down the cliff on our hands and knees to the stream to make it back to camp. The children and I took a vote, and their father was ousted as a leader of hikes too. We never let him be the leader again.

Exploring that campground was something we continued to do every year, because the harsh winter snow always changed the area a little. During our first year camping, we had followed a path upstream for about a ¼ of a mile when we came across a beaver dam. It was the coolest thing we had ever seen. Beavers were swimming all over the place, and the dam itself was huge by our standards; we'd never seen a beaver dam in the wild before, so we had nothing to compare it to. The following year, the dam and beavers were gone, and we never saw them again. But we were always on the lookout for traces of beavers and a new bigger and better dam.

We played a variety of games with the kids too. One year we had water pistols. No one knew I had brought them, and while we were all sitting around talking, I squirted one of my kids. It was so funny to see their face. They didn't know where the water had come from. One thing led to another, and we ended up with an all-out war. It was great!

We also played word games around the campfire at night. My husband and I played cribbage every afternoon. The best game for my kids, though, was Hide and Seek after dark. They ran through the trees, jumped, fell, hid, laughed, teased, got scared, but rarely fought. They had the time of their lives playing that game at night. They didn't use flashlights, so it's amazing that they never tripped and broke a bone.

Our worst camping experience came one Memorial Day Weekend at Mt. Madonna. A cloud hung over the top of the mountain the entire time we were there. In the morning, everything we owned was wet with dew. In fact, it was as if it was raining, because the dew dripped continually off the trees. The afternoons were overcast, so our clothes were never able to dry completely. We remained optimistic, thinking that on the following day the sun would shine and we would dry out. It didn't happen.

On Sunday morning, we decided we'd had enough. We were going home. We were tired of everything being wet and we were so cold. There wasn't a single thing we owned that wasn't soaking wet. All of our clothes, bedding, and shoes were wet. Even the camp stove was so wet that we couldn't light it to make breakfast. We drove out and pulled into a Denny's restaurant at the bottom of the mountain to eat. I can't begin to describe how we all looked. We were wet, dirty, and barefoot because our shoes were all wet. We were politely asked to leave the establishment by management. I began to cry. I felt like a little beggar.

"Please, sir," I began, "we've been camping up at Mt. Madonna for the past three days. The fog hasn't lifted from there. Everything we own is wet. We're soaked, tired, dirty, and very hungry. Can't you please sit us somewhere in the back and I promise we'll be quiet? We won't call any attention to ourselves. We just need some food. Please?"

The restaurant manager relented and let us stay to eat. That breakfast was one of the best breakfasts I had ever eaten. I don't know if it was because we were so cold and hungry or if the cook was better than most. I was so grateful that we were allowed to stay. It also taught me not to judge a book by its cover. We looked like homeless vagabonds without a dime to our name.

As it always does, time flew by and my children grew up. When Jennifer was 18 years old, she moved out of the house and into her own apartment. That same summer, I couldn't get off work for the whole week to go camping. Jennifer had a new job too and couldn't take that much time off from work. Don took all the other kids camping on Saturday, and Jennifer and I planned to meet up with them on Thursday evening at our favorite campground. Both Jennifer and I were able to get Thursday off from work at the last minute, so we took off to meet everyone Wednesday night after work. No one knew we were coming early. There were no cell phones, and they probably wouldn't have worked up in the mountains anyway.

Jennifer and I had a great time driving there, but it was late in the summer and it had been a dry year. The narrow, pot-holed, winding dirt road leading into the campground was also extremely dry and dusty. It was so dusty, in fact, that halfway into the campground the car stalled. Jennifer and I waited for quite some time, hoping the dust would clear and the car would start, but it didn't.

"Look, Jen," I said, as one with complete knowledge and authority, "we're about halfway to the campground. It shouldn't be more than a couple of miles. It's 10:00 P.M. I don't want to stay here all night. No one knows we're coming. Let's just leave the car here and walk the rest of the way."

Jennifer and I began to walk down the narrow dirt road to our campsite when a car drove slowly by. It was a station wagon with two men in it. They stopped and asked if the car back on the side of the road was ours. I told them it was. The man driving asked where we were headed and I told him. He then asked if we wanted a ride into camp.

"Sure!" I said, excited that I didn't have to walk a couple of miles through the mountains at night.

Jennifer and I got into the car with the two men, and we began the ritual of chitchat. I proceeded to tell them that we were surprising my husband and other children and that no one knew we were coming. That revelation just about threw Jennifer into a tailspin. Jennifer gave me an elbow in the side and put her finger to her lips to shut me up. We finished the rescue trip in silence. I took Jennifer's caution and asked to be let off at the entrance to the campground so that the nice gentlemen wouldn't know which campsite we were staying at.

When Jennifer and I got out of the car, she turned on me like I was her brainless daughter and she was my wise mother, "How could you tell complete strangers, whose car we were in and at their mercy, by the way, that no one knew we were coming? Didn't it occur to you at all that they might not be nice men, and that maybe, just maybe, they could hurt us? Why would you do that?"

Wow! It really hadn't occurred to me. I guess I was being pretty naïve, but I just assumed that anyone who was up there camping must be good people. I couldn't imagine a murderer or rapist in the great outdoors camping. Jennifer and I searched for the truck and the campsite our family was in. They were probably deep asleep and without a care in the world. We were able to find the campsite but the truck was nowhere to be found.

"They must have gone into the Village today and just aren't back yet," I told Jennifer.

We didn't have to wait long before we saw the truck coming our way. My husband practically jumped out of the truck and grabbed me. He didn't know whether to yell at me or hug and kiss me.

"We saw the car on the side of the road. I used my key and it started right up, so we thought something had happened to you. We were looking all down the side of the roads, down the hills and cliffs. I was scared to death that something had happened to you."

I explained to him what had happened with the car and the ride into the campground from the gentlemen. We all got back into the truck and drove back to the car. As soon as the car was in view, I got out and walked to it. My husband was at a spot in the road that was wide, so he was able to turn the truck around.

He headed back toward camp and I got into the car. I put my key in the ignition and — nothing. The battery in the car was dead. Evidently, when my husband and children had come upon the empty car, someone had turned the lights on inside the car and had failed to turn them off. I knew that my husband would be watching for me, and when he didn't see my headlights behind him in the distance, he would come back looking for me. He was back about fifteen minutes later, and we jump-started the car. By the time we got back to our campsite and into bed, it was well after midnight.

The following year was our last year camping trip as a family before the divorce. Don got rid of the camper, and no one went camping for several years. During the year which Jeffrey married Kristine, most of us went back to Yosemite and camped in the Village for just a couple of days. Jeffrey and Kristine didn't come because they were preparing for their wedding. My nephews, Johnny and Ben, came, as well as Jennifer, Manuel, Morgan, Joey, Jessica, her Steve, and her best friend Karen, whom Joey would later marry.

We had decided to take a bus to the top of Glacier Point and hike the eight miles back down to the Village. My children, nephews, and I had hiked the same eight miles years before when we were all a lot younger, so we looked forward to sharing the beautiful scenery with the others. But the winter had taken its toll on the trail, and we all paid for it dearly. The eight-mile hike was two miles down, two miles up, and four miles down. When we had gone on the hike several years earlier, the initial two miles down was like a stroll through the trees on a well-beaten path. That year it was full of boulders. We spent the first two miles climbing over those boulders, and it wasn't much fun. We were all out of water by the time we got to the end of the first two miles.

Joey had thought ahead and had ordered sandwiches for us to eat that we carried in our backpacks. When we finished the first two miles of the hike, we stopped to rest at the headwaters of Illilouette Falls, and we pulled the sandwiches out to eat them. They were disgusting. Between the heat of the day and bouncing in our backpacks, the sandwiches were not appealing at all. So we were now without water *and* food. We were grown adults, and we really did know better than to hike all day in the mountains without adequate food and water. The water flowing toward Illilouette Falls was extremely swift, so I filled my water bottle with that water. There are advisories posted all over the place not to drink the water, but fast flowing water is less likely to be contaminated. Plus, we really needed water.

When we had rested enough and were about to continue our hike, Joey made an announcement, "The next two miles are uphill. The one farthest behind must stay with my mother. She will be at the back of the pack. Under no circumstances is she to be left alone. Does everyone understand?"

Wow! My son knew me so well. Yeah, I knew I would be the slowest one in our group too. But in my defense, I was also the oldest by quite a few years. I was no longer in my 20s or 30s like they were. The next two miles were treacherous. The others seemed to make it fine, but I had difficulty. Manuel and Steve stayed behind with me. Manuel has bad knees from an old high school football injury and had difficulty climbing as well. I climbed fifty feet and had to rest a few minutes, then walked fifty feet and rested again. It was tough. Jessica tried to sneak up and scare us at one point, but it didn't work. I just looked at her in disappointment.

"I thought you were a bear coming to eat me and put me out of my misery," I sighed.

I didn't know it at the time, but I was walking on a clogged artery in my leg which was contributing to my difficulties.

By the time we made it halfway down, we were at the headwaters of Nevada Falls. We took another long break and basked in the beauty of our surroundings. We were hungry, tired, and thirsty, and we still had four miles to go. Thank goodness they were all downhill. Morgan, who was only 5 years old, had been a real trooper.

My nephew, Johnny, was holding Morgan, walking near the water's edge where a strong current was rushing the water over Nevada Falls, when Johnny's foot slipped and he and Morgan both fell into the water. Johnny was able to catch his fall and not get caught up in the current, but it had been all too close for everyone. The next four miles were pretty sobering as each of us contemplated the possibilities of what could have happened.

When we got to the top of Vernal Falls, I told everyone that the quickest way down was not along the mist trail. Everyone listened to me — except me. I had actually never hiked up or down the mist trail that goes along Vernal Falls, and I let Jessica talk me into going that way. I was in agony by that point. My leg muscles were killing me. I'm also afraid of heights, so I don't know what I was thinking. The mist trail is a series of stairs. They are not even or equal stairs either. They were cut from the side of the hill made of granite and wet from the mist of the waterfall. It was pretty scary going down those stairs. I wasn't even able to enjoy the beauty of the waterfall because of my pain and fear.

We all made it down the eight-mile hike in one piece. We complained about our aches and pains the entire night. We all had stories to tell of the adversities and struggles we had endured just to get to the bottom. Now, years later, when we all get together, we remember that hike with great passion. We all claim it was one of the best days of our lives. We laugh about what we did, how we survived, and we speculate if we will ever do it again. Time has a way of making a person forget the bad stuff.

My son Jeffrey called me about four years ago and said that he and Kristine were planning on going camping at our family campground that summer and wanted to know if my husband and I would also like to go. Tears filled my eyes. I often thought about that magical place. I had spent the happiest days of my life there with my husband and children, but I knew that I'd probably never see it again. I now lived in Florida. I didn't have any camping gear, and even if I did, I didn't have room in my luggage to bring it. I couldn't believe the opportunity presented to me.

"Yes!" I shouted into the phone. "I'd love to go! I can't wait to go! Jeffrey, I don't know when I've been so excited!" I was, in fact, elated.

Word spread throughout the family that a camping trip to our old place was in the works for that summer, and everyone wanted in on it. Lists were written, itineraries made, and it became official. Everyone, including my children's father and my husband of thirteen years, were going camping together. We planned the trip for early June, about nine months from the time we had decided to go. I hadn't looked forward to anything so much in many, many years.

My husband Dennis, Jessica, Rachel, Livvy, and I got to the campground first. We picked out a spot that had three campsites together next to the creek and in the shade. It was beautiful and just how I had remembered it. A few hours later, the rest of the gang arrived. We all helped each other set up the tents. As soon as everyone was settled, I grabbed my fishing pole and set out to find the perfect spot. I went upstream first. You could see

trout everywhere. The best place I found, though, was right by
my own tent. The water was shallow, but the fish were biting at
every cast.

My grandkids grabbed their poles too, and, before long,
they had each caught a fish. Jessica handed down the tradition
of "You catch 'em — you clean 'em." Morgan was the only one
willing to learn the art of cleaning fish. Jessica showed her step-
by-step how to clean them while Rachel looked on in disgust.
Rachel was appalled but couldn't take her eyes away from what
her Mommy was doing.

Allison and Livvy were just under a year old at the time.
Kristine brought a plastic fence that when connected together
made a large playpen for the little ones to play in. The girls
weren't big enough to walk yet, but they did crawl, so the
playpen made a place that was safe for them to move around
in.

We barbequed skirt steaks that first night, and everyone
pitched in to either cook dinner, clean up, or gather fallen wood
for the nightly bonfire. As night fell, the heat of the day quickly
disappeared and it became very cold. We all huddled around
the fire, telling stories of wonderful memories we all shared of
that same campground. Hunter was the first to ask me to tell
a story. They specifically requested I tell them a scary story. I
didn't want to give them nightmares, so I decided to tell them
stories about playing safely and what happens when people are
not safe. I started with the campfire and told the story of a young
boy named Hunter who ran around the campfire not watching
where he was going. He eventually tripped and fell into the
flames where his clothes caught fire. Everyone ran to his rescue
and rolled him in the dirt to put out the fire, but Hunter still
sustained severe burns. As I told the story, my grandchildren
slowly scooted away from the fire. I continued with the story by

telling them that the little boy was rushed to the hospital where the doctors treated his burns.

"After Hunter healed, he still had terrible scars all over his body," I finished.

Rachel and Morgan had heard me tell stories like that many times, so they were not bothered by it. Hunter and Christien, though, began to cry. Jennifer scolded me for making up such a scary story to the kids, and that put an end to my story telling.

We had all forgotten how cold it got in the mountains at night. Jessica was concerned about Livvy. Babies tend to kick off their blankets at night, and Jessica worried about her getting too cold. To keep that from happening, Jessica dressed Livvy in about ten layers of clothes. Livvy couldn't move with so many clothes on her. She reminded me of the little boy from *A Christmas Story* when he had on all his winter gear while playing outside. Livvy woke up crying all night long. Jessica thought it was because she was sick or cold. I told Jessica I thought it was because she is from Florida where it is hot all the time. At home, Livvy slept in a tee shirt and diaper every night without any blankets on. She had the freedom to move around as she pleased without getting cold. While camping in the mountains with all those clothes on, she was probably hot and frustrated that she couldn't move.

Allison, on the other hand, slept just the opposite. Jeffrey and Kristine swaddled Allison when they laid her down to bed at night. She was used to being confined and not able to move. But Allison cried all night too. Only those blessed with being sound sleepers were able to get any sleep that first night.

Jennifer woke the following morning running a fever. Hunter and Christien had both experienced nightmares of being on fire during the night. Jennifer was feeling so sick that Manuel took her into the nearest town to see a doctor. They were gone most of the morning. It was determined that Jennifer had strep throat, and she was put on antibiotics. By noon, everyone had forgotten the terrible night we had all experienced, and we were once again thrilled to be camping together. Jennifer stayed in her tent most of the afternoon, resting while the rest of us fished and played in the creek.

After dinner, as we all sat around the campfire, Livvy's nose began to run. The cold air chapped her face. When we all went to bed, Livvy began her crying once again. I went to Jessica's tent to see if I could help.

"Jessica, I think Livvy is crying because she can't move. Why don't you take some of her clothes off her?" I asked.

"Mom, she has a cold. I don't think it's a good idea to be taking clothes off her when she's sick," Jessica replied.

Livvy had another tough night as did anyone else who heard her. Allison, on the other hand, slept great.

The following morning, Jessica came to me and said that she couldn't handle another night with Livvy like the last two nights had been. Jessica wanted to leave. We had a family meeting, and we all agreed that if one person left, we would all leave. The vacation of my dreams had been short lived — two days. But in those two days, my grandchildren had caught fish, I had told smookie stories around the campfire, and we had all been together. We vowed to each other that we would do it again — maybe next year.

GRANDPARENTS

Spending time with my own grandparents was always a treat. They didn't live close enough so that we could see them anytime we wanted but close enough for my mother to take us there on a Friday night for the weekend. My sister, Dianne, and I usually went together. My grandparents were not called Grandma and Grandpa; we called them Mammy and Papaw. I have no idea why. I was number six of seven grandchildren, so their names were well decided before I came along. When I was at that awkward stage in life, around 12 years old, I was embarrassed to call them Mammy and Papaw in front of my friends. My friends would ask me what I was going to do over the weekend, and I had trouble saying that I was going to spend the weekend with my Mammy and Papaw. It never once occurred to me to say that I was spending the weekend with my grandparents.

However, they always made the time we spent with them special. Before we were even out of bed, Papaw usually got up early on Saturday morning and walked to the donut shop at the corner to get donuts for breakfast. Papaw loved jelly donuts! My mother never gave us donuts for breakfast, so it was a joyous treat! Sometimes Mammy would sew both Dianne and I a new dress while we were there. She was a wonderful seamstress, and occasionally we would go shopping on Friday night to pick out fabric for a dress. Other times, she made clothes for our Barbies out of scrap material left over from the last dress she had made for us. We had the best-dressed Barbie dolls in the whole world.

Mammy was also a great cook, a trait my mother didn't seem to inherit from her. She made homemade hot fudge for our ice cream and always, always had a container full of cookies. We actually invented cookies and cream ice cream fifty years ago at Mammy's house. When she gave us ice cream, she also gave us Oreo cookies. We always smashed them up in our ice cream like chocolate chips.

On Saturday nights, Mammy and Papaw would take us to Bob's Big Boy on the corner for a hamburger. It was about the only time we ever got to go out to dinner. I can't express enough what a treat it was for us to get to have a good hamburger, french fries, and even a coke. Mammy and Papaw always did what they could for all of us kids, even if it wasn't much by today's standards. For us kids, it was incredible.

The biggest treat of all was when they took us to Knott's Berry Farm. People outside of Southern California may have never heard of Knott's Berry Farm, but many years ago it was just that, a berry farm. It grew and became an amusement park like Disneyland. In fact, it's not too far from Disneyland. Once upon a time, in a galaxy far, far away, it was **FREE** to get into Knott's Berry Farm! You just had to pay for any rides you went on. But you could walk around all day while looking at exhibits, people, and the scenery. My mother would give Dianne and I each a $1.00 to spend, which was enough to go on two rides. Mammy and Papaw bought us a chicken dinner for lunch. Knott's Berry Farm is still famous for their chicken dinners. Usually they would spend an extra 35 cents and buy us an all-day sucker too. Those were some of the best memories of my childhood!

My grandparents were monetarily poor. They had no earthly possessions to speak of. They had been married nearly sixty-five years when they died, and during that time, they never owned their own home. They rented small houses or apartments their entire life. They never even owned a brand-new car. I want to make that distinction, because spiritually they were the wealthiest people I knew. They always put God first in everything. Their Bibles were never more than an arms-length away. They prayed at every meal, even when we ate out at a restaurant. They prayed together on their knees before going to bed at night. They read their Bibles to each other every night, too. God was always in their conversations. They spoke of Him all the time.

The unique thing about my grandparents was they had a very hard and very sad life. They personally didn't think so. They always considered themselves blessed. Near the end of their lives, they both told me often that they were ready to go and meet God. They couldn't wait. I was awestruck by their faith. Very shortly before her death, Mammy told me that she had been praying so hard for God to take her, but He wasn't ready for her to leave this world yet. Being in my late twenties, I so admired her faith and love that I wanted to be able to feel that way when my time came.

My grandmother was a very rare treasure. She was 4' 10" tall in contrast to my height of 5' 8". She was such a tiny woman. When I was a little girl, I remember thinking that she was really old. She was nearly 40 when my mother was born and in her mid 60s when I was born. She had the most beautiful thick, curly white hair I have ever seen. Even as a child, I prayed that I would inherit that particular gene, the one that would give me that same beautiful thick, curly white hair. Of course, I think my hair would have to be thick and curly for me to have a shot at it, which it isn't, so I think I'm out of luck with that gene.

Mammy was a gentle woman who only spoke well of others. I never heard a criticism or a derogatory, angry, or mean word escape her lips. She was a happy spirit, always smiling. I can still hear her in my mind saying, "Well, I'll say," when you told her something fascinating.

Mammy gave birth to four children. The oldest and youngest are still alive: my mother's older sister and, of course, my mother. Her other two children died during their own childhood. Every time I spent any time with my grandparents, they would tell me the story about Junior and Edna, their children who had died.

Junior died when he was two years old of multiple childhood illnesses such as measles and something else. I'm not sure what else he had. If losing your only son at the age of two wasn't bad enough, Edna had colitis. She was initially misdiagnosed, and by the time they changed doctors and received an accurate diagnosis, it was too late. Her colon had perforated and she had become septic. She died a few days after her 13th birthday in the hospital. That was over seventy years ago. Neither one of my grandparents could tell the story of Edna or Junior without tears filling their eyes. I heard their story for nearly thirty years, and both of my grandparents cried every time. Even as a child, I knew that their love for their children was so immense, and I couldn't imagine the pain they still carried after all those years. My own mother wasn't even born when Junior died, and she was five years old when Edna died. I think telling Edna's and Junior's story kept them both alive for my grandparents.

But it was my grandparent's faith that struck me the most then and is still striking today — their faith that someday they would see Junior and Edna again — their faith that the loss they felt was not the end, only the beginning. They both knew without a doubt that they would be with their children again someday. Thinking about that now, it is still so profound to me.

Papaw was born in the mid 1890s. As a child, I thought that was the coolest thing in the world — to be born in a different century. He only had a 3rd grade education because that's what you did back then. You went to school long enough to learn to read and write. Then you went to work to help support your family. As a young man, Papaw was unskilled and uneducated, so he never really had a high paying job. He eventually honed his skills as a machinist and made a modest living. And, of course, there was the Depression. It was such a different world back then. Papaw once said, "I've seen a man plow a field with an ox, and I've seen a man walk on the moon." What an extraordinary life!

My grandparents were happy people. They giggled with each other, held hands like young lovers, and still had pet names for each other. They were so much in love, even in their 80s! They had a humorous side to them as well. They laughed often and didn't seem to ever get bogged down in life's daily struggles or turmoil. They trusted God with everything.

I went to church with them one Sunday evening. Papaw was busy talking to people after church near the street in front. Mammy and I walked to the back of the church where the parking lot was. We got in the car and waited. Papaw still didn't come, so Mammy got behind the wheel and started the engine. I was a young child and had never seen Mammy drive a car before, so I was really scared. I honestly didn't think she knew how to drive. So many questions raced through my little inquisitive mind, *What was she thinking? Was she mad at Papaw? Had she ever done this before? Did she remember I was in the car with her? Where was Papaw anyway?* I prayed that he would hurry and come before she got some crazy idea about driving the car. My prayer was just a little too late. She put the car in gear and began backing it out of the parking space. I shut my eyes and started praying again, knowing that God would surely hear me. We were at church after all. While I was still praying, Mammy turned out onto the street. I couldn't help but wonder if she was crazy. I mean, really, what if another car came by going in the opposite direction? Would she even know what to do?

"Please, God! Please, God!" I prayed. We drove around to the front of the church where Papaw was still talking. When he saw the car, he said his goodbyes and got in. I remember chuckling to myself and thinking, *Boy, is Mammy in trouble now.* I had never known Papaw to raise his voice, but I just knew Mammy was going to get it big time. I couldn't believe it. Papaw didn't say a single word to Mammy about driving the car! Evidently, she had done this before.

Papaw was nervous and afraid to drive on the Los Angeles freeways, so wherever he went he drove city streets, and it took forever to get anywhere. Mammy was also a backseat driver, even though she sat in the front seat next to him. He never complained about her warnings. She always told him to watch out for things, and if he ever got too close to anything for her liking she'd say, "Eep, eep, eep!" She used to crack me up with that one. My bothers and sisters can all imitate her saying that.

Mammy wore dentures, but she could do a trick for us when she took them out if we coaxed her enough. After taking her dentures out of her mouth, she would touch her chin to her nose. It was just the funniest looking thing in the world to me. She looked like she only had half a face. Sometimes she would chase us around her apartment looking like that, as if she were a hideous monster.

When I became an adult and had children of my own, I took them to see my grandparents whenever I was in town. That tired, old, worn-out woman in her 80s got down on the floor and played with my children, her great grandchildren. Living in an apartment, we always had to be quiet when we were small, but when I brought my children, she got out pots and pans with spoons for them to bang on.

"Mammy," I said a little offended, "we always had to be quiet when we came to see you. Why don't my children have to be quiet too?"

She looked at me with those wise, old eyes, smiled, and said, "Don't you know that old people can't hear anything? We're all deaf! The kids won't bother anyone."

Papaw died of colon cancer shortly before his 90th birthday. While he was still alive and able to speak, I went to see him in the hospital. He remembered everything about my children, asking me specific questions concerning them. It so touched me that he would think of my children when it was a struggle for him to stay alive each day. His love for his family went far beyond the physical.

As a child, I knew, and I mean really knew deep in my heart, that if God were only going to let two people into heaven, it would be my grandparents. They loved God, their family, and their brothers and sisters in Christ. They looked after the widows at church and always took in a fellow brother or sister in need. They prayed for my father, especially after my parents divorced. They prayed for the safety of my brothers, my sisters, and I. We all credit our lives to Papaw because *The prayer of a righteous man is powerful and effective* (James 5:16 NIV). Papaw was the most righteous man I have ever known. He was also the most humble man I have ever known. I knew then as I know now that God listened to every prayer Papaw prayed.

We all also know that God still watches out for us for the same reason, even though my grandfather has been dead for about twenty-five years.

I looked up to them, respected them, and as I approach my golden years, I want my grandchildren to see in me what I saw in my grandparents. I want my grandchildren to be touched by my wisdom as my grandparents' wisdom touched me. And I want my grandchildren to feel the love I feel for them as I felt my grandparents' love. They were holy examples to me as a child — and even more so now. I want to be the same kind of example to my grandchildren. I remember the clothes, the food, the trips, the donuts, the talks, the prayers, and the laughter. I want my grandchildren to remember all those things about me, too. In years to come, when I am long gone from this life and they speak of me, I want a smile to cross their faces as they think of a moment in time spent together. That's how I want to leave this life — the same way as my grandparents did — as an example for my grandchildren. I knew of their love for God and how they strived to live for Him. I want my grandchildren to see that in me, too. I can't think of anything more important to do.

WHY GOD GAVE ME GRANDCHILDREN

A full year and a half after I finished writing this book, I added this chapter. I initially wanted to end the book with a chapter about my own grandparents, but through a tragedy and the wonderful uniqueness of each of my grandchildren, I decided to end this book about them. After all, they were the ones who inspired it to begin with.

As it always does, things changed. Life changed. In May 2008, Jessica moved from St Petersburg, Florida to Wyoming, taking Rachel and Livvy with her. People always ask me, "Why Wyoming? How does someone move from Florida to Wyoming? They're polar opposites. Florida is hot and humid, and Wyoming is cold and there's snow — lots of snow."

However, Wyoming has the mountains that Jessica so missed. She wanted and needed to go, and part of me envied her. I missed the mountains too. Dennis and I both understood why she had to leave. It took a little time on our part to get to that understanding, but we eventually got there. Although we would miss them all terribly and hated to see them leave, they left with our blessing.

We marveled at the irony of it all. We had finally succeeded in having children all over the United States. Jennifer was in Florida, Joey in Oregon, Jeffrey in California, Jessica in

Wyoming, and Dennis' daughter Cristy lived in Michigan. Boy was it going to be tough to orchestrate our vacations now!

After Jessica and her family left, Dennis and I talked about how much we would miss them. We had planned to go to Wyoming the following summer for Jessica's wedding, but next July seemed so far away. I wasn't sure if I could wait that long to see them all again. I was so accustomed to seeing Jessica, Livvy, and Rachel each week. After throwing ideas around and trying to do a little slight of hand with the money, we realized we would have to be content to see them at the wedding.

However, God had His own timetable and His own plans. For Dennis, going to Wyoming was not part of that plan. Dennis died on November 20, 2008. It was sudden and unexpected. Dennis went to the hospital for a minor outpatient procedure and had complications that eventually took his life. He was in the hospital for 2 ½ months, with the last six days spent in Hospice.

When I was finally told that Dennis would not recover and was going to die, I first went to my church to speak to our minister. Next, I went to Jennifer's house. Morgan, Hunter, and Christien were in school, so I was able to speak to Jennifer and Manuel openly. They promised to bring the kids to the hospital that night to see Grandpa.

Dennis was in the Hospice section of the hospital. It was a wonderful place, a place full of God's angels. Their only purpose was to make sure Dennis was comfortable and not in any pain, as well as making sure that any needs I had were met. They offered unlimited comfort, hugs, handholding, and prayers. There was a family section in Hospice where family could take a break, watch TV, talk, and eat. I had stopped by the store and stocked up on all kinds of food, wanting to make sure there was enough for anyone who came by and might get hungry. Plus,

I wasn't leaving and didn't want anyone to become concerned about trying to get me to eat or leave to get something to eat. I didn't want food to be an issue for anyone.

Later that evening, when Jennifer and Manuel brought the kids to see Dennis, Hunter just immersed himself in his father in complete grief. Hunter was 9 years old and took his grandfather's death very hard. Dennis was aware of their presence but could no longer speak or open his eyes. He responded in small ways that let us know he was still there and aware of what was going on around him. We sat in Dennis' room for a while, talking, praying, and crying. We decided to take the kids into the family area for a needed break. As Jennifer and I spoke about things that needed to be done and decisions that had to be made over the next few days, Hunter came and sat next to me.

"Grandma," Hunter began, "you said that Grandpa was dying because of a lot of illnesses."

"That's right, Hunter. Grandpa is so very sick," I replied.

"Does he have cancer?" Hunter asked with concern in his voice.

"No, baby, he doesn't have cancer," I responded reassuringly.

"Well... does he have Yellow Fever?" Hunter inquired

I burst into gales of laughter. I could see where this was going. I knew Hunter all too well. He was going to keep naming all the exotic diseases he could think of until he finally hit on the correct one. I figured malaria or typhoid was next.

"No, sweetheart, he doesn't have Yellow Fever. He had so many complications after his eye surgery, and his poor body just couldn't recover from them all. But thank you for making me laugh," I said, so grateful for the light moment at that particular time.

I thanked Jennifer for giving me such a lovely grandson and

told her that only a grandchild can make me laugh when my heart is breaking into a million tiny pieces. Only a grandchild can give me a moment of life when my own world is about to die. Later that evening, Hunter asked if he could be a pall hearer for his grandfather. He didn't know the term, but he wanted to help carry his grandfather to his final resting place. I told him Grandpa would be honored and privileged as I was. He was growing into such a wonderful young man. Dennis would have been so proud.

Jennifer didn't leave my side over the next few days. She went with me to choose a funeral home, select a casket, and pick out flowers. She sat with me for hours in Dennis' room, watching me cry, watching him die. My son, Jeffrey, flew in from California to be with me at a great sacrifice to his family. My daughter-in-law, Kristine, had just given birth to my newest granddaughter Hannah Banana the month before, and she was still recuperating from a little complication in the delivery. Jeffrey left Kristine, Allison, Elaina, Sophia, and Hannah to be at my side. He said he needed to come and be here for me, so I needed to let him. Dennis' daughter Cristy came from Michigan to say goodbye to her father also. We were all by his side, with Cristy holding one hand and me holding his other hand when Dennis took his last breath. It was both the saddest and most precious moment of my life.

During the 2 ½ month hospital ordeal, I had begun smoking again. I was weak and needed the indulgence. The day after Dennis' death, Jennifer's family came to my house. After feasting on the food that my church family had brought for us to eat, I wanted a cigarette. I was torn because I didn't want to disappoint my grandchildren that I had started the ugly habit again. The fact was, I was disappointed in myself that I felt the need for that crutch. I hated to tell them I had started smoking again, but I was too emotionally exhausted to care a whole lot. I sat my grandchildren down to break the news to them.

"The past couple of months have been really difficult with Grandpa in the hospital," I began. "Please don't be too disappointed in me, but I started smoking again. I promise that it is only temporary, and I have already started taking Chantix to help, so this is not a permanent thing. I love you and hope that you can cut me a little slack right now."

They were all so forgiving. It was Morgan's comment that took me by surprise, "Grandma, don't worry. If it were me, I'd start smoking too," she reassured me.

Jeffrey may have been caught off guard most of all. "What?" Jeffrey demanded. "Morgan, what are you saying?"

"Uncle Jeff, I'm just trying to be supportive," Morgan said through clenched teeth, giving her uncle a look showing a little irritation that he was slow on the uptake and hadn't picked up on her attempt to comfort me. We all broke into laughter.

It had been another lighthearted moment provided especially for me by my grandchildren in order to make me feel better. How lucky I was to have these precious treasures love me so much.

Most of my family had flown in from California, and all of my children were there. Jessica brought her entire family of six with her. She even brought the baby, my new grandson Joseph who was only five months old. My son, Joey, brought my 2-year-old grandson Jordan with him who provided his own form of entertainment for us. Jordan was at that age where his vocabulary grew by leaps and bounds on a daily basis, so he provided a substantial amount of comic relief when needed. Joey left his wife Karen and his brand new baby girl, my granddaughter, Rhea, in Oregon. Rhea was also a newborn, just 2-3 weeks older than Hannah. All of my children made great personal sacrifices to be there for me and to say goodbye to a man they had all grown to love.

There were other moments over the course of those first few weeks that I absolutely cherish and hold onto. At the conclusion of Dennis' funeral service at our church, Livvy wanted me to pick her up as I walked to Dennis' casket for one last goodbye. It had been a closed casket according to Dennis' wishes. He had been so sick and lost so much weight that I didn't want anyone to see him either. Since Dennis was a veteran, there was an American flag draped over his casket. I gently touched the flag and whispered my goodbyes. With tears rolling down my cheeks, I leaned over and kissed my husband's casket. At the same moment, Livvy, too, gave her grandfather one last kiss goodbye.

The following day was Sunday, and we had just gotten out of church and decided to go out to lunch at what I considered Dennis' and my place — a Mexican restaurant we had gone to about once a week for many years. I had frequented there more often, about three times a week while Dennis was in the hospital, since it was practically down the street. That Sunday afternoon, most of my family had lunch together. We had such a large group that we had to wait for them to put tables together for us. Almost everyone waited outside, but I sat in the small lobby with Livvy. A man walked in with a little boy. The boy was adorable, and he and Livvy struck up a conversation.

"What's your name?" Livvy asked.

"Michael," the boy replied. "What's your name?"

"My name is Livvy. How old are you?" Livvy continued with her questioning.

"I'm 4," Michael said. "How old are you?"

"I'm 5. I don't live here anymore. I live in Wyoming. I came back because my Grandpa died. His funeral was yesterday." Livvy just didn't have any secrets.

Michael's father had been listening to the conversation as well, and suddenly it became an awkward moment. I was so used to that with Livvy. She made many moments awkward for me during her brief time on earth. However, that happens to be one of the things I love most about her. Michael's father offered his condolences, and the server who said our table was ready rescued me from the tears that were beginning to well up in my eyes. Jessica confided to me later that Livvy, too, had struggled with Dennis' death. Every time anyone mentioned Grandpa around her, she broke into tears, so maybe her talking openly about it was good for her. I marveled at her understanding of her loss and her own grief at such a young age.

Time went on as always, and on December 23rd our anniversary came, one month and three days after Dennis' death. It was a difficult day. Dennis and I always went out to dinner on our anniversary. It was our day: the anniversary of the day we promised our love to each other until death. I still wanted to celebrate. I wanted to remember. I wanted to talk about that day. Jennifer and Manuel asked if they could come to dinner with me. We went to the restaurant Dennis and I would have gone to on that day. We had a great time. The food was great as always, and we talked about Dennis and our wedding day. It was good.

The following day, on Christmas Eve, Jessica called to see how I was doing and to ask about my dinner the night before. After the preliminaries, Rachel wanted to speak to me. "I'm going to miss Grandpa tomorrow," Rachel said.

"I know, Goobie Doo. I'm going to miss him, too," I replied.

"But, you know, Grandma," Rachel continued, "Grandpa is going to have the best Christmas of all of us. He gets to spend Christmas with Jesus."

How profound and insightful was that? No one could have said anything to lift my spirits as much as that one simple little message from my 9-year-old granddaughter. I said a little silent prayer, thanking God for my wonderful granddaughter.

On Christmas Day, I got up early and went to Jennifer's house to watch the kids open their presents from Santa. After everything was opened and the mess cleaned up, we went to the cemetery. Jennifer's family always went to the cemetery on Christmas. Manuel's father had died when Manuel was a teenager, and his birthday had been on Christmas day. Dennis and Manuel's father were buried at the same cemetery for this very convenience. I was still in the state of mind that I needed a lot of alone time, time for just me and my own thoughts, so I didn't want to ride with Jennifer and I drove my own car. On the way home, Morgan asked if she could ride with me.

As soon as my car was put into drive, Morgan began asking questions, "So, Grandma," she started, "how are you *really* doing?" She sounded so concerned.

My usual knee-jerk response to that question was, "I'm fine." I wasn't, but that's how I normally responded. Most people don't really want to know. But Morgan had asked how I really was, so I thought I might just throw some feelings out there to see how she responded, to see if she could handle a little of my grief.

"Well, sweetheart," I started, "I'm having a tough time. I cry for him everyday. I miss him so much that my heart actually aches. Sometimes I feel like I can't breathe. Other times I talk to him, and that seems to make me feel better."

"You… talk to him?" Morgan responded, a little unsure of how to react to my revelation. "If you don't mind my asking… what do you say to him?"

"I usually tell him how much I love him and how much I miss him. Sometimes I tell him I need him to come home to me," I continued. "Being here at the cemetery doesn't seem to bother me, because I don't feel he's here. I feel him at home. That's why I always want to be there. The other night, when we went out to dinner for my anniversary, I asked him if he wanted to come. I don't know why I feel that he stays at home all the time and misses all the fun. So I asked him to come along. I told him it was too bad that he doesn't eat anymore, because I knew the food would be great and he would have loved it."

Morgan was fantastic. She even chuckled at my attempt at humor. She's becoming a mature young lady now. I wanted her to know that although my grief was profound, I was getting through it all, even if it meant that I talk to a person who is no longer there. I wanted her to know that it was normal to grieve for what she might consider to be a long time but that I would someday be okay. She seemed to understand what I was saying to her. Then again, for all I know, she may secretly think I'm ready for a mental hospital.

My children usually call me to ask how I'm doing. I answer that I am fine. Occasionally they will delve a little deeper, and occasionally I will open up and tell them how I really am doing. Morgan is 13 years old, and she wanted to know how I *really* was.

Morgan also spent the night with me on New Years Eve along with Christien. They didn't want me to be alone. We went to their favorite restaurant for dinner, stayed up until midnight, slept late, and then I took them to breakfast in the morning. Jennifer has confided that Hunter still mourns for his Grandfather and has difficulty talking about him without crying, but Morgan worries about me.

My grandchildren inspired me to write this book, so, as I said, it is only fitting that I end it with them. Through all the years that I have been a grandmother, my grandchildren have surprised me, thrilled me, lifted me up, been my cheerleaders, my advisors, my conscience, brought out the best in me, made me laugh like no one ever has, and, most of all, have given me unconditional love. These past few months have been the most difficult of my life, and although I still grieve for my husband every single day, the joy these innocent children continue to bring into my life is why God, in His infinite wisdom, gave me grandchildren.

July 2009
Front Row: Elaina, Morgan, Hannah, Sophia, Rhea,
Myself, Jordan, Josie, Rachel, Joseph, Hunter
Back Row: Christien, Livvy and Allison

www.ingramcontent.com/pod-product-compliance
Lightning Source LLC
LaVergne TN
LVHW051458080426
835509LV00017B/1804